PRAISE FOR DR. JIM TAYLOR AND
Your Children Are Listening

"Dr. Jim Taylor's strengths are his compassionate voice,
his insights into parents' and children's psyches, and his 'boots on
the ground' approach to helping parents send healthy messages to
their children. In a world filled with harmful messages, *Your Children
Are Listening* will resonate with all parents."

—MICHELE BORBA, EdD,
author of *Parents Do Make a Difference* and
The Big Book of Parenting Solutions

"In a world where children are surrounded by negative messages,
Dr. Jim Taylor gives parents the tools they need to effectively
communicate healthy, positive messages that will infuse their
childrens' hearts, minds and souls."

—MICHELLE LAROWE,
author of *A Mom's Ultimate Book of Lists, Working Mom's 411*
and the *Nanny to the Rescue!* Parenting Series

THE EXPERIMENT

BECAUSE EVERY BOOK IS A TEST OF NEW IDEAS

Your Children Are Listening

**NINE MESSAGES THEY
NEED TO HEAR FROM YOU**

Jim Taylor, PhD

THE EXPERIMENT

NEW YORK

The Experiment, LLC
260 Fifth Avenue
New York, NY 10001–6408
www.theexperimentpublishing.com

The names of some people, and identifying details, have been changed to protect their privacy.

The Experiment's books are available at special discounts when purchased in bulk for premiums and sales promotions as well as for fundraising or educational use. For details, contact us at info@theexperimentpublishing.com.

Many of the designations used by manufacturers and sellers to distinguish their products are claimed as trademarks. Where those designations appear in this book and The Experiment was aware of a trademark claim, the designations have been capitalized.

Library of Congress Control Number: 2011925091
ISBN 978-1-61519-034-8
Ebook ISBN 978-1-61519-135-2

Cover design by Michael Fusco | mpulsedesign.com
Cover photograph by Stuart Cobue | Shutterstock
Author photograph by Gary Yost
Text design by Pauline Neuwirth, Neuwirth & Associates, Inc.

Manufactured in the United States of America
Distributed by Workman Publishing Company, Inc.
Distributed simultaneously in Canada by Thomas Allen and Son Ltd.
First published June 2011
10 9 8 7 6 5 4 3 2 1

DEDICATED TO . . .

Carol Mann, literary agent extraordinaire, for taking a chance when others wouldn't and finding the best home for my book.

Matthew Lore, my publisher at The Experiment, who, even in today's challenging book publishing environment, got my message. Your vision, editorial input, and collaborative spirit made Your Children Are Listening *a reality.*

Gerry Sindell, my mentor, friend, "book doctor," and officiant at my wedding, whose faith, perspective, and insight have helped make my journey through the unpredictable world of publishing a passion, a joy, and one of constant discovery, wonder, and fulfillment.

My father, Shel; my late mother, Ceci; and my sister, Heidi; for their love, support, and acceptance.

My daughters, Catie and Gracie, who never stop sending me messages on how I can be a better father and whose calls of "Daddy!" and hugs and kisses each day make parenting oh-so worth it. And, of course, for their daily contributions to this book. How much do I love you? Sooo much!

Finally, Sarah, my bride and the mother of our two daughters, for her support of the sometimes crazy career I have chosen, for leading the way in raising Catie and Gracie so well, and, ultimately, for making my life complete. I love you madly!

Contents

Introduction

Consider the toddler. Having made it through the year of infancy, a year of almost complete helplessness, toddlers are entering a radical new phase of life. They are learning to stand on their own (a nice metaphor, don't you think?) and are on their way to taking their first steps. Soon they will be feeding themselves. Toddlers will be exploring speech and making themselves understood. Two years from now, when this period of learning is complete, children will understand that they are separate beings from their parents. They will be able to say, "Yes!" "No!" "Thank you," and even "I love you," and know what they mean. Toddlerhood is that magical time when children learn the beginnings of personhood.

Now consider the preschooler. In many ways, preschoolers appear to be little adults, having mastered many of the basics of personhood. They can talk (and be mostly understood) in an ever-growing vocabulary, dress and feed themselves, walk, run, climb, and jump. Yet, preschoolers are still just starting on their journey toward personhood, along which their personalities will become more defined and their values, attitudes, and beliefs about themselves and the world will form and become ingrained in their minds.

Finally, consider the elementary schooler entering that big and exciting world beyond their home. It's a world they are not fully prepared to navigate. Nonetheless, they are thrust out the front door into an intense maelstrom of messages, both positive and negative, which they are still largely ill prepared to assimilate in any kind of reasoned fashion. Over the next few years, their personalities and their self-perceptions and views of the world will become more established and will guide the direction that their lives will take.

Toddlerhood, preschool, and the early elementary school years are also the time when you have your best possible chance to have your say about what kind of person you would like your child to become. Perhaps eight years max. After that, your influence slowly but inexorably diminishes.

I'M A "PARENTING EXPERT"

I have a PhD in psychology and am the author of two previous parenting books, I have a consulting practice that involves working with young people and their parents, and I regularly speak to gatherings of parents, educators, and students around the world. For many years I've been a "parenting expert." But here's the hitch: I wrote those parenting books and became a so-called parenting expert before I had children.

The instant my first daughter, Catie, was born, I went from being an authority on parenting to just another baffled parent trying to muddle through raising my children. In fifteen years I may write another parenting book titled *I'm Sorry, They Seemed Like Good Ideas at the Time.*

That said, my professional experience has demonstrated that my ideas about raising children do stand up to the test of real-life parenting. Now that I am the father of two young girls, five-year-old Catie and three-year-old Gracie, I have firsthand experience to support the value of my approach to raising children. Plus, being a parent has helped me to better understand what actually works and what doesn't in the real world of raising children.

HOW DO CHILDREN BECOME WHO THEY BECOME?

The key question that intrigues me as both a parent and a so-called parenting expert is: How do children become who they become? Certainly, genetics plays a formative role; intelligence, physical attributes, and temperament all have been found to have a strong hereditary component. Evidence is equally strong that the environment also contributes significantly. It is no longer a dispute between nature *versus* nurture, but rather a collaboration of sorts involving nature *via* nurture: How children are raised and the environment in which they live influence which genetic predispositions emerge as they develop.

So what aspects of the environment affect children's development? Some have argued that parents have much less influence than they like to think and that peers and popular culture affect children more. However, I believe that during these early years, you have a window of opportunity before your children become integrated into the larger social world—and that, during this period, your impact on your children is greater than that of outside forces.

Consider this: During this period your children are absolutely ravenous for every morsel of information they can ingest, and you control most of the developmental "nourishment" they receive. You control the physical, daily social world in which your children live, which plays an increasingly important role in their later development. You determine the house they live in, your neighborhood, and the childcare or preschool your children attend. You decide what they eat, when they sleep, and their daily activities. You choose their playdates and the peers with whom they interact and the type and frequency of exposure to popular culture. In other words, during those early years, you have the opportunity to control the messages your children get. Other messages, many not as nourishing for the development of young children, will arrive soon enough.

THEY GET THE MESSAGE

At the heart of *Your Children Are Listening* is this message: *Children become the messages they get the most.* Given the inherent power that you have in shaping your children through your messages, the core question you should ask yourself is, "How can I be sure I am sending the healthiest messages to my children?" The answer to that question has two parts: First, you need to be clear about what messages you want to communicate to your children. And second, you must develop your own skills in conveying those messages.

The messages that come early in your children's lives are particularly significant because, before long, your children will be getting messages from many much less controllable and less benign sources. Peers and popular culture will inexorably introduce children to all kinds of information and attitudes—good, bad, and downright dangerous. All you can do is attempt to transmit positive messages early in your children's lives as a form of immunization against the onslaught of harmful messages they are certain to receive as they get older.

THE GIFT OF MESSAGES

What values and beliefs do you want to instill in your children? What kind of people do you want your children to become? How can you prepare them for a future that is largely unforeseeable? These are fundamental questions that all parents ask. The answers that you come up with will determine how you raise your children.

From my work I know that the vast majority of parents come up with similar answers. We want our children to thrive, to be kind and generous people, to find success, happiness, and meaning in their lives. We want our children to feel good about who they are, to pursue meaningful goals, and do well in school and their careers. We want them to be thoughtful, respectful, and responsible. We want them to develop healthy relationships, feel connected with the world in which they live, and find love. Ultimately, we all want our children to become decent human beings. And the way to realize these hopes for our children is to send them the right messages. Your hopes and your messages are the gifts that you can give your children every day of their lives.

YOUR CHILDREN ARE WORKS OF ART

Children are like paintings that start at birth with only broad genetic strokes on an otherwise blank canvas. During infancy, more distinct shapes and colors add to the complexity of the canvas. Then, in toddlerhood and during the preschool and elementary school years, more precise strokes, textures, and colors allow us to begin to see what the final work of art might look like. You are the principal artist at this stage. Eventually, your children will take over and continue to refine the work of art until it becomes a genuine self-portrait. Your messages during your children's early years are the most important contributions you will make to the masterpiece that they will become.

You begin to make your contributions to the painting by sending messages to your children long before you think they might actually understand the messages. For infants as young as one day old, eye contact, tone of voice, physical contact, affection, and responsiveness to their needs all communicate messages of love, security, and connectedness.

The work of art becomes more interesting in toddlerhood, when children begin to walk, acquire language, and develop complex cognitive and motor skills. Toddlerhood is also the time when children start to really get parents' messages. In some ways, toddlers are still more baby than child; they are needy, pure, and unprepared for the world. In other ways, they are gaining the complexity and understanding of the adults into which they will grow. They enter this stage as largely helpless little beings and leave it with most of the major tools necessary to evolve into fully functioning adults.

The canvas gains in richness and complexity in your children's preschool and elementary years. The basic skills they mastered in toddlerhood evolve into more sophisticated expressions of who they are and what they can do as they prepare to enter and progress through their elementary school years.

If you're reading this and your children are already beyond elementary school, rest assured that it's never too late to begin sending cogent messages to your children. I've worked with parents who had sent confusing and even unhealthy messages for most of their children's lives into their late teens. But, even at such a seemingly late stage by which you might think that young people are fully formed and no longer malleable, parents who altered their messages saw their teenage children change for the better. Though your impact on your children will ebb as they progress through elementary and high school, you will still have a tremendous influence on them for many years to come. As a result, you must continue to send them healthy messages that will help them resist the unhealthy messages that will ever be present in their lives.

The specific strategies that I discuss in *Your Children Are Listening* focus on the toddler, preschool, and elementary school years and may not always be applicable to older children. At the same time, everything else in this book, from the ways in which messages are communicated to your children, to the obstacles that prevent messages from getting through, to the essential messages I describe, is relevant to the entire spectrum of young people. You should never stop sending positive messages to your children, and the information in *Your Children Are Listening* can help you to shape your messages to the unique needs of your children at their particular stage of development.

A WORLD OF UNHEALTHY MESSAGES

In earlier generations, being a good parent was easier. Parents could trust that most of the institutions that composed their society—schools, communities, youth sports, and popular culture—sent mostly good messages, messages that aligned with those of the parents. The cumulative effect was that children were inundated with healthy messages from just about everyone and everything around them, and that unhealthy messages were by far the exception rather than the rule.

Times have changed. Now, many schools are so focused on test scores and budget deficits that they either don't have the time or energy to devote to healthy messages or they are sending the wrong messages. The student culture is frequently toxic: Pressure to grow up too soon, peer pressure, cyberbullying, and the emphasis on physical appearance, affluence, and popularity create additional unhealthy messages for children. Communities that were once tight-knit are now often transient and disconnected. Youth sports, which were once about fun, fitness, and love of sport, are now often about fulfilling the frustrated dreams of parents, earning college athletic scholarships, or preparing for professional or Olympic success, fame, and fortune, however unrealistic these goals might be. Finally, although popular culture has always had a rebellious dimension, it did, in times past, send primarily good messages to children. Television and radio, for example, had a Congressional mandate to act in the "public interest"—in other words, to provide programming that was positive and healthy. Whatever the public interest may once have been, it no longer governs the media. The sole purpose of popular culture now is to make money, with little consideration of its corrosive effect on children.

Because of these powerful negative influences on your children, you have to be, as they say in the political world, "on message 24/7." If you're not, your children will not only fail to get your messages, but they probably will get the unhealthy messages to which they are going to be increasingly and continually exposed.

MESSAGES EVERYWHERE

The idea of the power of messages on children didn't actually come to me from my work and experience with children. The reality is that we hear about messages constantly these days. In politics, the goal is to control the message and stay on message. Why? Because, in the political world, the party that controls the message has the most influence over the electorate. And cable-news channels, talk radio, the blogosphere, and party "war rooms"predictate their very existence on identifying and consistently conveying messages and responding to conflicting messages.

The communication technology landscape of the twenty-first century is also rife with messages. There are voicemail messages, e-mail messages, text messages, and instant messages. Think about all of the messages we send and receive every day and you'll understand how messages influence us in ways both trivial and significant. And you'll see that messages will also shape your children in ways predictable and unexpected, healthy and harmful.

DO YOU NEED A CRYSTAL BALL?

As parents, we want our children to be prepared for the future. There was a time, not too long ago, when parents could make some sensible assumptions about the future and how their children might best be prepared to flourish in it. But with the pace of change in our society ever-increasing, can we still trust those assumptions?

Will what worked in the past continue to work in the future? What should our messages to our children contain that will adequately prepare them for a future no one can predict with any reasonable degree of certainty? The uncertainty can sometimes feel paralyzing given the immensity of the task we face as parents and the consequences of failure for our children.

But preparing our children for the future doesn't have to be terrifying, because, despite the profound and fast-paced changes occurring now, raising children doesn't have to be very different than in the past. Yes, parenting is more difficult now, because we lack the social supports we once could rely on and the resulting feeling is that we have to "go it alone" more than ever before. And yes, the world continues to change technologically, socially, and politically in unpredictable ways. But the fundamentals of child rearing haven't changed much because people haven't changed much; we are all driven by the same motives that have driven people for centuries, even millennia: to find meaning, happiness, and connectedness in our lives.

And what children need to thrive hasn't changed much either. Children still need a loving and safe environment. They need support, encouragement, and important life skills. And they need guidance from their parents to help them navigate the world in which they are growing up (which has, admittedly, gotten much more complex). In fact, because of the rapid changes and profound uncertainty they are experiencing every day, our children need these messages from us more than ever before. If we can give our children a solid foundation of the right messages, they will have the maturity and capabilities to handle all of the unforeseeable changes that lie ahead.

THE BIRTH OF *YOUR CHILDREN ARE LISTENING*

Your Children Are Listening is based on my own professional knowledge and experience as one of those so-called parenting experts. As a former full-time academic and published researcher, my work has always been informed by the latest scientific theory and research on child rearing. The last decade has been a fertile time for the study of children, and it has brought new understanding and insights into how children develop. In fact, it may be that this book could not have been written earlier.

But, equally, *Your Children Are Listening* is based on the real-life parenting experiences my wife, Sarah, and I have had in raising Catie and Gracie. As Catie is just now in kindergarten and Gracie is knee-deep in her preschool years, our memories are sharp, our concerns are fresh, and our joys continuous. These in-the-trenches experiences provided me with the inspiration and the lessons to write *Your Children Are Listening*. I also sent out a survey to almost 5,000 parents in which I asked them to share their experiences with communicating messages to their children. The response was overwhelming; I received a wealth of new, interesting, and sometimes surprising strategies from parents, just like you and me, on the what and how of the messages they send their children.

NINE ESSENTIAL MESSAGES

Your Children Are Listening will describe nine essential messages that your children need to get in their early years to have a life of meaning, connection, happiness, and success. This book is divided into four parts. Part One, Get the Message, will introduce you to the importance of messages; all the ways that you send messages to your children, whether consciously or otherwise; and, equally important, what prevents your messages from getting through to them.

Part Two, I Like Myself, focuses on the messages that help build self-esteem, which is the foundation of children becoming confident and capable people. This section will examine the role messages of love, competence, and security play in developing self-esteem and the best messages to send to instill this all-important positive perception in your children.

Part Three, I Like Others, explores the messages that will help your children develop the ability to relate to and connect with others. This section considers how compassion, gratitude, and the Earth play essential roles in this relationship.

Part Four, Others Like Me, looks at the messages that your children need to understand so that the world at large can connect with them. Respect, responsibility, and emotion are the messages that are highlighted.

Your
Children Are
Listening

PART I

Get the Message

1

The Why and the What of Messages

For you to send the healthiest possible messages to your children requires that you fully buy into my notion that *children become the messages they get the most.* Though I think it is a pretty intuitive and reasonable concept, I feel the need to thoroughly convince you of the profound value of messages to your children's development. To really win you over, I want to explain the why and the what of messages.

WHY MESSAGES?

I've always been a bit of a tech geek and first adopter and, for some time, I've been blogging on the psychology of technology for a variety of Web sites. One concept that I come across frequently in the technology world is "default." For those of you not familiar with what a default is in tech-speak, it's defined as a "preset option: an option that will automatically be selected by a computer if the user does not choose another alternative." Although I didn't understand why for some time, the idea of defaults has always resonated with me and struck me as meaningful on a psychological level.

You may be wondering what a computer default has to do with raising children. Well, in raising your children, whether you realize it or not, you're creating a set of default options for just about every aspect of their lives. To paraphrase the computer definition above, these defaults are "automatically selected by children if they do not deliberately choose another option." In other words, your children's defaults are reflexive responses to their life experiences, including their first thoughts, emotions, decisions, and actions in any given situation. Defaults, whether healthy or unhealthy, are very important for children because they are the first options that will arrive in their "inbox" when they are faced with a choice. If you can "install" healthy defaults in your children, you are increasing the chances that they will choose the healthy option over other alternatives that might be more attractive to them, but would also be potentially harmful.

The Importance of Defaults

There are several reasons why defaults are so important for children. The cognitive sciences have demonstrated that people in general attempt to be as efficient as possible in choosing and taking courses of action. This means that whatever mechanism will enable children to come to a decision most quickly will likely determine the course they choose. Defaults provide that efficient mechanism.

Also, recent neuropsychological research has shown that the prefrontal cortex, the part of the brain associated with so-called executive functioning—such as impulse control, risk/reward comparisons, future planning, and decision making—is still developing well into children's teenage years. This means that, without proper defaults, children are not only more likely to act without thinking, but also more readily swayed by external forces, such as peer pressure and popular culture. In other words, children will usually have knee-jerk reactions to, rather than make deliberate decisions about, the situations they face. Whether children have healthy defaults, unhealthy defaults, or no defaults at all will, to a large extent, dictate what their reactions will be.

How Defaults Develop

Defaults develop early in your children's lives from several sources. Role-modeling from parents, peers, and other people visible in the lives of young children provides them with their earliest exposure to defaults. When your children see influential people in their lives—and you are, by far, the most important people in their lives—act a certain way in various situations, they internalize those reactions as their own defaults. You can see the power of this role-modeling effect in simple ways, such as the body language and vocabulary your children pick up from you. Once your children develop language skills, you can shape their defaults by discussing appropriate behavior after teachable moments that arise in situations and in conversations. Ultimately, defaults are instilled through sheer repetition; the more your children see and hear the same messages, and act and react in the same way themselves, the more deeply ingrained those defaults become and the more likely those defaults will direct their behavior in the future.

Types of Defaults

The values that your children internalize can act as defaults because values will be the first "gatekeeper" in choosing a particular course of action. If your children's default values include honesty, responsibility, and generosity, then when they are faced with situations that trigger these value defaults, they will be more likely to, for example, tell the truth, accept blame, and help others. And, given all of the bad values in the messages that they are getting from popular culture these days, it is an immense challenge to instill healthy values in your children. Unfortunately, once your children leave the nest, most of the values to which they are exposed, for instance, those conveyed by popular culture, will not be healthy ones. If you can inculcate positive values through good messages early in your children's lives, you'll be setting value defaults that will make them more impervious to the unhealthy values they will confront once they enter the larger social (and digital) world.

The attitudes that your children develop about themselves— self-esteem, self-respect, confidence, willingness to take risks, patience, and hard work—will become defaults when they face challenges in different aspects of their lives, such as in school and relationships. These attitudes are initially created through the quality of your relationship with your children and the messages you send them about your attitude toward them.

Defaults related to children's physical health become habits that guide their physical life. Eating, exercise, and sleep defaults can set the stage for their long-term physical health (or ill health). When you look at the unhealthy diets and lack of physical activity among so many children these days, and the unhealthy defaults that get established at such a young age, you can understand why obesity among children has reached epidemic proportions.

How children occupy their free time (For example, do they read or watch television?) and how they play early in their lives (Do they play tag in the backyard or video games indoors?) can set their default for how they spend their playtime and respond to boredom in their later childhood years. Early use (or overuse) of entertainment and social media—for example, television, computers, smartphones, and video games, all of which have become so prevalent in recent years—is creating an entirely new set of defaults that were simply unavailable in generations past.

Early social patterns also become defaults that will affect their relationships in later childhood and into adulthood. The messages young children get about how they interact with others determine whether their social defaults trigger, for example, kindness, compassion, respect, and cooperation, or selfishness, antipathy, rudeness, and contention.

No Guarantees, But . . .

Even if your children develop healthy defaults, does this ensure that they won't do anything stupid, mean, or unhealthy? Of course not. Just as computers have bugs, glitches, lockups, and crashes no matter how well they are programmed and maintained, your children will need to be refreshed and updated periodically. But if your children are well programmed from the start, then you can be hopeful that those darling little "computers" will function productively and happily for many years to come.

Defaults for Parents, Too

The notion of defaults doesn't just apply to children. They can also play a big role in your parenting as your children get older. Think of it this way. In the first years of parenting, you send a variety of messages to your children through many different conduits. The quality and quantity of messages you send and the specific conduits through which you send them become internalized and, as a result, become your defaults for what messages you send and how you send them as your children develop.

Let's be realistic. Sending positive messages is, in many ways, easier when your children are young because they remain inside the "family bubble" with few outside influences, either on them or on you. But once they enter the social and cultural world of school, the number and intensity of messages from the "real world" ratchet up a great deal for both of you. Your children are exposed to many messages from their peers and popular culture that aren't healthy. That is obviously where the importance of early positive messaging from you comes in; those messages establish healthy defaults that will help your children resist the later noxious messages.

But you, too, are exposed to many messages from your peers and popular culture that are equally harmful. You will feel pressure from these messages to "keep up with the Joneses," for example, to push your children to get better grades or win more in sports, which may leave you vulnerable to sending them messages that you don't really believe. Here is where the real benefits of early beneficial messaging and creating healthy defaults in *you* come in. When you create positive defaults for the messages you communicate to your children and the conduits through which you send them, you gird yourself against the toxic messages that you will surely receive as your children get older.

WHAT MESSAGES?

The most important thing that you can do to ensure that your children get the right messages is to know what those right messages are. This understanding is not a given for new parents. To the contrary, expectant and new parents often don't give much thought to this aspect of their young children's development simply because they have other more pressing priorities in caring for their children, namely, managing their sleeping, crying, feeding, and pooping. Before parents know it, their infants become children and, because raising children doesn't get any easier, other priorities arise and parents still don't seem to have the time or energy to devote to these all-important developmental concerns. Without deliberate consideration of what messages you want to communicate to your young children, the result is that, at best, the messages you do send will be random and largely missed by them. And at worst, you will send an entirely wrong set of messages to them.

The question that you have to ask yourself is: How do we figure out what the right messages are? Before I share a process you can use to flesh out those messages, I thought that you might find interesting the findings of a survey that asked children four to eleven years old what they wanted from their parents. First, they wanted more attention from their parents and for their parents to be more available. The children wished they had more solo time with each parent and that they could choose what they did with them. They said that they definitely wanted rules even though they often resist them. The children in the survey wanted their parents to protect and love them in more noticeable ways, so they would feel safer in a world which they feel is out of control. For example, they really liked spontaneous expressions of love and being checked on at night. These children did not like being yelled at by their parents. Finally, they said that they enjoyed "family rituals, routines, and predictability." As the saying goes, "Out of the mouths of babes . . ."

In-depth discussions about parenting philosophies and styles should be prerequisites, ideally, before couples have children (or even before they get married), but realistically, if you have these conversations any time before your children reach toddlerhood, you are ahead of the game compared to most parents. In my practice and my group of friends with children, I'm amazed at how little discussion there is about parenting approaches and the lack of consensus that many couples have in how they want to raise their children.

A good place to begin this discussion is to each share your own experiences as children, since most of us either copy or try to do the opposite of what our parents did with us. Examine what messages each of you received as children, how those messages played out in the formation of who you are in adulthood, and how they might affect your parenting:

- What was the emotional tone and style of your family life when you were a child? For example, was it calm and re-served or expressive and chaotic?
- What values were expressed in your family, such as faith, charity, achievement, or fitness?
- What attitudes or beliefs were evident in your family, for example, humility, compassion, hope?
- What activities and experiences did your family share, for instance, sports, games, or gardening?

- What healthy messages did you receive as a child that you want to pass along to your children?
- What unhealthy messages did you receive as a child that you don't want your children to get?

Note that I used rather positive examples, but the above list could just as easily include anger, bigotry, selfishness, and alcohol abuse.

Then, talk about the messages that each of you believe are most important to instill in your children. Ask yourselves the following questions:

- What values do you most want to instill in your children?
- What beliefs about themselves do you want your children to gain?
- What attitudes toward others and the world do you want your children to develop?
- What values, beliefs, and attitudes do you want to protect your children from?
- What activities and experiences can you share with your children to communicate healthy messages and obviate unhealthy messages?

Based on both my professional experience and the answers that Sarah and I arrived at in response to these questions, *Your Children Are Listening* offers what I consider to be nine of the most important messages that young children need to get from you: love, competence, security, compassion, gratitude, Earth, respect, responsibility, and emotion. At the same time, I encourage you to explore messages that may differ from mine. Though I believe that my nine messages transcend individual and cultural differences, the reality is that people's values, beliefs, and attitudes, which act as the source of the messages, can vary based on upbringing, culture, faith, and any number of other factors. As your own ideas about the messages you want your children to get become clear, you can substitute or complement those that I have offered. Regardless of the messages you decide to emphasize with your children, you can use the information and strategies that I offer in this book to convey them in the most effective way.

Of course, this discussion won't conclude in one sitting, but rather should be an ongoing conversation as you gain new information and perspectives, have fresh ideas, and as your positions shift and the messages that you value most become clarified and prioritized. Your goal is to establish an agreed-upon set of messages and create a powerful and united front that will increase the chances of your children getting the messages that you want them to get.

One important benefit of having this discussion early and often is that you can frequently resolve conflicts before they arise. For example, before we had Catie and Gracie, Sarah and I read a lot of parenting books and talked to many parents about how they were raising their children. Though we were of like minds on most things, we didn't agree on everything at first—for example, how much popular culture to which we should expose our girls. Where there were differences, we discussed them and found consensus. We were able to prevent a lot of potential disagreements and create a unified front about how to raise Catie and Gracie before they were even born. Once they were born, when conflicts arose, we reminded each other of our earlier discussions and considered any new information or experiences that might have changed our views, which minimized our disagreements about our messages.

There may not always be middle ground or compromises on message issues; you and your spouse may just disagree. In this case, someone has to give, otherwise your children will get mixed messages, which will not do them a bit of good. One of you should accede to the other in the name of a cohesive message if one feels strongly about an issue and can offer a compelling argument for his or her position. This kind of conflict can be particularly touchy on fundamentally important messages, for example, those related to religious belief (e.g., Christian vs. Jewish), exposure to popular culture (video-game player vs. book reader), and health and eating habits (vegetarian vs. omnivore). There is not necessarily a right choice in these types of message disagreements. What is most important is to place the interests of your children ahead of your own and to consider each position as it relates to their long-term health and development.

Sarah and I have found that when we set our ideologies and stubbornness aside, one of us can convince the other that one message will be better for Catie and Gracie. Though it always hurts to "lose" these arguments, it also feels good to do the right thing for our girls. Thoughtful and dispassionate discussion, an atmosphere of mutual respect, and the shared goal of finding solutions to the message conflict that best serve your children can ensure that the two of you minimize the conflict and maximize the good messages you are sending to your children.

This open line of communication also enables you to adapt to situations in which, as the poet Robert Burns reminds us, "The best laid schemes o' mice an' men gang aft agley" (often go awry). Parenting theory often doesn't jive with parenting reality mainly because, although you've read all of those parenting books, your children haven't. Reality has a way of throwing cold water on both the specific messages we want our children to get and the way we send them. The frequent disconnect between what parenting books tell you will work and what actually works demands that you remain flexible in your messaging.

You may want to develop some practical guidelines about the messages you want to communicate based on these discussions. For example, Sarah and I agreed that before telling Catie or Gracie that something is okay to do, we will first speak to each other to find out what is going on and to ensure that the girls aren't trying to play us off each other. And we agreed that when a particular situation arises, for example, Gracie hits Catie, we will always send a specific message, that Gracie must not only apologize for hitting her sister but also say precisely what she is sorry for ("I'm sorry for hitting you, Catie") and give Catie a gentle touch.

You can also assign particular roles depending on your temperaments and styles. Some parents are better suited to be the bad cop (meaning a little more firm; that's me in our family) and others to being the good cop (meaning a little more nurturing and patient; that would be Sarah). In other words, play to your strengths. If you're just not good at sending the message that you both have agreed on, it's better to send no message at all and send your children to your spouse for the message. In fact, different parenting styles can be a strength in families because couples can provide a wider range of message conduits and styles to get a message across to their children.

GOOD VERSUS BAD MESSAGES

Of course, you love your children and want to send them the very healthiest messages so they internalize the most positive values, beliefs, and attitudes about themselves and the world. But, as many adult children know in looking back on their own parents and upbringing, "The road to hell is paved with good intentions." Parents send many wonderful messages to their children, but they also often send less-than-healthy messages that children may adopt and carry with them into adulthood. Let's be realistic. Because we are, first and foremost, human beings with strengths and flaws, we can expect to send our children messages that are both healthy and unhealthy. We don't mean to send bad messages, of course; we all want what's best for our children. But whether out of lack of awareness, misguided intentions, self-interest, baggage, or just plain unhealthy values, we are vulnerable to sending messages to our children that can interfere with their healthy development. And the real concern is that our children will pick up those less-than-admirable messages and make them their own.

I realize that I'm wading into sensitive territory here, because this discussion involves making judgments about the messages we send to our children. And I don't want to suggest that I am the final arbiter of what is good or bad, healthy or unhealthy for your children. At the same time, I don't think it's that controversial to say that there are messages that we can all agree are beneficial to children. Messages about the values of integrity, compassion, hard work, and accountability would seem to fit nicely into this category. I also believe that there would be widespread agreement that some messages are harmful to children. I would place messages that convey the values of greed, selfishness, callousness, and mean-spiritedness in this category. Yet I don't think I would be going out on a limb by suggesting that parents today (not to mention popular culture) often communicate "bad" messages to their children.

And believe me: You are not alone in sometimes sending unhealthy messages to your children. In a survey of more than 1,600 parents with children between the ages of five and seventeen, the substantial majority said that it was "absolutely essential" that they teach their children to develop self-control, save money, be honest, be independent, do their best in school, have good eating habits, and be well mannered. Yet when asked if they succeeded in sending messages that affirm these beliefs, the discrepancy between the belief and success in conveying the message ranged from 22 percent (e.g., 84 percent of parents believed that they should teach their children to be polite, but only 62 percent felt they had succeeded at sending that message) to 49 percent (e.g., 83 percent believed in the value of self-control, but only 34 percent see themselves as having succeeded in giving that message). As one father who was interviewed put it, "My challenge is I need to be more focused on discipline and all that. Life is so short; I want to have fun."

As you are reading this section, I recommend that you consider what messages you may have received during your childhood or later in life that you may inadvertently be passing on to your children. This process of "looking in the mirror" can be painful because no one likes to look at their baggage and weaknesses. At the same time, it is an act of courage, resolve, and unselfishness to be willing to face your demons for the good of your children. Many of the parents I work with make this commitment, and the result is life-changing for the children. You give your children a lifelong gift when you don't send them unhealthy messages that your parents may have sent you (or that you picked up elsewhere along the way).

To be a good role model for you, I'll share with you (with Sarah's permission) two bad messages that Sarah and I worry about passing on to my daughters. I have control issues. Though I'm not precisely a control freak in the generally accepted sense of the term, admittedly, when things don't go as expected, for example we're running late or Catie and Gracie aren't being cooperative, I can get stressed out and be pretty darned stern. When our girls push my "control button," I send them messages of inflexibility, frustration, and disapproval, no doubt tinged with anger (though I am not a yeller).

In turn, one of Sarah's "hot buttons" is worrying about being judged by other people, particularly as it relates to her parenting. This sensitivity to what others might think about her can cause Sarah to get angry and be overly controlling with the girls because she's worried that they will be too loud or rude, even when they aren't by most standards. Such "out of control" behavior would then reflect badly on Sarah as a mother. The messages that the girls might get include feelings of shame for disappointing Sarah, and the idea that they have to be perfect or they won't be valued by their mother and others. These messages could then quash their playfulness and spontaneity.

Both Sarah and I are painfully aware of these and other types of baggage we carry, and we do our best to resist these personal demons. But as we are decidedly flawed human beings, we accept that if we can keep our unhealthy messages to a minimum and the healthy messages to a maximum, our girls will not only survive but also thrive. In these efforts, we may just finally figure out how to unpack our baggage, which will make all of the Taylors much happier people.

The upside to knowing your baggage is the realization that you have the power to change the messages you convey to your children. Once you accept the fact that you, like all people, have flaws that might cause you to communicate unhealthy messages to your children, you can learn to be conscious of those messages, take control of them, and stop sending (or at least send fewer) messages that may not be healthy for your children.

There are no magic steps to recognizing the unhealthy messages that you may be predisposed to communicate to your children. Perhaps it's looking back on your childhood and recalling how bad it felt when your parents sent you certain messages—for example, messages of needing to be perfect to earn their love. Or seeing another parent send the same unhealthy message that you have been conveying to your children and being appalled by the message and saddened by their children's reaction, for instance, seeing another parent get angry at their child when he makes a mess. Or putting yourself in your children's shoes and seeing their reaction to your message, for example, imagining how they feel when you constantly correct their language mistakes. In all these cases, insight is likely to hit you like a ton of bricks and motivate you to change your messages for the sake of your children.

Another thing you'll realize as you become more conscious of your messages is that you won't be able to recognize and preempt all of the bad messages you may be communicating to your children. I can assure you that both Sarah and I were shocked with some frequency by the messages that we would send to Catie and Gracie that we either hadn't predicted in our many earlier discussions or that we didn't think we were capable of conveying. Parents can even say what would seem to us to be fairly innocuous things and still send a powerful message to their children that they won't forget. For example, on several occasions while shopping in the downtown district of a nearby town, Sarah has expressed concern about getting a parking ticket. Now, Catie, at five years old, worries about getting a parking ticket whenever we visit that part of the town. As I'm sure you have already discovered, because parenting can be so overwhelming and stressful, it can bring out the worst in us and highlight the darkest parts of who we are. But you shouldn't beat yourself up over that epiphany; it's just part of being human. Thankfully, most of the time, parenting brings out the best of who we are because we are driven to love, protect, and do right by those little beings who are our children.

Another problem with "bad" messages involves not just the content of the messages, but also how they are communicated to your children. You may have the best intentions to convey a very positive message, but the way that you send it can change that message into something very different that is not healthy for your children. For example, you may want to send your children a message about the admirable value of hard work and achievement. But the way you send that message is by constantly nagging them to do their homework, materially rewarding them for good grades, and showing disappointment and frustration when they fail to live up to your expectations. Given these surface messages, it's likely that your intended message will be masked by the more explicit messages of mistrust, conditional love, and anger.

The important thing to remember is that your influence over your children is a two-sided coin. Yes, you can do great harm to your children by sending them bad messages. At the same time, with the right message, you have the power to do wonderful things for them. If this discussion raises any red flags for you, don't take it as an indictment of you or your parenting. Instead, take it as a call to action to do what is best for your children.

LET GO OF PERFECT MESSAGING

You may now be thinking how much pressure there will be on you to always send the right messages to your children—to be on message 24/7. Fortunately, I don't believe in perfect parenting—a truly unattainable goal—because before we are parents we are human beings, flaws and all. Also, kids are very resilient. They can have a lot of bad stuff thrown their way, and they still turn out just fine most of the time. Gosh, children have survived and thrived for ages under much harsher conditions than those found in twenty-first-century America. So accept your humanity and realize that the occasional outburst of anger, show of impatience, or act of expediency won't hurt your children. I hope the message you're getting is that even if you send the wrong messages sometimes you won't be a bad parent and you won't scar your children for life. The key is to make sure the *preponderance* of your messages are good ones. If you can maximize the healthy messages and minimize the unhealthy messages, your children will turn out just fine (all else being equal, of course).

META-MESSAGES

When you communicate a message to your children, you're actually conveying two messages. The first message is overt and clear to your children, for example, be nice to your sister or clean your room (messages of kindness and responsibility, respectively). The second more subtle meta-message underlies the obvious message and communicates more elemental lessons about the world. For instance, when you get into a battle of wills with your children over bringing their dishes to the sink after dinner, the message may be "You have responsibilities that you must fulfill." The meta-message may be "Ultimately, I am the boss, and you must do what I say sometimes even when you don't want to do it." Or, when you require that your children donate some of their allowance to a charity of their choice, the message is "We value compassion and helping others less fortunate than us." The meta-message is "We should be grateful for what we have."

Behind almost every message is a meta-message. As you think about and formulate messages for your children, you should also be aware of the meta-messages that lurk just below the surface of your messages. You want to ensure that your meta-messages are both healthy and supportive of the overt messages you send to your children.

YOUR CHILDREN SEND MESSAGES, TOO

Though my focus in *Your Children Are Listening* is on how you can send healthy messages to your children, the message highway is not one way. Your children are constantly sending you messages that you may or may not be getting or interpreting correctly. Your ability to receive and understand those messages can help you send your children the best messages in the best way (and to know when to stop sending or to change your messages).

Children are incredibly good at sending their parents messages about how they are doing at any given moment in time. If your children are anything like our girls, they are very good at sending the message that they are cranky, but parents often miss the meta-message. For example, when Catie or Gracie throw a tantrum, it's easy to conclude from that very loud message that they are being babies or brats. But the meta-message is, more often than not, that they are feeling scared, unsupported, hungry, or tired. Clearly, how Sarah and I interpret this very emotional message determines, for instance, whether we respond with our own frustrations and harsh tones or with empathy and kindness.

Your children will also tell you how well your messages are getting through to them. You can judge the effectiveness of your "message transmission" by seeing whether your children's words, emotions, or behavior are consistent with your messages. For example, if they are saying please and thank you, responding constructively to feelings of frustration, or bringing their dishes to the sink after meals, then you are getting a pretty clear message that they are receiving your messages about manners, emotional maturity, and family responsibility, respectively. If they aren't sending you such affirming messages or are, in fact, sending contradictory ones, that is another powerful message in itself, namely, that something is blocking your messages from getting through, they are not understanding your messages as intended, something is motivating them to act counter to your messages, or they just haven't gotten your message enough. You can use this information to figure out how to alter the message so it will get through and produce the desired change in them.

Your children will often send you a message that it is time to change your message. Think about it this way. The point of sending a message is to get it in their heads. But when you send the same message too often, it can get crowded in their heads and that is really annoying for children. In fact, when I work with young people, I know they are getting my messages when they tell me that I'm really irritating them. It's the same with my girls. I have to admit that I can get pretty heavy handed and preachy in my desire to get a message across to them. When I send a message one too many times, Catie will look at me with an exasperated look, give me the "talk to the hand" sign, and say "DAAAAD, I know!" So I get her message and back off or send a different message. Her message is one of irritation, but her meta-message is, "I got the message, you don't need to keep sending it!"

2

Are Your Messages Getting Through?

By this point, I hope you have bought into the power of messages in your children's lives. The question you may now be asking is: "So how do I get these messages across to my kids?" Before you can take actual steps to convey specific messages, you need to understand the various ways in which you communicate them to your children.

A recent study compiled a list of the top ten competencies that, according to decades of research, lead children to positive outcomes, specifically, healthy relationships with their parents, health, happiness, and success. This study supports my belief that it is not

MESSAGE CONDUITS

- What you say
- What you feel
- What you do
- Who you are
- What your children do

only what you do for your children, but also who you are that makes a difference.

In the category of what you do directly to your children, the research found that, not unexpectedly, love and affection are the number-one predictors of raising healthy children. Also, not surprisingly, the study reported that parents are generally quite good at expressing love and affection. Other "parenting techniques" that emerged were teaching children to be become independent, promoting learning and education, using behavior management strategies to reinforce good behavior, exposing children to a spiritual life, and ensuring their safety.

Yet just as important as anything you specifically do to your children, the study highlighted the importance of messages you send through modeling who *you* are. In fact, after love and affection, the second and third most important parenting competencies are your ability to manage stress effectively and to have a positive relationship with your spouse. It seems that how you handle crises and maintain relationships send powerful messages to your children that translate into whether they develop those capabilities as well. A worrisome finding, though, was that parents rate themselves rather poorly on these two essential competencies. Other skills that affect your children include providing for their basic needs, planning for the future, and leading a healthy lifestyle that combines exercise and good eating habits. A final result of the study worth mentioning is that parents who actively seek to educate themselves about child-rearing "best practices" tend to produce better outcomes. Such parents have better relationships with their children, and their children are healthier, happier, and more successful.

MESSAGE CONDUITS

What you say. Your messages come from what you say to your children directly. For example, "What you did was not kind!" or "You were so generous in sharing your toys with Sofia." Before you tell your children something that you believe has an important message in it, be sure to consider what the real message you want to communicate is and if your words will best convey that message. For instance, a key message that I believe all children should get early and often is the need to be helpful around the house (see chapter 11 for more). In response to their children being helpful, most parents say something like, "You are such a good boy (or girl)." What message does this impart? That when your children do good, they are good and when they don't, they are bad? This is not a great message because it focuses on who the child is, not on what he or she did to deserve that positive message. The purpose of messages is to encourage attitudes and behaviors you want them to absorb and repeat in the future. If you want your children to learn to be helpful, a better message might be, "You were so helpful. Mommy really appreciates what you have done." Could your messages be any simpler or more direct? Be aware, though, that verbal messages have their limits with younger children because their language skills are still quite rudimentary. If they don't have a great command of language yet, they won't understand what you are saying and won't get the message. In this case, other message conduits, such as those described below, will be more effective.

What you feel. You send messages to your children through your emotional content, such as tone of voice, facial expressions, and body language. In fact, your emotional messages may be the most powerful because children, as not yet fully developed verbal beings, are highly attuned to their parents' emotions. Make no mistake about it, your children will pick up your emotional messages more quickly and effectively than any other message. If you are angry, they will get that message. If you are sad, they will know it. If you are happy, they will feel it. No matter what you say! Even if you say or do something to cover up your emotions, it's likely your feelings will come through. And, if your children get different messages through your words, emotions, and actions, your emotional messages will take precedence in your children's psyches.

That's why it's so important to make sure that your verbal, behavioral, and emotional messages are aligned. Especially with young children with limited language capabilities, you can say something, and even if they don't understand the words, if the message is infused with the appropriate emotional content, then they will nonetheless get the deeper message. And if you can use multiple conduits, that is, combine words, actions, and emotions, you send a truly resonant message that your children won't be likely to miss.

What you do. The cliché "actions speak louder than words" is as true with children, if not truer, as with anyone else. Young children are incredibly alert to what you do. They are watching and listening even when you don't think they are. I'm sure you've been in a situation where your children mimicked your facial expressions, body language, words, and behavior before you even realized how you were expressing yourself in those ways. Put simply, your children want to do what you do. That influence bestows on you extraordinary power as a role model. But, as the saying goes, with great power comes great responsibility. Yes, this realization might instill in you great fear that your children might pick up some of your less admirable messages. At the same time, you also possess the ability to model wonderfully positive behavior.

Who you are. When I talk about communicating messages to your children through your words, emotions, and actions, I don't just mean the messages that are aimed at them specifically for their consumption. In fact, the way you interact with the world outside your direct relationship with your children, and the messages that you send to them inadvertently just by being who you are, may have an equally influential effect on them. For example, your relationships with others in your life; your work, avocations, and interests; your emotional reactions; and your conversations with others during which your children are within earshot all convey powerful messages to your children.

This influence of the messages you send to your children by just being you can be a two-sided coin. The positive side of the coin is shiny and smooth, and gives you the ability to convey really wonderful messages. For example, if you devote your free time to working at a homeless shelter, are a voracious reader, stay calm in emotional storms, or are an affectionate spouse, you send your children really healthy messages.

The other side of the coin, however, is more tarnished and rough. As I have mentioned previously, one thing that people often forget is that parents are, first and foremost, human beings who bring lots of good stuff to their role as parents but also probably bring some baggage that can prevent them from sending the most positive messages to their children. These less-than-healthy messages are also expressed in the totality of who you are: how you describe the world, the emotions that dominate your life, and the behavior you engage in day to day. For example, if you are critical and catty toward others, yell when angry, or treat your mother badly, you are sending decidedly unhealthy messages to your children. Your goal and challenge is to highlight and communicate the positive aspects of who you are and be aware of and mitigate the less attractive qualities that you, like all parents, possess.

Recent neurological research is shedding light on the incredible power parents have as role models, why their influence is so potent, and what areas of development are influenced by role modeling. The "mirror neuron system" is believed to be an area of the brain that is activated when children simply watch others. It has been implicated in the healthy development of empathy, nonverbal communication, emotional recognition, social behavior, motor skills, and language. Damage to the mirror neuron system has also been suggested as a possible contributor to autism. What this research tells us is that the messages that your children get from you are not just "psychological," but rather can become hard wired into their brains and affect them for their lifetimes.

What your children do. Your actions speak louder than your words, but your children's own actions speak louder than your words or actions. What this means is that the more you can get your children to engage in words, emotions, and actions that represent the message you want to communicate, the more directly and powerfully they will and adopt it as their own. In other words, when your children talk, feel, or act in ways that convey a message—for example, being loving to you, sharing with a sibling, or cleaning up their bedroom—they are actually sending a positive message to themselves that they can't misinterpret. These messages carry extra weight because children are both the sender and the recipient of the messages, and action is the best way for these messages to become deeply embedded.

MESSAGE STRATEGIES

Within the general types of conduits I just described through which you communicate messages to your children, there are specific strategies that are the actual means by which the messages are transmitted. The aim of each strategy is to provide a pathway for your messages into your children's minds.

MESSAGE STRATEGIES

- Catchphrases
- Routines and rituals
- Activities
- Outside support

Catchphrases. For just about every message we want to communicate to Catie and Gracie, Sarah or I create a catchphrase or, even better, the girls come up with a catchphrase (e.g., for patience, "It's great to wait"). These catchphrases are usually jokey or goofy, easy to remember, and tangible; they're not ethereal theories or concepts, but down-to-earth ideas and actions. They're also "sticky," meaning the girls retain them. Our catchphrases are also often created spontaneously based on something one of us says or does. For example, Catie came up with "The Look" (see chapter 10). Because they are memorable and playful, Catie and Gracie enjoy repeating and making games out of them (e.g., returning to the patience catchphrase, "It's crate to gate. It's blate to nate. It's tate to zate!"). All of these qualities mean that the girls remember and connect the catchphrases to the underlying messages we want them to get. Each of the nine messages described in *Your Children Are Listening* has a catchphrase associated with it, and I offer several catchphrases in each chapter, so as you progress through the book, you'll see plenty of examples of how to connect a message to a catchphrase.

Routines and rituals. As I mentioned earlier, repetition is an essential part of transmitting messages, and rituals provide that consistent replication. Routines and rituals communicate messages not only by what you say or do but also, more powerfully, by the actions your children themselves take. Plus, when they engage in routines and rituals and experience the positive consequences, your children gain "buy-in" and ownership of the messages, which is essential for their long-term adoption of those messages.

There is a significant body of literature that supports the importance of routines and rituals in children's intellectual, emotional, social, linguistic, and academic development. Routines, such as those at meals and bedtime, have a practical focus that involves accomplishing necessary daily tasks. They offer children a predictable framework that helps them to organize and make sense of the steadily growing world in which they live. Routines allow children to practice important competencies such as dressing, bathing, and grooming. They also provide children with a sense of familiarity, control, and comfort that instills the sense of security and stability that is so fundamental to development.

Rituals, such as Sunday dinners and holiday celebrations with extended family, carry with them a deeper meaning, sending messages of connectedness and spirituality to children. They are often seen as special activities that are unique to individual families and, as such, encourage love, closeness, and support. Rituals create an emotional tone in a family that shapes how children experience, interpret, and express emotions. Rituals such as religious ceremonies, family camping trips, or cultural pursuits convey messages about what families value most.

We regularly establish routines and rituals that further emphasize the messages we want Catie and Gracie to get from us. For example, we want to send them the messages of tidiness and responsibility for their belongings, so every evening before they go to bed, our girls pile their books on the coffee table in our living room and put away their toys in their bedrooms. Their morning routine involves making their beds and getting dressed before breakfast on school days. The messages embedded in this routine are preparedness and cooperation on busy school mornings.

Rituals that we practice regularly are moments of gratitude before dinner, Tuesdays with their grandmother, and regular hikes on a nearby mountain. These rituals, which are special to Catie and Gracie, convey messages of appreciation, connection to extended family, and reverence for nature and fitness, respectively.

I have noticed that our routines and rituals seem to emerge, transform, and ultimately fade away, to be replaced by others. Out of no conscious decision on our part, they appear to run their course as new capabilities, thought processes, or experiences trigger new routines and rituals that replace the old ones. When you recognize that old routines and rituals have limited "shelf lives" and new ones evolve naturally, you can ensure that the messages that underlie them stay fresh and compelling for your children. *Your Children Are Listening* will offer a variety of routines and rituals that may be associated with important messages.

Activities. Because what you and your children do has a greater effect on them than what you say, the most direct way to communicate messages is to engage your children in activities in which the messages are embedded. These message-laden activities exist everywhere in your family's lives: when you cook a meal, do chores around the house, play games, read books, go on outings . . . The list is almost endless. When you provide opportunities for your children to participate in activities that convey meaningful messages, you allow them to experience firsthand the messages' inherent value while observing their many benefits.

Outside support. You can't communicate all of the messages you want to send to your children by yourself. You need to enlist help from the world around you so that your children are enveloped in a cocoon of healthy messages before they leave that protective nest and venture out into a world that is full of anything-but-healthy messages. Outside support can come from your extended family and friends, the schools your children go to, the houses of worship your family attends, and the extracurricular activities in which your children participate. The more sources from which your children receive positive messages, the more likely they will be to see their value and adopt them as their own. Research demonstrates the value that outside support provides parents in sending healthy messages to their children. For example, a study of children who participated in Boys and Girls Clubs of America, as compared to others who did not, had stronger self-concepts and better social skills, received more reinforcement for positive behaviors, engaged in fewer problem behaviors, and were less vulnerable to unhealthy influences.

USE MULTIPLE CONDUITS

Research has shown that children possess different learning styles, typically categorized as visual (by watching), auditory (by listening), kinesthetic (by doing), reading/writing, and tactile (by feeling). Ideally, you should send messages through the conduits that play to your children's learning strengths, thus increasing the likelihood that your messages will get through. At the same time, despite children's specific learning styles, when you send messages through multiple conduits that engage their dominant and nondominant learning styles, you will get the messages through to your children in more and different ways. And when these multiplied and diverse avenues embed the message in your children through different psychological and physiological systems, the message will be grasped more deeply and completely.

LOUDSPEAKER VERSUS STEALTH MESSAGES

You can convey messages to your children either directly or indirectly. "Loudspeaker" messages include telling your children the message you want them to get, pointing it out in other people, or telling stories with the specific message in mind. These straightforward messages ensure that there is no confusion about your intent and that your children are paying attention and are focused on the message. The risk with direct messages is that your children may get fed up with all of your messaging and resist the messages out of sheer irritation with you.

In contrast, "stealth" messages are those which leave your children completely unaware that what they are doing is connected with a message, for example, participating in activities or playing games. Let them think they are having fun or just helping you out. You know that your message is sneaking past them into their little minds.

LET YOUR CHILDREN HELP
SHAPE YOUR MESSAGES

Children have an amazing ability to send their parents signals about the messages they might need at any given time or the best way to send a message so that they will be receptive. It's up to you to "have your radio tuned to their frequency" so you pick up on those signals. Your children will have experiences, challenges, and reactions every day that should alert you to great opportunities to communicate messages to your children.

Let your children guide you in how best to send your messages. Listen and watch for opportunities that can be turned into catchphrases, routines and rituals, and activities that convey the messages you want. Kids are also creative and playful, and as a result, can turn a serious message into serious fun, which increases their attention to the message and their desire to act on that message.

FOUR KEYS TO MESSAGE SUCCESS

Your greatest challenge in sending healthy messages to your children involves getting those messages to really sink in. Patience, repetition, persistence, and perseverance are the most powerful tools you have for meeting that challenge. Effective message retention, defined as your children receiving, assimilating, and expressing the desired messages, depends on communicating messages over

FOUR KEYS TO MESSAGE SUCCESS

- Patience
- Repetition
- Persistence
- Perseverance

and over and over again. I have found that the best way to tell that our messages are getting through to Catie and Gracie is when the messages begin to irritate them. Their irritation indicates that they are paying attention and we are getting into their heads. Of course, when they send this signal to us, we try to respond by easing up on that message or perhaps switching to another message so they don't get totally annoyed with us.

Patience acts as the foundation for the other three keys to successful messaging. When you make a commitment to deliberate messaging, your first acknowledgment is that, as a parent, you are in it for the long haul. Also, the more experience you gain as a parent, the more you realize that few things related to your children happen overnight (or over a few nights). Just about everything about children takes time, lots of time.

Unfortunately, we live in a culture where we are told that nothing in life should take time or be difficult; "instant" and "effortless" are central to its zeitgeist (celebutantes, microwaves, and Web searches come to mind). Yet, when you buy into this attitude as a parent, you pretty much guarantee a parenting experience replete with frustration, anger, despair, and failure, because this attitude simply can't coexist with the child-rearing universe.

So it all starts with patience, knowing that most of your efforts will not be rewarded for a long time, perhaps months, perhaps years, but it is also grounded in the belief that your commitment and hard work will bear fruit sooner or later. When you begin with this Zen-like patience, you accept obstacles, setbacks, failures, and resistance as part of the long journey of raising your children. Although, because you are human, you will certainly feel some of those less-pleasant emotions associated with raising children, your overall attitude will be one of equanimity in the face of the many challenges that are parents' constant companions. The result is greater resolve, more level-headedness and empathy, less frustration, and most important, a very clear meta-message to your children that "*I am never giving up!*"

Repetition addresses the simple fact that children won't get most messages the first or second or tenth or hundredth time we send them. I read a study not long ago that found that it takes 2,000 repetitions to gain a sports skill. I don't know whether this finding would apply to children absorbing messages from their parents, but, given the number of times we have asked Catie and Gracie to set the table or bring their dishes to the sink or take their shoes off when they enter the house, I'm going to guess that 2,000 is a vast underestimation of the number of repetitions needed for messages to sink in.

And I don't think there is a parent on Earth who would say that it is easy getting to that large number of repetitions. In fact, I would guess that many parents give up long before they hit that magic number. Why? Well, does the image of beating your head against a wall ring any bells for you? That's what it sometimes feels like to us when Sarah and I keep sending Catie and Gracie messages and they just don't get them. What emotions do we typically experience in these situations? Frustration, anger, exhaustion, and despair sum it up pretty well. And when you hit despair, the next reaction is to give up, but there is no place in parenting for surrender, because when you throw in the towel you're really giving up on your children. The result? They lose. That's where the next three keys come into play.

That is why persistence may be the single most necessary tool for getting messages across to your children. Even when your children seem not to be listening (though they actually are), when they don't seem to be getting the messages (the blank stare), when they are acting contrary to your messages (just to test your limits), your commitment to those messages and your willingness to persist against such discouragement will ultimately determine whether your children truly get your messages. You must be doggedly persistent; you just have to stick with it no matter how little appears to be getting through those thick skulls of theirs.

Your children may not seem to be listening to anything you say. It's easy to get frustrated and give up: "Why should I put so much time and energy into positive messages if my kids aren't paying attention?" But let me assure you that your children are listening, they are watching, and those messages are getting through to them. It may take years for them to finally "get it" enough to act on those messages, but it's worth the wait.

But persistence isn't enough because, more often than not, you are going to hit bumps in the road that will test your mettle. You'll feel like your children are not only missing the messages you send them but also getting their exact opposites. For example, after months of sending your kids the messages "Be nice to your siblings" or "Please don't interrupt when I'm speaking to your mother," they continue to be mean and butt in. Oh, the frustration!

That's where perseverance comes into play. I see perseverance as different from mere persistence. The latter involves just continuing to send the messages under normal conditions. The former means continuing to send the message in the face of setbacks and discouragement. There is no magic to developing perseverance. It starts with an unwavering commitment to do what's best for your children, no matter how tiring, frustrating, or just plain galling it gets. It continues with an ever-conscious awareness of when your children are pushing you to the edge—recognition alone will help prevent you from giving up—and a reaffirmation to continue to send the messages no matter what. Perseverance concludes with a deep faith in the value of your messages to your children. This steadfast conviction that your efforts will eventually be rewarded will provide you with the intestinal fortitude to step back from the precipice, turn around, and continue your journey of healthy messaging for the sake of your children.

MESSAGE RULES

Here are a few simple rules to help ensure that your messages get through loud and clear to your children:

- Be clear: Make sure that your words, emotions, and actions unambiguously communicate the message you want to convey.
- Be simple: Tailor your message to fit your children's level of development.
- Be active: The best way to convey messages is through your actions and the actions of your children.
- Listen to your children: Let them help you decide what messages to communicate and how to send them.
- Immerse your children in messages: The more conduits through which you can send messages to your children— through words emotions, actions, activities, and outside influences—the greater the likelihood they will get the messages.

3

What Can Block Your Messages?

Have you noticed that sometimes your children only need to hear a message once and they get it? And, frustratingly, you can send a message dozens upon dozens of times and it is as if you had never sent the message at all? Well, welcome to the real world of parenting, where nothing goes as expected, what is supposed to work doesn't, what isn't assumed to work does, and what does work only works intermittently or only works for a limited time. It takes detective work and a real understanding of your children to figure out why some messages get through easily and others, despite your best efforts, don't seem to get through at all.

MESSAGE BLOCKERS

- Overly complex messages
- Disconnect between send and receive
- Too many messages
- Inconsistent messages
- Conflicting messages
- Different conduits, different messages
- Fatigue
- Unhappy marriages or divorced parents
- Siblings
- Extended family
- Social world
- Popular culture

Even if you understand the messages you want to communicate to your children, even if you know the conduits through which those messages are conveyed, and even if you have strategies for sending those healthy messages, you can't be sure that those messages will get through. Every time you send a message to your children, it will probably have to navigate its way through a maze of "message blockers" that can deflect, weaken, contaminate, or outright destroy your intended messages to your children. If you can understand these message blockers, you can lessen their impact and increase the chances that your messages will make it into your children's psyches.

OVERLY COMPLEX MESSAGES: "HUH?"

One of the challenges of communicating messages to your children is ensuring that they actually understand the messages you send. The key to this understanding is conveying messages in ways that are appropriate for your children's level of development. I see many parents who send messages that seem perfectly clear to them and then can't understand why their children aren't getting those messages. Even worse, parents then blame their children for not getting their messages. The problem is that parents see their messages through their own eyes rather than through those of their children. But your children don't think the way you do. You have had years of experience during which you have honed your ability to interpret and understand the world. In contrast, your children are still relatively undeveloped when it comes to how they perceive, interpret, analyze, and make decisions about their world, whether they are toddlers, preschoolers, elementary schoolers, or beyond.

This is why you have to walk in your children's shoes. If you were them, what message would you be getting? Consider what unique aspects of their current stage of development will influence how they get the messages you send them; for example, are they more receptive to speech, emotions, or actions? If you can understand their true capabilities at their current age, you will be better able to tailor your messages in ways that are developmentally appropriate and to maximize the chances of their understanding your messages.

DISCONNECT BETWEEN SEND AND RECEIVE: "BUT I DIDN'T MEAN THAT."

A disconnect between sending and receiving can occur in several places. You may intend to send one message but end up sending another. The disconnect here is between your intention and your action. For example, you may intend to communicate to your children the message that they should eat their vegetables because vegetables will help them to grow big and strong, but the actual message you send is that "I get mad at you when you don't eat your vegetables."

The disconnect can also occur between what you send and what your children receive. Don't think about the message you mean to convey, but rather the message your children will probably get. Ask yourself: How clear is my message? If I were three years old, for instance, what message would I get? Here's an example. You work very hard at a job for which you earn a good living that affords your family a comfortable lifestyle. You want to send your children the message that you love your work and taking care of your family is important to you. But the message they get is that "my momma cares more about her job than she does about me." These two very different messages have very different ramifications for your children's perceptions of your work and how you feel about them.

To clarify the messages you send about your work, you could ensure that your children get your real message about taking care of your family by talking to them about why you work so hard and how difficult it is to be away from them. You can also be sure that you spend as much quality time as possible with your children so they get the real message loud and clear: You love them more than anything. You're also modeling the meta-message of how life works: When you grow up there are things you want to do (e.g., be with your children) and there are things that you must do (e.g., support your family).

Also, as mentioned earlier, children have different learning styles that will affect their receptivity to your messages. As your children develop, you will get a sense of what their learning strengths are. With this knowledge, you can tailor your messages to fit their particular style. For instance, let's say you want to send your toddler the message to bring his bowl to the sink after a meal. For an auditory learner, you might explain to him what you want, whereas with a visual learner, you might show him what to do. A disconnect in these areas can doom your message even before it is sent.

Your children also have different temperaments, each of which can affect whether and how they pick up the messages you send them. You should consider your children's inborn temperament when you send messages; are your children stubborn and controlling, or do they have difficulty paying attention? For example, an emotionally sensitive child may be more vulnerable to conflicting, inconsistent, or emotional messages than one who is more stoic.

These examples illustrate the importance of using as many conduits as possible to communicate messages. Because there are so many factors that affect whether your children get the right message, increasing the number of ways you express a message improves the chances that your children will get the message you intend.

INFREQUENT MESSAGES: "HOW MANY TIMES HAVE I TOLD YOU?"

Messages can have a powerful impact on children, if they get through. Some messages are so potent they can get through with just one or two expressions. For example, children don't need to touch a hot stove twice to get the message to stay away from it. But with most messages, the more you "click the send button," the better the chance your children will get them. So if you don't send your children a message with sufficient frequency, it may not sink in.

Everyday life, for most parents, is incredibly busy, with a long list of daily priorities including work, meals, housekeeping, family care, and shopping. And because you're so busy, it's easy for your messages to fall through the cracks. As you're dashing around with too long a to-do list and not enough hours in the day, you might fleetingly think that you'll get to those important messages. But, because family life rarely slows down, such messages continue to be pushed further down the priority list until they are no longer on it.

Here's what is necessary to keep your messaging on track and consistent: You need to keep your messaging on your radar screen as much as possible. Clear the clutter off your fridge and post the important messages that you want to send your children. On your smartphone, set an alarm to remind you throughout the day. Have your spouse prompt you on a regular basis and do the same for him or her.

The nice thing about the catchphrases, routines and rituals, and activities that I'll describe later in *Your Children Are Listening* is that you will have many tools in your "message toolbox" readily available with which to communicate your messages. These tools also allow your messages to become so woven into the fabric of your family's lives that the messages become automatic. You don't need to constantly remind yourself. You don't have to think about them at all. It's just what you do.

TOO MANY MESSAGES: "DO THIS, THAT, AND THE OTHER THING."

One thing you have to be careful of when you commit to conscious messaging is message overload, in other words, trying to convey too many messages to your children at one time. You may get so excited about all of the great messages you can communicate to your children that you start hurling as many messages as possible at them at once. Several problems arise when you become over-zealous about sending messages to your children. First, the messages, rather than being distinct, may amass into an incomprehensible jumble that loses all of its value. Second, your children may be so bombarded by messages that they won't be able to focus adequately on any single message. The worst-case scenario is that, to avoid being overwhelmed by the messages, your children actively resist them and may actually do the exact opposite of what your messages tell them.

The best strategy is to choose and focus on a few messages that are most appropriate to your children's current level of development and life situation. Life has a way of letting parents know what their children need to learn at any given time. For example, if your son isn't sharing with his younger sister or your youngest daughter is hitting her older sister, you are presented with a ready-made "teachable moment" in which to send messages about generosity and kindness, respectively.

INCONSISTENT MESSAGES: "YOU CAN THIS TIME."

Though we may not like to admit it, many of us as parents aren't as consistent as we should be. Too often, we allow our children to do some things sometimes—usually when it's expedient—but not other times. What's the message that your children are getting with these inconsistent messages? At best, they don't get the messages at all. At worst, the contradictory messages confuse them so much that they choose whichever message works best for them, even if it isn't the one you want them to get. Or even worse, they get the meta-message that being inconsistent is okay.

You may find it helpful to ask yourself in what situations you become inconsistent in your messages. It may be when you are under stress, such as when you are trying to get your children out the door in the morning, when one of your children is throwing a tantrum because you don't initially give her what she wants, or when you are trying to get dinner on the table on time at the end of the day. This awareness alone can trigger an internal alarm that reminds you of the need to send messages consistently. You can also develop strategies, such as taking a deep breath or having a keyword that will help you remember the importance of consistency in your messages as you enter those situations that are difficult for you. Both approaches will buttress your resolve during those difficult times when it would be so much easier to send a contradictory message or no message at all.

CONFLICTING MESSAGES: "BUT DADDY SAID . . ."

If you and your spouse send conflicting messages, you pretty much guarantee that your messages won't get through to your children. Not only will your children not get a clear message, but they will be confused by the contradictory messages from such credible sources and may become paralyzed with uncertainty about what your message really is and what you want them to do.

Another problem with conflicting messages, aside from the obvious fact that children won't get a clear message, is that children are amazingly adept at learning which parent will give them what they want. Even as young as age two, children can be incredibly manipulative and capable of playing each parent off each other to get what they want. At the very least, if they don't like the message from their mother ("No, you can't have any candy"), children will try to get a better message from their father ("Here you go, dear").

Conflicting messages arise for a number of reasons. Parents may be carrying different mental templates of what constitutes good parenting from their own upbringings. They may, as a result, have divergent parenting philosophies and styles. Parents may have different personalities and temperaments; for example, one is laid back and one is more intense. They may also have different values, such that one parent thinks certain messages are important and the other parent doesn't. One parent might simply not believe that the other's message is all that important. Or perhaps worst of all, parents may do what is expedient rather than what is in the best interests of their children.

To reduce conflicting messages, parents need to look at their parenting beliefs and explore where the conflicting messages are coming from. As I mentioned in chapter 1, in-depth discussions about parenting philosophies and styles should be prerequisites to identifying and resolving possible conflicts in the messages that you send to your children. In an ideal world, you want to arrive at an accord long before you communicate any messages to your children. In the real world, the sooner you can craft a consistent message, the better it will be for your children.

DIFFERENT CONDUITS, DIFFERENT MESSAGES: "DO AS I SAY, NOT AS I FEEL."

Messages are conveyed through a variety of conduits, whether consciously or otherwise. We usually first think about messages that are expressed verbally because speech is adults' primary means of communication. But children are still in the early stages of mastering language. Although they may understand a great deal of what you say, they are only beginning to grasp the complexity of your words. At the same time, children are very intuitive and have been honing their emotional radar since day one of life. In fact, this intuitiveness to emotional messages dates back to the earliest human beings. In our cavepeople days when our vocabulary consisted of inflected grunts, parents communicated with their children nonverbally, so the survival of little ones depended on how well they could pick up on their parents' messages through their tone, facial expressions, and body language. That adeptness is still evident today and plays an important role in your children understanding you and getting your messages.

This greater sensitivity to emotions than words means that if you communicate a verbal message that conflicts with the emotional content of the message, chances are your children will get the emotional message. For example, let's imagine you're trying to be calm and patient although you're soon going to be late dropping your son off at preschool because he is dragging his feet about getting ready. You force a smile and say in what seems like a calm voice, "Let's move along, dear. We don't want to be late for school." But inside you are totally frustrated and stressed out. What message does your child get? "Gosh darnit, we're going to be late! Hurry, hurry, hurry! You make me sooo mad!"

The only way to prevent this disconnect between what you say and what you feel is to acknowledge and accept your emotions. You may try to cover up your feelings because you don't want your children to see how upset you are. But your emotions will leak through whether you like it or not. The best way to ensure that your words and emotions align is to be genuine. It's not only okay to communicate to your children that you are frustrated or angry, it's actually beneficial to them. They won't be confused by your conflicting messages. They will get the message that they should get, namely, that you're mad and frustrated with them because they aren't being cooperative. Of course, you don't want to yell at them. That sends an entirely different message, namely, that yelling is okay when you're mad. It also sends a meta-message that it's okay to lose control of your emotions. Your children will also benefit from several other meta-messages from your emotional honesty. They will learn that it's okay to feel negative emotions and express them appropriately, and they will learn the powerful lesson that their actions affect other people.

FATIGUE: "I AM SO TIRED."

An almost unavoidable part of parenting—unless, I suppose, you have a cadre of full-time nannies—is exhaustion, both physical and mental. Too little sleep, too few respites, and too little time dedicated to your own needs can all contribute to a state of deep fatigue that leaves you, at best, lethargic and unmotivated, and at worst, depressed or physically ill. Exhaustion leaves you without the energy to send healthy messages.

Even worse, fatigue leads to expediency—one of the most harmful words in parenting—which means acting in your self-interest rather than what is best for your children. Unfortunately, "self-interest" and "good parenting" don't play well together. If you're exhausted, you're naturally drawn to doing what requires the least amount of effort and energy. If you're being expedient, you have probably given up on sending healthy messages to your children. So, for example, you give your daughter a cookie before dinner to stop her from whining even though it will ruin her appetite, or you buy your son that toy in the supermarket checkout line because you don't want him to make a scene. Easiest short-term solution? Definitely. Best long-term message? Definitely not.

A real test for all parents is whether they are able to send positive messages when they don't want to, when they're tired, stressed, or rushed. You don't want to be a "fair-weather messenger," meaning you only send healthy messages when it's convenient. A fair-weather meta-message is that you only stick to what you believe in and only do the right thing when it's easy or opportune. That's certainly not a message you want your children to get. The survey of 1,600 parents I referred to in chapter 1 showed that about 17 percent describe themselves as "softies" and say that "I'm sometimes too tired to be firm with my child even when I know I should," "I sometimes let too many things go," and "I sometimes give in too quickly." Fifty-four percent say their children waste money shopping, 48 percent believe they are overindulging their children, 81 percent bribe their children, and 53 percent worry that they are raising rude children.

Another meta-message you send when you are exhausted and being expedient is that your needs are more important than those of your children. And children pick up on that meta-message like bloodhounds on a scent because at a deep level they feel unvalued and neglected. Still another meta-message your children may get when you act expediently is that when life gets difficult, it's okay to take the path of least resistance.

There is no easy answer to how to reduce your fatigue. The unfortunate reality is that you have been and will continue for the foreseeable future to be very tired; it's called being a parent. At the same time, you can't possibly be a good parent if you are in a constant state of exhaustion; a dog-tired parent makes for an unhappy child. As a result, you must find ways to recharge your batteries. Whether it involves your spouse letting you sleep in once a week or getting some exercise or quiet time or an evening out with friends, such "selfish" pursuits can keep total exhaustion at bay (as can the hope that you will some day get a decent night's sleep, perhaps when your children go off to college!).

When you're really tired, it's difficult to think clearly, weigh options, and make good choices. In other words, it's just too hard to think, so you will probably fall back on your default reactions. If you don't have a clear idea of what messages you want to communicate or a strong commitment to those messages, then your default will be not to send positive messages at all when you're exhausted. But if you have given considerable thought to the messages you want to convey to your children, have established a steadfast resolve to send those messages, and have sent them so often that they are second nature, then sending those healthy messages will be your default, and doing what is expedient will actually require more thought and effort on your part. When you know what is right, you will have a healthy dose of guilt for even thinking about acting in your own self-interest and a healthy dose of resolve to send the right message no matter how exhausted you are.

I'm not saying that you have to send the right messages to your children 100 percent of the time. That is a burden that no parent could ever shoulder. Sometimes doing what is expedient is necessary for your own health and sanity (if you don't have those, there's no way you can be a good parent), and that's fine as long as it's the exception and not the rule. So don't feel guilty if you slip up periodically; welcome to parenthood! In fact, a key meta-message that your children need to get is that you have needs, too, and that they can't always be the center of the universe. As long as the preponderance of messages you send to your children are healthy ones, they will get the messages and meta-messages they need to get.

UNHAPPY MARRIAGES OR DIVORCED PARENTS: "WHOSE SIDE ARE YOU ON, MY DEAR?"

Parents with marital problems or who are divorced have unique challenges to sending clear and consistent messages to their children. Where unified messages of every sort are so important, the very nature of troubled or broken marriages makes creating unity extremely difficult. But that shared purpose has to start with this: No matter what your feelings about each other may be, you have a responsibility to place the needs of your children ahead of your own and work together to present cohesive, consistent, and healthy messages to them. And it's important to get this right early, because it will affect your children throughout their lives. If you work together to send a coherent message, the marital discord or divorce will probably have a less negative effect on your children.

Creating a unified message between parents in conflict is difficult but essential, because the quality of the relationship between spouses has a significant impact on the health and well-being of children. Research has shown that children exposed to parental conflict feel their parents were less emotionally available and loving; these children have lower self-esteem and more emotional problems, and they feel less competent. Additionally, this conflict causes stress that hurts children's physical health, including their sleep, diet, and susceptibility to illness.

You will need to have open discussions with your spouse or ex-spouse that enable each of you to find ways to separate your own issues and needs from those of your children. Despite the lack of unity the two of you may have as a couple, it is incumbent on you in the best interests of your children to create that unity as parents. If the two of you require the help of an outside professional to facilitate these discussions, then seek one out. All that matters in your role as parents is to ensure that your children get the best messages possible. That objective must supersede any difficulties that exist in your marriage.

SIBLINGS: "I WAS TALKING TO YOUR BROTHER."

If you consider that the average American family has 3.14 children, then your children are probably not growing up in a vacuum at home. Instead, they are exposed to all kinds of messages related to their older and younger siblings. Not only are your children getting the messages you direct toward their siblings, they're also receiving the messages that their siblings communicate to you and to one another. This means that you have a whole lot of different messages flying around your home, some appropriate for all of your children and others less so.

There are several problems with having many and often conflicting messages at home. The reality is that your children, whether younger or older, have different temperaments, personalities, and learning styles and are at different levels of development. So your children are getting many messages that aren't suitable for them individually. Also, they may not be sophisticated enough to readily discriminate between those that are for them and those that aren't. Plus, your older children may have little regard for the messages they are sending to your younger children, however bad they may be, and may even gain some perverse pleasure out of "corrupting" their younger siblings. As any parent knows, young children often revere their older siblings and are easily persuaded by any messages from them.

Younger siblings can also be message blockers or send the wrong messages to your older children. For example, because infants are so needy and receive immediate attention whenever they cry, their older siblings may get the message that they too can get all the attention they want by crying.

Your sensitivity to this message chaos is paramount. Put yourself in your children's shoes to see how unfair it all appears to them. Their younger sibling gets all the attention he wants; he just has to cry and Mommy comes running. Your older children think: "Why can't I do that?" Or perhaps their older sibling gets to stay up late or play outside by him- or herself. Your younger children think: "Why can't I do that?" Sure, you can get frustrated when your children continue to not get your messages and even push back against them, but consider where they are coming from and imagine how frustrated they must be, too.

So how do you deal with all of this message confusion? You start by having a set of messages that apply to all of your children. Basic values of honesty, responsibility, and kindness, for example, are relevant for children of all ages. Conduct messages, such as "no hitting" (underlying message: kindness) and "put your toys away" (underlying message: responsibility) are also meaningful for all of your children. These "blanket" messages can be conveyed with your entire message toolbox to your whole brood. For these messages, older siblings can actually be message facilitators; as role models they can help send healthy messages to their younger brothers or sisters. For example, Gracie was a fast learner of dinnertime chores because she saw Catie set the table before dinner and bring her dishes to the sink after she finished eating. So positive messages you send to your older children will also be on their younger siblings' radar screen at an early age and will, at a minimum, begin to be absorbed, and at a maximum, be fully assimilated.

You can also do your best to separate your messages by separating your children when you have a specific message to send. If your younger children aren't around their older siblings you send a certain message, there can be no confusion about who the message is for. Of course, in the usually full and hectic life of any family, separation isn't always possible. So you have to make clear, when sending a message, who it is for and why. If you call your children by name and look them in the eye, you can at least be assured that they understand that you are talking to them.

The reality is that there will in evitably be some message confusion if you have more than one child. You must accept that, until your younger children develop greater language and cognitive capabilities, they are not necessarily going to be able to distinguish messages that are aimed at them from those aimed at their siblings. This means you must ensure greater message clarity with the messages you do send, by giving your children more time to let the messages sink in, and being patient if they don't get the messages as quickly as you would like.

EXTENDED FAMILY: "YOU MEAN I'M NOT ALLOWED TO SPOIL MY GRANDCHILDREN?"

Though some extended families, including grandparents, aunts, uncles, and cousins, are on the same page when it comes to the messages they all want to send to their children, others are not. Some of your extended family members, for example, aunts, uncles, and cousins, may simply assume that you share their values and attitudes. As a result, they may not realize that they are sending messages that you might not approve, whether, for example, it's exposing your children to too much media or giving them too many sweets or not expecting them to clear their dishes after meals.

Other extended family members, most notably grandparents, may simply not feel an obligation to support the messages you want your children to get because they feel that they paid their dues in raising you and should get a free pass when it comes to their grandchildren.

Grandparents sure have it good when it comes to our children. They get all of the perks and none of the burdens that we have as parents. Grandparents get to do all the fun things with their grandchildren, but then get to return the children to us at the end of the day when they are tired, hungry, or cranky. And grandparents are usually absolved of responsibility when it comes to things like discipline and setting limits ("I have earned the right to spoil my grandchildren," states one of our girls' grandmothers).

The degree to which extended family can affect your children through the messages they send depends on their proximity. If your children's grandparents, aunts, uncles, and cousins live far away and see your family infrequently, then little harm can be done. For the sake of family peace, it's probably best to just accept that your children may get some less-than-healthy messages during visits and realize that your ever-present messages will probably override any they receive during the rare visits from extended family.

If, however, you have extended family nearby, they are a frequent presence in your children's lives, and you find them sending messages of which you do not approve, then you have to make a difficult choice: either accept those unhealthy messages and hope that your messages take precedence or have that potentially difficult discussion with your extended family members about the disconnect between the messages they are sending your children and the messages you want your children to get. This conversation can be difficult because all parents believe that they are sending their (and your) children positive messages; what parent would consciously do otherwise? Your suggestion to the contrary might not be accepted in the best light; in other words, your extended family might take offense. As a result, this conversation requires sensitivity to and respect for your extended family's values, and, most important, some compromise on your part so your extended family doesn't feel judged or put upon. The goal of this discussion is to show that you value your extended family's presence in your children's lives while, at the same time, doing your best to ensure that your children receive mostly good messages from them, so that everyone can feel comfortable during family visits.

With grandparents in particular, this conversation might be easier because you won't be offending their parenting sensibilities; their parenting is far behind them. I have found that the best approach is to start by being appreciative beyond a doubt for the grandparents' spending time with your children (and giving you a break!). Then, discuss the values you want to instill in your children; the grandparents will probably find it difficult to argue against them. Next, provide guidelines to the grandparents on what messages you want to send to your children—for example, limiting gifts and sweets and expecting your children to be respect-·ful and cooperative—while giving the grandparents some latitude in appreciation for all that they do for your children.

SOCIAL WORLD: "IT'S A JUNGLE OUT THERE."

Your children don't live in a vacuum outside your home either. There is a wide world out there in which you're not their only influence. As soon as your children walk out the front door, they are receiving messages of all sorts from their immediate social world, including from their friends, other children, other parents, caregivers, schoolmates, and teachers. This social world can be an immense message blocker because you can't control everyone to whom your children are exposed outside the home.

You can't protect your children from their social world, but you can do your best to minimize for as long as possible their exposure to messages that you don't want them to get. The best way to do this is to thoughtfully create a social world that will communicate the messages that you want them to receive. You can accomplish this by carefully choosing your children's childcare (e.g., babysitters, daycare), preschool program, elementary school, extracurricular activities, and playdates to ensure that most (all is unrealistic) of the influences in your children's world support your messages.

From that social world that you have created, your children's social world of peers will emerge. The majority of their friends will come from their daycare, school, and the neighborhood in which you live. When you make deliberate choices about the social world that your children inhabit, you increase the chances that the friends they make and their friends' families will also convey healthy messages. You can further ensure that your children's peer group sends the right messages by getting to know your children's friends and their parents. You can see whether they will be supporting or undermining your messages.

I'm not saying that you should reject your children's friends just because they or their parents do something with which you don't agree. At the same time, you should be open with the parents of your children's friends about the messages you do and don't want your children to get, and ask those parents to respect your limits. For example, when our girls have a playdate, we tell their friend's parent or caregiver that the girls don't eat candy regularly and ask that they not be given sweets. We've never had a bad reaction to our request and have never heard that our request was ignored.

POPULAR CULTURE: "NO, YOU CAN'T HAVE ANOTHER DORA THE EXPLORER DOLL."

Popular culture can be another significant obstacle in communicating healthy messages to your children. From relatively old media (e.g., television, DVDs, and magazines) to the explosion of new media (e.g., mobile phones, the Web), popular culture has become an ever-present, intense, and unrelenting vehicle for sending messages to children, and many of those messages are not healthy (e.g., those on junk food, and those that emphasize wealth, celebrity, and beauty).

Popular culture does offer a variety of entertainment that conveys positive messages to young children. For example, *Dora the Explorer* communicates messages of kindness, diversity, exploration, family, cultural tradition, friendship, compassion, and physical activity. At the same time, just about all TV shows and DVDs aimed at children have strong merchandise tie-ins that send messages of consumption. Also, while Dora and her friends are out in the world exploring, the children watching *Dora* (or any other TV show) are sitting idly in front of a screen. In fact, research by the Kaiser Foundation has found that two thirds of children under two years of age use screen media (e.g., TV, DVDs, video games) for more than two hours a day, despite the recommendation of the American Academy of Pediatrics that young children should have *no* exposure to screens until they are two years old. Those hours of "screen time" increase dramatically as children progress through preschool, kindergarten, and elementary school.

Contrary to conventional wisdom, early exposure to technology such as home computers actually hurts academic achievement. For example, a study of elementary school students found that test scores declined when computers were introduced into homes and that children with readily accessible computers scored lower than peers who did not use computers regularly. The research concluded that lack of parental monitoring and guidance and time spent on non-educational computer use were the primary reasons for the test-score disparity.

Beyond popular culture devoted to young children, the landscape seems far bleaker. If you deconstruct the messages in popular culture aimed at older children and young adults, you will uncover values of superficiality, materialism, disrespect, irresponsibility, greed, voyeurism, and selfishness. You may be thinking, "But my children are still so young. They aren't exposed to that sort of popular culture." In fact, your young children may be exposed to adult-oriented popular culture far more than you realize both in and away from your home. For example, at home, you are probably exposing them to whatever popular culture interests you, the TV shows and movies you watch, the music you listen to, the magazines you read. The same holds true for their older siblings. Away from home, your children are bombarded by popular culture through billboards and store advertising and displays. For example, at the supermarket, child-oriented products (read junk food) are deliberately placed at the height of children in grocery carts. In fact, recent research has shown that children demonstrate brand recognition and loyalty as early as three years of age. As one executive of a cereal company noted, "When it comes to targeting kid consumers, we . . . follow the Procter & Gamble model of 'cradle to grave.' We believe in getting them early and having them for life."

Parents often recognize the dangers of popular culture, but don't always take action against it. In the survey of 1,600 parents I referenced earlier, parents overwhelmingly expressed the belief that popular culture sends truly harmful messages to children. For example, about 75 percent said that they are concerned about the negative impact of peers and the media on their children. And many of these parents expressed greater worry about the negative influence of popular culture on raising children with healthy values than about practical concerns such as paying the bills. As one mother noted in the survey, "It's basically exhausting. What's hard is . . . keeping the world at bay until you've formed these kids, so that they can learn to make their own decisions and live in the real world."

These early messages can have a profoundly negative effect on children's behavior as they develop. For example, several studies found that children who were exposed to adult media were more likely to engage in sensation-seeking and risk-taking behavior.

Other research reported that children whose access to adult media was restricted by their parents were not as likely to drink, smoke, have sex, or act violently as compared to children whose parents set no limits on exposure to adult media.

You might argue that, because you can't keep your children in a bubble forever, they should be exposed to some popular culture. Certainly, small doses of popular culture will not hurt them. And, yes, children do need to learn how to defend themselves against popular culture at some point. But young children are at such an important and impressionable stage of development that exposing them to too much popular culture so early could be harmful. Wouldn't you rather send your children out into that world after you have prepared them?

For its sheer pervasiveness and inescapability, popular culture is the most difficult message blocker confronting you. In fact, you will never be able to fully safeguard your growing children from the unhealthy messages sent by popular culture. Your only real hope is to delay their entrance into popular culture until they are prepared. In the meantime, you can immunize them with positive messages so that when they are faced with popular culture in full force in the next few years, the defaults formed from those healthy messages will protect them.

You can limit your children's contact with popular culture by first looking at what aspects of popular culture they are exposed to in their daily lives. Then, deconstruct what messages your children may be getting from those media and decide whether you find them acceptable or not. This decision is a personal one based on your own values and interests. I would recommend that you read up on the impact of popular culture on children and make an informed decision about what is appropriate for them. Finally, make deliberate choices about what parts of popular culture you are comfortable having your children experience.

PART II

I Like Myself

4

Message #1:
Love Is Your Child's Wellspring
("Sooo Much")

Love is the wellspring from which everything your children become emerges. It is the foundation from which your children develop their most basic beliefs about themselves and the world that will guide their thoughts, emotions, and behavior throughout childhood and into adulthood. And love is the most powerful force at your disposal in shaping your children's development.

CONTINUUM OF LOVE

Children who are given appropriate love grow up with a sense of acceptance and security that is the basis for their ability to value themselves, explore their world, take risks, strive for goals, and connect with others. Children who feel love learn that their world is a friendly and safe place that they can trust to shield them and meet their needs. These benefits express themselves in very real ways including self-love (of the healthy variety) and love toward others, happiness, healthy relationships, and academic and career success. One of the most robust findings of research on parent-child relationships is that the most well-adjusted children say they feel the most love from their parents.

At the other end of the continuum are children who grow up feeling unloved, due to abuse or neglect. They learn that the world is to be feared, an inhospitable and menacing place. Children who feel unloved suffer myriad problems, including low self-esteem, stress disorders, unhealthy relationships, a higher incidence of substance abuse, and struggles in school and career.

In the middle of this continuum of love, there are children whose parents express their love in less healthy ways. These children, by far the most common I see in my practice and social world, develop a conflicted view of the world. They receive love from their parents, so they gain some of its benefits. At the same time, because that love is often unpredictable, inconsistent, and laden with conditions, these children develop the belief that the world is the same way. As a result, they can't feel genuine security, comfort, or trust in themselves or the world.

These parents, though certainly well intentioned, heap love on their children, praise them unceasingly and unrealistically ("You are the most wonderful boy in the world!"), reward them out of proportion to their accomplishments, and attempt to fast-forward their development, all in the name of love and the best interests of their children. Unfortunately, these parents' efforts are often counterproductive to their goal and end up doing more harm than good. These children face difficulties that include feelings of worthlessness, sadness, anger, guilt, shame, and internal pressure to succeed. This can manifest itself in outwardly positive ways—for example, academic or athletic success—but their inner worlds are governed by turmoil and angst. The sad reality is that while you can't love your children too much, you can love them in the wrong way.

MODERN LOVE

Loving your children has gotten a bad rap in recent years. Helicopter parents, Velcro parents, Little League fathers, and stage mothers exemplify inappropriate and potentially unhealthy love. At the heart of this "modern love," more commonly referred to as conditional love, is the parents' overinvestment in their children's lives. Parents' self-esteem becomes enmeshed in their children; how parents feel about themselves becomes dependent on whether their children meet their expectations. In response to this overinvestment, whether intentionally or unwittingly, parents overwhelm their children with love, attention, praise, and gifts when they meet their parents' expectations. When children fail to do so, their parents either withdraw love through coldness and distance or express disappointment, frustration, and anger toward them. In either case, the message that children get is that their parents' love depends on their achievements. And this entanglement of parents' and children's selves can be a crushing weight on children, particularly in today's culture of high expectations and hyperachievement.

Messages of conditional love are usually subtle when children are young. They can be conveyed by the disappointment of parents when their children aren't as developmentally advanced as their peers (despite the fact that early development isn't highly predictive of later achievement). As children get older and become immersed in school, sports, and the arts, the danger is that the overinvestment on the part of parents mixes with the children's vulnerability to those cultural messages of extreme achievement. The purity of the unconditional love parents feel toward their children when they were young can change into the toxic brew of conditional love for children school-age and beyond as they enter the results-oriented world in which we live.

The harmful consequences of loving your children conditionally have been demonstrated over and over again in research. For example, children who believed that their self-worth was dependent on how they performed were highly self-critical, showed strong negative emotions, judged their performances severely, and demonstrated less persistence following setbacks. Additionally, children who received conditional love from their parents said that their joy in their successes was short lived and that they experienced considerable guilt and shame for their shortcomings. Adding insult to injury, children resented and disliked their parents for the way they treated them. And to show you the generational power of conditional love, mothers who said that they received conditional love from their own parents felt unworthy in adulthood, and, in spite of their hurtful experiences with conditional love, these mothers were more likely to treat their own children the same way!

THE "DARK" MESSAGES OF LOVE

The challenge for you when your children are young is not that you consciously reward your children with love and attention when they, for example, first sit up or walk, or punish their failures with anger or rejection. The challenge is to become aware of the unconscious, and often unhealthy, messages of love you may be prone to send to your children. Your goal is to convey positive messages of love, not the messages that are being sent from your "dark side," the side of you that is driven by your baggage.

It's completely natural to get excited when your children achieve some developmental milestone, particular if they reach it sooner than most children. And you may very well feel a twinge of disappointment or frustration when your children aren't as far along in their development as their playmates. That, too, is a normal reaction for parents who want their children to be the best they can be. Plus, few of us are entirely immune to the feeling that we will be judged based on our children or to the messages from our parenting culture that earlier and faster is better. But if your reaction in either direction is too extreme, then your children will probably get those messages of love from the "dark side." The goal is for the expression of your love to be appropriate to the situation and in your children's best interests, not extreme or unfitting for what they did.

I experienced my own dark side of love when helping Catie learn to ride her bike without training wheels when she was four years old. While I was pushing and supporting her, she wasn't looking where she was going, trying to pedal, or steering straight ahead. After several gentle reminders, I became increasingly frustrated and irritated by what I perceived to be her lack of effort and expressed this in a clearly angry tone. Within minutes Catie was in tears, and I experienced the worst parenting moment of my fatherhood. I had done exactly what I counsel others not to do; I allowed my baggage, in this case my perfectionism, to dictate the messages I sent Catie about her biking. Of course, I felt absolutely horrible that I had hurt my daughter. And I was afraid that I might have "scarred" her biking experience and that she might not ever bicycle again! In fact, Catie didn't ride her bike for several weeks, but then one day she asked if I would go out with her for a ride. As we headed to the garage, she stopped, looked me in the eye, and, with an earnestness that only children can express, asked me if I was going to be nice to her this time. With my heart in my throat and tears in my eyes, I gave her a big hug and promised her that I would be very nice, and I was.

This period early in your children's lives is so important because the defaults you set for how you express your love may very well determine the kinds of messages that you communicate to them if and when they board that runaway train of achievement that may be such a big part of their lives. Your early messages of love will be received by your children, helping them to establish that wonderful foundation of love for the future. And those early messages of love will become ingrained in you in the form of defaults that will make it easier for you to avoid the "dark side" of love and give your children the healthy love they will need when they venture out into that "big, cruel world."

LOVE AND TECHNOLOGY

New communication technology has enabled parents to send all kinds of messages to spouses, family, and friends, literally and figuratively. There are mobile phone calls, voicemail, e-mail, and texting. These technological advancements have, in theory, allowed parents to be more efficient, and as a result, spend more quality time with their children. But the reality is very different from the theory. The 24/7 connectivity that now exists has created a new breed of parent who seems to pay more attention to their mobile phones than to their children (probably a slight exaggeration, I admit).

The next time you go to a playground, for a walk, or grocery shopping, take note of how many parents are talking on their mobile phones, checking their e-mail, or responding to a text message . . . and thoroughly ignoring their children! What message are these parents sending to their children? The message that children get, however untrue it may be, is that "My phone and all it offers is more important than you." The meta-message is that the child feels "You must not really love me because you wouldn't put your phone ahead of my needs if you did."

LOVE THROUGH YOUR CHILDREN'S EYES

Loving your children isn't as clear-cut as "conditional love is bad and unconditional love is good." When I share the contrarian notions that unconditional love may actually be bad and conditional love might actually be good, I provoke very strong reactions from parents arguing otherwise. They just don't believe that they could ever send the message that they don't love their children wholeheartedly and without reservation. The mistake these parents make, though, is looking at their love through their own eyes rather than through the eyes (and hearts) of their children. They confuse what they feel with what messages might actually be sent and what messages their children might actually receive about love.

From your children's perspective, you constantly use love to reward or punish their behavior. When your children behave badly, for example, when they are selfish, whiny, uncooperative, or mean, I'm going to guess that you don't lavish them with love and affection. In fact, I will bet you get pretty darned annoyed with them, perhaps even angry. You may even yell at them (not recommended, mind you). Are you truly withholding your love in these situations? Of course not; you still love them, so you see your reaction as simply expressing disapproval.

But remember that this experience isn't about what you believe or intend, but rather what your children perceive and experience. Until they are approaching middle school, children are not sophisticated enough to tell the difference between "We disapprove of your behavior" and "Because of what you did, we are taking away our love." Your child's perception is that love has been temporarily suspended. To your child, it feels like, "I did something wrong, and my parents don't love me now." Why do you think parenting experts tell you that, after you have given your children a time-out, you should tell them how much you love them? My point is that, whether you want to admit it or not, you are constantly giving and withholding love from your children's perspective. In reading this section, please think about my ideas about unconditional and conditional love from the perspective of your children, not yourself.

UNCONDITIONAL LOVE

The basic idea behind unconditional love seems quite reasonable. You should love your children just for who they are, regardless of what they do. Children shouldn't have to worry whether their actions will cause you to love them less. They should be able to count on your love no matter what.

But, if you look at unconditional love carefully, you can see why it isn't all its cracked up to be. By taking away conditional love, you lose your ability to influence your children. With unconditional love, you lose your ability to approve of good behavior or disapprove of bad behavior. You give your children carte blanche under the misguided belief that this freedom will somehow build their self-esteem and foster maturity and independence. But what it actually does is create immature, insecure, and irresponsible children, ill prepared for life in the adult world.

CONDITIONAL LOVE

At some point many parents realized that unconditional love wasn't working. Many children were lazy, disinterested, disrespectful, and out of control. Children raised with unconditional love weren't good people, and they weren't successful or happy. Clearly, a change needed to be made. Many parents decided to return to conditional love.

Unfortunately, those parents reinstated the wrong kind of conditional love, what I call "outcome love." Perhaps because of the economic uncertainty in recent times or the aspirational and competitive nature of popular culture today, parents decided to direct their conditional love toward their children's achievement activities, believing that this approach would motivate their children to work hard and become successful. Parents began to make their love conditional on how their children performed in school, sports, or the arts. If Johnny got an A or won a tennis match or earned first violin in the school orchestra, his parents heaped love, attention, and gifts on him. When he received a D or lost that tennis match or didn't make the school orchestra, they withdrew their love by expressing disappointment, hurt, embarrassment, or anger. As a result, children's self-esteem became overly connected to their achievement efforts. This conditional love caused achievement to become threatening to children because success and failure was too intimately linked with whether their parents would love them.

At the same time, parents maintained their unconditional love for their children's behavior and the kind of people they were. Parents gave their children unfettered freedom and few responsibilities, didn't hold them accountable for their actions, provided no consequences, impressed no good (or bad) values on them, and continued to express their love for them no matter how they behaved—so long as they did well in school, sports, and so on. The mistake parents made was that they got this love thing backward. Parents must reverse their use of unconditional and conditional love.

THE RIGHT KIND OF LOVE

Yes, folks, conditional love can be good! As much as you may have been led to believe that unconditional love is the Holy Grail and that conditional love is Satan (no religious connotations intended), I am telling you that they are not. Like most things in life, unconditional and conditional love are neither good nor bad; it is what you do with them that makes them so. You can use love as a tool for your children's healthy growth or as a weapon that can harm your children's development. Rewarding children—love is really the ultimate form of reward—regardless of their behavior robs children of one of their most important lessons, that their actions have consequences. What more powerful inducement to good action is there for your children than the perceived threat of losing your love?

Unconditional Love for Achievement

You need to give your children unconditional love for their achievements so that they will be free from the fear that you will not love them if they fail to meet your expectations. This means whether they win or lose, succeed or fail, you still support and encourage them (assuming they tried their best; more on that shortly). This unconditional love liberates your children from the specter of lost love and encourages them to push themselves, take risks, give their best effort, and achieve at the highest level of which they are capable.

Conditional Love for Values

Love should have strings attached. Most things of importance in life are earned, whether they are values like trust, respect, and responsibility, or substantial things such as an education or a career. Why should love be any different? But the key is to attach the right strings to your love.

Instead of outcome love, you should use *value love*, in which love is conditional on your children's adopting essential values and acting in socially appropriate ways. Value love nurtures the development of positive values and moral behavior and fosters healthy growth. You can instill values such as respect, responsibility, empathy, compassion, and generosity by giving approval (which children perceive as love) when your children demonstrate these values and showing disapproval (which children perceive as withholding love) when your children don't demonstrate these values.

You can also encourage your children's achievement efforts using conditional love without resorting to outcome love. You do this by offering conditional love for values and life skills that will support their academic, athletic, or artistic aspirations—for example, hard work, discipline, good decision making, time management, patience, and perseverance.

There are several important differences between these two very different forms of conditional love. First, value love is about the overall development and well-being of children; it's about creating well-rounded, capable, and decent human beings. In contrast, outcome love may create the opposite. Yes, children raised with outcome love will probably achieve some degree of success—they had better, or their parents won't love them!—but because their parents focus so much on achievement, rather than on the whole person, these children are more likely to miss out on all of those great values and healthy life skills that make just plain good people.

Second, outcome love is outside children's control. They don't always have control over whether they can meet their parents' expectations; they may simply not be good enough to clear that bar, or another child, such as an opponent in a sport, may simply be better, which is no fault of their own. Conversely, all of the values and life skills that are fostered by value love are within children's control. They have the power to act in valued ways and gain the benefits or not do so and suffer the consequences.

Third, with outcome love, children sense that their parents are acting on their own needs and interests rather than on what is best for the children. This perception can create several harmful results. It causes conflict between children and parents that can generate anger, resentment, and resistance on the part of the children. Parents, in turn, probably unaware of their use of this unhealthy form of conditional love, are bitter toward their children, whom they perceive as ungrateful for their efforts to help them succeed. The ultimate result of this conflict is that children may sabotage their own efforts as a way to exact revenge on their parents. And, sadly, the relationship between parent and child is severely damaged, sometimes irreparably.

Finally, children raised with outcome love internalize their parents' style of love and use it as the basis for loving themselves. In other words, they come to love themselves only when they live up to their now-internalized expectations, and they hate themselves when they fail to do so. Children raised with value love, by contrast, learn that form of love and are able to love themselves independent of their achievements and gain healthy self-love from their deeply felt values.

MESSAGES OF LOVE

The messages about love that you send to your children at a young age are important because love, as the many books, poems, plays, movies, and songs have described, is a powerful, complex, often wonderful, and sometimes painful emotion that will play a central role in their lives. The messages you communicate in your expressions of love toward your children provide the context for the relationship they develop with love: their feelings of love for themselves and others, how they give and receive love, and their willingness to communicate their love to you and others. In the purest sense, your early expressions of love are the first inputs your children receive that will shape their view of themselves. Am I loved? Am I safe? Am I worthwhile? Your love molds their perceptions of the world in which they live. Is it safe? Is it hospitable? Is it supportive? Your early messages of love also lay the foundation for teaching your children the nurturing values, attitudes, and beliefs that will guide them toward being kind, thoughtful, and responsible people.

Your children get their first messages about love from you in the very first days of their lives and beyond. Physical contact, eye gaze, bodily warmth, your voice, a mother's milk, and responsiveness to their needs are all early messages of love. This initial love, so simple and pure, lays the foundation for your love as your children get older and love (and life) gains complexity. Your ability to continue that simplicity and purity of love in the context of an increasingly complicated and demanding life will ultimately determine the relationship they develop with love throughout their lives.

You want your children to feel your love and for love to become woven into the very fabric of your family life that envelops and protects them every day. You want your family life to be so imbued with love that your children feel your love in everything you do with and for them. This feeling provides a solid foundation of comfort and security that frees them to experience love deeply within themselves, reciprocate your love openly, and express their love for others.

So please, love your children fully and openly, but don't send messages of love that are unwise or indiscriminate. It's never too early to start expressing love in the most healthy ways possible. When you send your children messages of healthy love when they are very young, you provide them with a template of what love should be. Just as important, you are training yourself to give healthy love to your children so that when they get older and life becomes more complicated and demanding, you will continue to communicate messages of love for them that will be as sweet and pure as when they were babies.

CATCHPHRASES FOR LOVE

Pretty much from day one of each of their lives, every night before Catie and Gracie went to bed, I would softly whisper in their ears the question, "How much do I love you?" Obviously, when they were infants, I didn't expect an answer, and the question was intended to be rhetorical; I hoped they could feel how much I loved them. Then, one evening at bedtime when Catie was about two and a half, in response to my question, she said, "Sooo much!" The message had gotten through! And "Sooo much!" has been our catchphrase for love ever since.

CATCHPHRASES FOR LOVE

- "Sooo much."
- "Bigger than the world."
- "Big love!"
- "Explosion of love."
- "My love, my lovette, my loveling."
- "I love you."

A catchphrase used by one mother, Susannah, is "Bigger than the world." She wants to give her love for her children a physical dimension that they can literally and metaphorically grasp. They have a globe in their living room that, when her three children were young, seemed immense. Susannah would say "bigger than the world" and point to the globe. They would then wrap their arms around it to feel the size of her love for them. She would also point to her heart and the globe to send this message a different way. As her children got older and really understood how big the world was and learned about space and the solar system, they got to have some fun with the catchphrase. She would say "bigger than the world" and they would get into a competition to see how big their love could be, for example, "bigger than Saturn," "bigger than the sky," and "bigger than the stars." When Susannah gives her love physical dimensions, she is able to make very tangible the immensity of her love for her children.

Jake, the father of two boys, plays a lot of basketball, a sport with its share of catchphrases (e.g., "slam dunk") and physical expressions of emotions (e.g., chest bump). After a basket, players on his league team often shout "big shot" and pound their chests with their fists. While he was shooting baskets in his driveway one day with his young boys watching nearby, he made a shot and spontaneously shouted "Big love!" and pounded his chest over his heart with the L sign (thumb out, pointer finger up). His boys cackled with joy and "Big love" became his catchphrase for them. Now nine and seven years old, his boys, both of whom are now passionate basketball players, shout "Big love" and pound the L sign on their chest after they sink a basket at home.

Catchphrases don't even have to be words, but can be sounds, too. Another father, Dave, told me that when he first laid eyes on his newborn daughter, Patrice, at her birth he thought he was going to explode (and he made this explosion sound effect). From the time she came home from the hospital, his little "explosion of love" became his catchphrase. While she was still an infant, he would give her a hug and let out a little explosion, and as she got older, he would stand in front of her, clutch his heart and, with a big smile on his face, let out a big explosion sound while spreading his arms wide. When he related this story, I was worried that his daughter might think Dave was having a heart attack, but she has always gotten a kick out of it, so who am I to judge? And now, at age four, she has her own little explosions of love for him.

Terms of endearment are another type of catchphrase that can send powerful messages of love to your children. Ty, a father of two girls I know, has different love-related names for each of the "ladies" in his family. He calls his wife, "my love," his elder daughter, "my lovette," and his younger daughter, "my loveling." These terms of endearment express his love to all three, yet offer a unique and special expression to each.

Finally, don't forget the most reliable catchphrase for love that has stood the test of time: "I love you!" It may be old-fashioned and a bit sentimental, but nothing expresses your feelings of love more unambiguously, directly, or powerfully. And "I love you" is just plain warm and fuzzy. Tell your children (and your spouse) "I love you" early and often—with hugs and kisses attached, if possible (more message conduits)—so it becomes a part of your family vocabulary.

ROUTINES AND RITUALS FOR LOVE

The "How much do I love you? Sooo much!" question and catchphrase have been an enduring ritual for us. At bedtime, Catie and Gracie will turn the tables and ask me the question, and I answer. This give-and-take has become a part of our nighttime routine. It has gotten to the point where, thoroughly spontaneously at some point during the day, the girls ask me, "Daddy, how much do

ROUTINES AND RITUALS FOR LOVE

- Catchphrases at bedtime.
- Sign language for love.
- Notes of love.
- "Woobie" (blankies) love.
- Run & Hug.
- Express love to your spouse.
- Skype with extended family.
- Spontaneous expressions of love.

I love you?" And I say, "Sooo much!" They respond with smiles and giggles. By making this catchphrase and ritual their own, Catie and Gracie have become active participants in our family's love. They also learn how to express their love for me, Sarah, and each other.

As soon as Catie and Gracie began to understand language, but were still a ways away from talking, we taught them rudimentary sign language to help them communicate their needs, for example, signing for sleep, hunger, thirst. We also taught them how to sign "I love you." By around fifteen months, both girls were signing back to us. I doubt they knew precisely what the signing meant, but I'm sure they got the idea that whatever we were "saying" was a good thing because of the "warm fuzzies" we communicated in our facial expressions and body language.

Sign language gives children another conduit through which to receive and send messages of love, particularly for young children who haven't yet developed their language skills sufficiently to express their feelings. Also, because love is such a visceral experience, the physicality of sign language provides a direct path to the feelings associated with love. It also enables them to send messages of love beyond arm's length and carry of voice. To this day, our girls use the "I love you" signs as a means of expressing their love, for example, from our living room looking down to our driveway when Sarah or I are driving away, or when they are speaking to their grandparents on Skype.

Martha, mother of Amanda, missed her baby daughter mightily when she returned to work after a four-month maternity leave. To ensure that Amanda knows that she is always in her momma's heart, every morning for what is now more than five years, Martha gives her a Post-it note with some variation of a red heart and "I love you" written on it. Amanda's grandmother, who cared for her while Martha worked, kept the notes without telling Martha, and on Martha's latest birthday, Amanda (with her grandma's help) presented Martha with a handmade book of every single one of those Post-its. Suffice it to say that many tears of love were shed at that birthday party.

Steve and Caitlyn gave their twin boy and girl, Kyle and Sophie, soft and cuddly little "woobies" (another name for blankies) when they were born. Now that they are four years old, Kyle's and Sophie's woobies are an ever-present source of comfort in their lives. These woobies also became a first spontaneous and then ritualized expression of their love for their parents. As told to me by Steve, every night when Kyle and Sophie were put to bed, the twins would each take the most worn corner of their woobies and give their parents "woobie love," by brushing their cheeks gently with it. And just to show you the power of ritual, when one of the twins was upset, the other would offer woobie love as comfort, or the sad twin would give him- or herself woobie love as a form of self-soothing.

Blake, the father of three—ages six, four, and two—isn't allowed to leave the house for work each morning until all three of his children do "Run & Hug." This morning ritual involves his kneeling down by the front door and each of his children standing about ten feet away, counting down "three, two, one, go," and running into his arms for a hug and kiss. His kids have gotten very creative and modified "Run & Hug" to "Dance & Hug," "Hop & Hug," "Crawl & Hug," and many other variations thereof.

Ritual expressions of love shouldn't be exclusive to you and your children, but can (and should) also include your spouse and others as role models. A ritual that Sarah and I developed, more out of our love for each other than by conscious decision, is that every time we leave or enter our house, we give each other a kiss. We have similar rituals of love for extended family and close friends. Catie and Gracie see love being modeled in these different ways with different people and get the message that love is something that can be appropriately expressed toward others for whom we share deep feelings of affection.

As I just suggested, it is a very positive message to expand the circle of love beyond your immediate family. One of our neighbors, Nancy, has a ritual for her son that every Sunday, he "Skypes" his grandparents on both sides of the family. This new video-calling technology has been a boon for distant grandparents who are now able to remain much more connected to their grandchildren now through the combined visual and voice medium. It allows children to build and maintain loving relationships with extended families whom they might not see often. And it has the added bonus of sending the meta-message that family is important.

Beyond ritualized expressions of love, spontaneous expressions of love send a dramatic message to children. Unexpected words of love, hugs and kisses, or even just a gentle and reassuring touch can cause children's eyes to brighten, smiles to widen, and moods to rise. You can think of these surprising shows of love as sort of reverse scares. Let me explain. You know how it feels when someone jumps out from behind a door and yells "BOO!" Your heart stops for a second, then starts racing, and adrenaline surges through your body. The unexpected expressions of love create an inverse sudden reaction of calm, joy, and love. Your unanticipated love is like a special treat that your children didn't expect and, as a surprise, is especially sweet.

ACTIVITIES FOR LOVE

One of the most powerful ways you can express love for your children is to give them a gift that is, sadly, in short supply for many families, namely, time. The message you send when you are with them, mind, body, and spirit, is that you love them enough to make them your number-one priority. Unfortunately, as for most families, our life can get pretty hectic, to the point that there seems to be little down time when Sarah and I can really

ACTIVITIES FOR LOVE

- Special time with each child.
- Establish traditions that express love.
- Make special things for them.
- Make up stories about love.
- Remove activities that send bad messages of love.

connect with our girls. So we make sure that we set aside "special time" during which we separately share a fun activity with each of our girls. The specific activity matters less than the time you spend together, but something out of the ordinary conveys an especially powerful message to your children. For example, Sarah and I have alternated taking Catie to *The Nutcracker* ballet the last several years. And we take turns taking Gracie to the zoo (which she loves).

But special time doesn't have to be a major affair. It can involve playing a game, going for a walk, or just sitting and cuddling. Sarah allows Catie and Gracie to decide how they want to spend this special time. Catie loves to do artwork with Sarah. Gracie likes to play with her stuffed animals and have Sarah read to her. Because my work can be time-consuming, I make an extra effort to have special time with each of the girls as well. I take them individually in the baby jogger when I go for runs. I take Catie on a "trail-a-bike" when I go mountain biking. And Gracie zips around on her pedalless bike with me. But the most special special time for me, though it is also the simplest, is when I take each girl for a walk around the neighborhood just holding hands, talking, and exploring nature.

Activities that turn into traditions are a wonderful way to send the message of love to your children. A friend of ours, Eliana, has established a tradition of taking her daughters for tea on Valentine's Day. They dress up, she makes Valentine's Day cards for each of them, and they spend an afternoon celebrating this day that represents love.

Ted was definitely not the artsy type, but one day while his son Arnie was painting with his watercolors, Ted started using them, too. When he showed his "work of art" to his son, Arnie went bonkers with joy. And Ted found that, despite his very limited artistic capabilities, he enjoyed producing his little creations. So before work trips, he creates a painting, a drawing, or even a small piece of Play-Doh sculpture that he leaves for Arnie to find after Ted has left. Arnie treasures these gifts and has a bookshelf devoted to his dad's art collection.

Renny's mother was a real storyteller. When he was a boy, she would create the most amazing tales that entertained him for hours. So he figures that explains why he loves telling stories to his two children. And Renny has found that his storytelling is a great way to send messages of his love for them. He creates elaborate yarns of adventure and excitement in which his sons are the main characters, to ensure that they are paying attention. Then he incorporates love and support into the narratives, between his two boys and with the characters' parents. The stories end, of course, with triumph over the bad guys, but also with the characters' families together hugging and kissing.

Sometimes removing an activity that is sending unhealthy messages about love is an expression of love. Marcy used to be so disdainful of her friends with children who were always chatting it up on their mobile phones with their kids around. But then she had two children of her own, and before she knew it, Marcy had become one of those mothers. She saw the attraction of the phones. However much she loved her children, being with them full time was often boring. To entertain herself, she would call or text friends, check her e-mail, or surf the Web. Then one day, her three-year-old, Sami, and one-year-old, Jessie, wanted her attention, but Marcy was talking to her mother on her mobile phone. After several attempts at getting their mother's attention, both of her daughters started crying, and Sami yelled, "You love that phone more than me!" Well, that cry was a slap in the face for Marcy, and she got the message from Sami. Thereafter, she made a rule that she wouldn't use her mobile phone when she was with her children except for short and necessary communications.

For Sarah and I, that activity was checking our e-mail or searching the Web on the laptop computer on our kitchen counter when we were with the girls. Sarah or I would often open the laptop while Catie and Gracie were eating, figuring we were being very efficient in our use of time.

But after a while, our girls started to complain, telling us that we were ignoring them. And they were right. We realized that we were with them in body, but not in mind or spirit. Neither Sarah nor I had the willpower to resist the siren song of the laptop calling out to us every time we entered the kitchen, so we took drastic measures. We removed the laptop from the counter and placed it around the corner on a high shelf with Sarah's cookbooks. It was close enough for Sarah to conveniently pull it out to access online recipes or for either of us to check e-mail or surf the Web when the girls weren't around, but not so ever present that we were constantly drawn to it. Our belief was "out of sight, out of mind," and it worked!

5

Message #2: Competence Is Your Child's Strength ("I Did It")

Competence is the most neglected contributor to self-esteem. The "self-esteem movement" that began in the 1970s placed so much emphasis on ensuring children felt loved that the role of competence in developing self-esteem has been ignored, minimized, and misapplied.

Competence is important because it provides the foundation on which children feel able to act on and control their world. It is, in many ways, what separates adults from children. The latter haven't developed a large "toolbox" of skills yet and are still dependent on others, namely their parents, to survive in the world. In contrast, adults possess most of the competencies necessary to navigate the world on their own.

Competence is such an essential attribute because it affects children's personal, social, physical, and achievement-oriented worlds. A well-developed sense of competence gives a child the confidence to leave the safety of their family, explore, take risks, overcome challenges, and strive for goals. Without a fundamental belief in their competence, children will probably be doubtful, feel insecure in uncertain situations, and experience reluctance and fear when put in unfamiliar circumstances. This sense of competence will give your children the strength and determination to confront and persevere in the face of the many challenges—physical, intellectual, emotional, and social—that they will surely encounter as they progress through life. And, in a somewhat surprising twist, research has shown that competence is highly related to happiness. This is why it's so important for you to send the right messages of competence to your children early and often.

COMPETENCE IS POWER

Children need to develop a sense of competence in their actions, an understanding that their actions matter and that their actions have consequences: "If I do good things, good things happen, if I do bad things, bad things happen, and if I do nothing, nothing happens." This sense of competence and the self-esteem that accompanies it are two sides of the same coin. If children don't accept their mistakes and failures, they can't take responsibility for their successes and achievements. Yes, they're going to feel bad when they make mistakes and fail. But you want your children to feel bad when they mess up! How else are they going to learn what not to do and what they need to do to improve in the future?

Competence provides children with belief in their ability to set high goals, persevere in the face of obstacles and setbacks, and strive for success in all aspects of their lives. Without this competence, children feel incapable of mastering the many challenges with which they will be confronted in their lives. Research shows that children with a low sense of competence are less likely to engage in and persist at activities. They also can't ever really feel good about themselves or experience the meaning, satisfaction, and joy of owning their efforts. Without this sense of competence, children are truly victims; they believe that they are powerless to change the things that might happen to them. With a sense of competence, children learn that when things are not going well, they have the power to make changes in their lives for the better.

MESSAGES OF INCOMPETENCE

Our always well-intended but often misguided parenting culture has sent messages to parents that actually undermine children's sense of competence. When you set the bar for competence too high in the name of instilling competence in your children, you cause them to view that bar as too high to clear. With this feeling of "I can never be that competent," children come to believe that whatever competencies they do have, which are probably more than sufficient to be a successful, happy, and contributing member of our society, simply pale in comparison to the impossibly high standards that have been set for them.

These messages of incompetence arise from three sources: the unrealistic expectations that parents set for their children, perfection as the benchmark for competence, and a fear of failure that develops in children from the realization that they will never live up to those out-of-reach thresholds of competence.

EXPECTATIONS

Setting expectations for your children is an essential responsibility of parenting. Expectations communicate messages to your children about what's important to you and establish a standard toward which your children can strive. But expectations can be double-edged swords. They can be a tremendous benefit to your children's development or they can be crushing burdens that destroy their self-esteem, depending on what types of expectations you set.

But it isn't just the messages you send about expectations that are important, but also how they are received and interpreted. As I noted in chapter 3, there can be a disconnect between the messages that you send your children and the messages they receive. And research has demonstrated the harm that can be done to children when the messages they get from their parents are different from those that their parents intended to send. One study found that students experienced anxiety about their ability to perform in school, which can hurt self-esteem and make adapting to school more difficult. But, as I mentioned previously, the findings showed that students' perceptions of their parents' expectations were exaggerated. Specifically, students thought their parents' expectations of academic achievement were much higher than those actually held by their parents.

Unhealthy Expectations of Competence

There are two types of expectations that you shouldn't set for your children: ability and outcome expectations. *Ability expectations* send children the message that you expect them to achieve a certain result because of their natural ability, "We expect you to get straight A's because you're so smart" or "We expect you to win because you're the best athlete out there." The problem with these messages is that children have no control over their ability. Children are born with a certain amount of ability, and all they can do is maximize whatever ability they are given. The fact is that if your children aren't meeting your ability expectations, you have no one to blame but yourself—you didn't give them good enough genes! Another problem with ability expectations is that if children attribute their successes to their ability—"I got an A because I'm so smart,"—they must attribute their failures to their lack of ability—"I failed because I'm stupid."

Popular culture also conveys the message that results matter above all else. As a consequence, parents often set *outcome expectations* in which the message is that their children must produce a certain result—"We expect you to win this game" or "We know you'll be the soloist in your dance school performance"—if they want to be seen as competent. The problem is that, once again, children are asked to produce an outcome over which they may not have control. They might perform to the best of their ability but still not meet their parents' outcome expectations because other children just happened to do better than they did. So they would have to consider themselves as incompetent despite their good performance. Setting outcome expectations also communicates the meta-message to your children that you value results over everything else, so they'll come to judge themselves by the same standards. Contrary to what you may believe, ability and outcome expectations actually hinder your children's development of competence.

Results Matter!

Now you might be thinking, "Wait a minute! I can't push my kids to get good grades or do their best in school, sports, and other activities? No way I'm buying this one." Before you jump all over me, give me some latitude to bring all these ideas back to the real world.

Here is a simple reality that we all recognize in our culture: results matter! No two ways about it, in most parts of our society, the message that children get is that their competence is judged on the results they produce: grades, victories, test scores, rankings. Though it would be great if children were rewarded for their good intentions or efforts, that is not the way the world works. Unfortunately, this societal message can cause parents to place their desire for their children to excel in the short run ahead of their desire to instill a sense of competence in the long run, and the result is interference with, rather than encouragement of, their children's growth.

I would recommend that you give up outcome expectations altogether but still give your children outcome "somethings." These somethings are outcome goals. Goals are very different from expectations. Outcome expectations are often set by parents and placed in front of their children without their consultation or "buy-in." For example, "We expect you to get straight A's in school," or "We expect you to win the state tennis championships." There is almost always an implied threat with outcome expectations: "If you don't live up to our expectations, we won't love you." And kids often feel dragged—sometimes kicking and screaming—toward those expectations. Children have no ownership of expectations and little motivation to fulfill them, apart from that implied threat from their parents. When I ask children about expectations, they usually grimace and send a very clear message, "That's when my parents get really serious, and I know they're gonna put pressure on me," or "They're telling me what to do, and I better do it or I'll get into trouble." Not exactly "feel-good" parenting! The message of outcome expectations is also black and white; your children either meet the expectation and succeed or they don't and they fail. So there is very little opportunity for success and lots of room for failure.

Goals are very different. Humans are wired to want to pursue goals; this instinct has contributed to our survival. And one of the great joys in life is to set, work toward, and achieve a goal. Children have ownership of their goals and want to set and strive toward goals for themselves, with guidance from parents, teachers, and coaches. For example, "I want to aim for straight A's this semester," or "I'm going to do everything I can to get the lead in the school play." One great thing about goals is that they aren't black and white, but are about degree of attainment. Not every goal can be achieved, but there will almost always be improvement toward a goal, and that progress defines success. So if children give their best effort, there is little chance of failure and great opportunity for success. When I ask kids about goals, they convey a very different message. Their faces perk up and they say things like, "It means I decide to do something, and I really work hard to do it," or "I feel like my parents are really behind me, and I'm psyched to do it."

For example, if a child's parents establish an outcome expectation of raising her math grade from an 80 to a 92 during the school year, and she only improves her grade to an 89, then she will have failed to meet the outcome expectation. But if she had set an outcome goal of a 92, even though that goal isn't fully realized, she will still see the 89 as a success because of the substantial improvement she made over her previous grade.

Many parents believe that results at a young age are imperative, so they send a meta-message that results are important by placing outcome expectations on their children. Yet childhood is about learning, improving, developing, and gaining the values, attitudes, and competencies necessary for later success. When you send messages about goals rather than expectations to your children, you foster rather than inhibit their sense of competence.

But even outcome goals aren't ideal. Many parents think that focusing on the outcome will increase the chances of that outcome occurring, but the opposite is actually true. Here's why. When does the outcome of a performance occur (e.g., in an exam or a sports competition)? At the end, of course. And if children are focusing on the end of the performance, what are they not focusing on? Well, the process, obviously. Here's the irony. By focusing on the process rather than the outcome, your children will more likely perform better, and if they perform better, they're more likely to achieve the outcome you wanted in the first place. Also, why do children get nervous before a test, sporting event, or recital? Because they're afraid of the outcome, more specifically, they're afraid of failure. So if they are focused on the outcome, they're going to get nervous and, as a result, will be less likely to perform well and achieve the outcome you wanted for them.

So if you're going to send messages about outcome somethings, make sure they are outcome goals, but then immediately send other messages that encourage your children to focus on the process—that is, what they need to do to demonstrate their competence and achieve the outcome goals.

Effort Expectations

If you want your children to develop that essential sense of competence, you should communicate messages about effort expectations, over which they have control. This will actually encourage them to do what it takes to achieve the outcomes you want. If your children feel that they have the tools to experience competence, they are much more likely to embrace and pursue their goals. Think about what your children need to do to gain competence, and create effort expectations that will lead to that competence: commitment, positive attitude, hard work, discipline, patience, focus, persistence, perseverance. "Our family expects you to give your best effort," or "Our family expects you to make your studies a priority." In doing so, you are also communicating to your children the meta-message that hard work matters most.

Notice that I use "our family" instead of "we, your parents." This subtle change in language communicates several important messages and meta-messages. It removes the parent as the source of the message, focuses it on the children, and establishes the message as a collaboration between you and them. This cooperative messaging ensures that your children, as members of the family, have ownership of the expectations rather than feeling that you have forced the expectations on them. You want your children to get the key message that connects their efforts and their competence. The meta-message is that the messages you send to them are a part of your family and all members must abide by them.

If your children meet your effort expectations, they will, in all likelihood, gain competence and experience, the intrinsic rewards garnered from their efforts. If your children don't meet the effort expectations, they won't experience that sense of competence and will also be disappointed (they should be). But rather than being crushed by the failure, they will know that they have the power to fulfill the expectations in the future.

PERFECTIONISM

Perfectionism is one of the most destructive messages that children are getting these days. The problem is that perfectionism has a great allure to parents, particularly in our perfection-driven culture at a time when being good doesn't seem to be good enough. Who wouldn't want their children to be perfect? And in these uncertain economic times, parents may feel that perfection is the only way to ensure their children's success in life. Unfortunately, perfection is, at best, a double-edged sword. One edge of the sword drives parents to urge their children to be perfect. These children push themselves to get straight A's, be top athletes, and save the world on weekends, all of these efforts directed at demonstrating their perfect competence.

But the reality is that perfection is unattainable, so such an expectation will guarantee failure. The message that children who are expected to be perfect get is that, no matter how competent they are or strive to be, they will never be competent enough.

What Is Perfectionism?

Perfectionism involves parents communicating to their children messages of impossibly high standards that they will never attain. And these parents believe that anything less than perfection is unacceptable. When children internalize these messages from their parents and popular culture and then fail to meet such ridiculously high standards, they berate themselves unmercifully for their self-perceived incompetence (despite the fact that they are viewed by others as highly competent). Perfectionistic children are never satisfied with their efforts no matter how objectively well they perform, and they punish themselves for not being perfect. For example, after I spoke to a group of high school students recently, a girl from the audience described to me how she had gotten a 100 on a recent test that also offered ten extra-credit points. She got seven out of the ten points correct for a total of 107 out of 100, yet missing those three extra-credit points ate at her for days because she felt completely stupid!

At the heart of perfectionism lies a very threatening message that children receive from their parents (almost always unintentionally): if they aren't perfect, their parents won't love them. This threat arises because children connect being perfect with their self-esteem; if they are perfect they see themselves as worthy of love and respect. The message of perfection and competence is clear for perfectionistic children: "If I am not perfect, I am not competent, and if I'm not competent, my parents won't love me." The price these children believe they will pay if they are not perfect is immense, and the research shows that the toll can be devastating: depression, anxiety, eating disorders, substance abuse, and suicide.

Perfection and Popular Culture

We live in a culture that reveres perfection. Our culture has elevated competence to absurd heights where being good is no longer sufficient. Children must now aim for the Ivy League or the pros. They must become wealthy and have the perfect house and the perfect car. Our culture also worships at the altar of physical perfection. Children, particularly girls, are bombarded by images of perfect people with perfect bodies, perfect faces, perfect hair, and perfect teeth, as evidenced by the popularity of cosmetic surgery and "reality" TV shows that feature only beautiful and thin women.

Where Does Perfectionism Come From?

After almost every talk I give, a parent says to me, "I swear that my child was born a perfectionist." Yet there is no scientific evidence that perfectionism is inborn. The research indicates that children learn their perfectionism from the messages that their parents send them, most often their same-sex parent. Through their parents' words, emotions, and actions, children get the message that if they want to be loved, they must be perfect.

Parents communicate messages of perfection to their children in three ways. Some perfectionistic parents create perfectionistic children by actively rewarding success and punishing failure. When children succeed, their parents lavish them with love, attention, and gifts. But when they fail, their parents either withdraw their love and become cold and distant or express strong disappointment and anger toward their children. Thankfully, in my twenty-five years of practice, I have only come across a few parents who were this overtly perfectionistic.

Other parents send unintentional messages of perfectionism to their children through role modeling; parents are perfectionists, so their children get the message that they must be, too. Children see how their parents hate themselves when they're not perfect, so they feel they must be perfect so their parents won't hate them. These parents unwittingly communicate messages to their children that anything less than perfection won't be tolerated in the family.

The final type of parents that convey messages of perfectionism are not perfectionists at all; in fact, they are the antithesis of being perfect. But they are going to make sure their children are perfect! These parents project their flaws onto their children and try to fix those flaws by giving love when their children don't show the flaws and withdrawing love when they do. Unfortunately, instead of creating perfect children and absolving themselves of their own imperfections, they pass those imperfections on to their children and remain flawed themselves.

Excellence: The Antidote to Perfection

You should remove the word "perfection" from your vocabulary. It serves no purpose other than to make your children feel incompetent and miserable. You should replace it with "excellence." I define excellence as *doing good most of the time* (I use poor grammar intentionally because that's how most children talk—and I'm not perfect either!). Excellence takes all of the good aspects of perfection (e.g., achievement, high standards, disappointment with failure) and leaves out its unhealthy parts (e.g., connecting achievement with self-esteem, unrealistic expectations, fear of failure). Excellence still sets the bar high, but it never connects competence with the love you give your children (or the love they give themselves). Messages of excellence actually encourage your children to explore, take risks, and yes, fail periodically because those messages communicate another essential message: that without some failure, competence isn't possible.

FEAR OF FAILURE

Fear of failure among children in America today is at epidemic proportions. Fear of failure causes children to feel debilitating doubt and anxiety when they face anything that might challenge their competence or cause them to fail. It leads them to avoid the challenge altogether, not take risks, give little effort, give up when they struggle, and, ultimately, deprive themselves of opportunities to gain competence.

Parents and Fear of Failure

Many parents send the painful message to their children: "If you fail, I won't love you." In receiving this message, children come to see failure not only as a threat of loss of love from their parents, but even worse, a fundamental attack on their value as people. Research has shown that parents with a high fear of failure punish failure, but don't reward success. Other studies have found that parents who set unrealistic expectations and withdraw love when those expectations aren't met produce fear of failure in children.

The bottom line is that children who fear failure are taught by their parents to do so.

Popular Culture Makes Things Worse

Unhealthy messages about failure are ubiquitous in our popular culture—on television, in the movies, on the Web, in magazines. And these messages reinforce those communicated by parents. The basic message that children receive these days through all the different forms of media is that "if you fail, you are a loser" who will be demeaned and rejected by all. This message of failure creates a culture of fear and avoidance of failure that prevents children from developing a vital sense of competence that, ironically enough, would reduce the chances of failure.

Avoiding Failure

When children absorb this message of failure being unacceptable, they are driven to avoid failure and the specter of incompetence at all costs. There are three ways in which children can prevent themselves from failing. First, children can simply not engage in an activity in which they fear failure. If children don't even try, they can't fail. Young children will simply tell their parents that they don't want to do it. I have seen children as young as three years old who were unwilling to even try to do something as seemingly unthreatening as walking on a beam at a playground or putting together a simple puzzle.

When children get older, they manufacture reasons why they can't participate, for example, injury, illness, damaged equipment, forgotten or lost materials, apparent lack of interest or motivation, or just plain refusal to take part. Unfortunately, when children avoid even the remotest chance of failure, they deprive themselves of vital opportunities to gain competence. And their reluctance to even try hurts their sense of competence even more, making them more resistant to trying in the future.

Second, children can avoid failure by engaging in what is called self-defeating behavior in which, paradoxically, they cause themselves to fail, but have an excuse that protects them from the stigma of failure—"I would have done well, but I just didn't feel like trying my hardest" or "I would have done just fine, but the teacher was totally unfair." Because these failures are not their fault, children can't be held responsible, and they can't be labeled as failures with the associated personal and social repercussions that they believe accompany such failure.

Third, many older children don't have the luxury of not taking part or coming up with excuses, for example, children can't just not go to school. So another way that children can avoid failure is to get as far away from failure as possible by becoming competent and successful. But children who are driven to avoid failure (rather than pursue success) are stuck in limbo between failure and real competence and success, a place I call the "safety zone," in which the threat of failure is removed, for example, they have a B+ average or finish in the top 10 in their sport. They are far from failure, so no one can call them incompetent. But they are unwilling to intensify their efforts and take risks to fully demonstrate their competence and achieve real success because doing so would increase their chances of failure, which they must avoid at all costs.

The Value of Failure

For those children afflicted with a fear of failure, failure is a ravenous beast that pursues them every moment of every day. There is no rest from the approaching specter of failure, and their primary motivation is to avoid failure no matter what, because the perceived consequences of failure are devastating.

The problem is that children who suffer from a fear of failure have a skewed view of failure. The reality is that failure is an inevitable—and essential—part of life that offers far more benefits than costs. Failure can bolster children's motivation in the future to overcome the obstacles that caused the failure. It shows children what they did wrong so they can correct the problem in their subsequent efforts. Failure connects children's actions with consequences, and that connection helps them gain ownership of their efforts. Failure teaches important life skills, such as commitment, patience, determination, decision making, and problem solving. It helps children respond positively to the frustration and disappointment that they will often experience as they pursue their goals. Failure teaches children humility and appreciation for the opportunities that they're given.

Of course, too much failure will discourage children. Opportunities to successfully demonstrate competence and experience success are also needed for their ability to bolster motivation, build confidence, reinforce effort, and increase enjoyment. As children pursue their life goals, they must experience a healthy balance of success and failure to gain a deep sense of competence.

Reframe Failure

To protect your children from the destructive messages of failure, you need to communicate healthy messages about the meaning of failure. You should define failure in ways that encourage children to value rather than fear it and that will actually encourage their sense of competence by giving them control over it so they can avoid it in the future. For example, when children experience a failure in their lives, such as a bad grade on a test or poor performance in a sports competition, they personalize it as an attack on their value as people. That reaction can be truly hurtful and damaging to them. And it can be further reinforced by a strong reaction of disappointment, frustration, and perhaps even anger on your part.

Your reactions to your children's failings (and even your own) send powerful messages about failure that can relieve your children of feelings of guilt and shame and make failing an inevitable and healthy part of their lives. You can convey these messages through role modeling, responding to your own failures with calm and aplomb. You can also be supportive and encouraging when you see your children "fail," for example, when they spill their milk at the dinner table, fall down while walking, struggle with a puzzle, or do poorly on a test in school.

You can also help your children to reframe failure not as a judgment on their competence or their worthiness as people, but as information and a lesson to be learned. The information might be that they didn't prepare well enough or they made some poor decisions in how they used their time. The lesson that they can learn is how to prevent that failure in the future by doing something different the next time they are faced with the situation.

When you communicate positive messages of failure, your children gain an understanding of failure that liberates them from fear of failure. It also frees them to strive for competence without reservation, to explore, take risks, and vigorously discover their competencies. Children will know in their hearts that some failure is okay and is in no way a negative reflection on themselves as people. This early and frequent messaging will lay the foundation for healthy attitudes toward failure that will serve them well when they get to the age when "results matter."

DEVELOPING COMPETENCE

In recent years, our parenting culture began to send the message that competence is important for building self-esteem and that parents need to do everything they can to convince their children of how competent they were. All very reasonable, to be sure. However, that same parenting culture made a big mistake by telling parents that the way to instill competence in their children was to *tell the children* how competent they were. Parents bought into this message and started telling their children how smart and talented and wonderful they were. But here's the problem: Children can't be convinced that they are competent.

When parents try to convince their children of how competent they are, they often have the exact opposite effect. There is this little thing called reality that children have to confront on a daily basis; life has a way of sending messages about competence that can be in sharp contrast to the outsized messages of competence that parents send their children. When children are faced with the conflict between what their parents have told them about how good they are and what reality is telling them, the result is the bursting of the "you are the best" bubble that their parents inflated for them. The result: disappointment, hurt, and an actual loss of the sense of competence. Let me be clear here: The only way for children to build a true sense of competence is through firsthand experience that includes travails, triumphs, struggles, setbacks, and successes.

So to reiterate, only your children can build their sense of competence. You can, however, do several things to encourage them to develop their own competence. First, you can give them opportunities in their daily lives to gain a sense of competence. Your family life is rife with situations that are just calling out for you to allow your children to "get their hands dirty" and find out what they are capable of.

These daily experiences allow your children to develop specific competencies that will be helpful to them as they progress through childhood and into adulthood. These include dressing, eating, drawing, reading, cooking, doing chores, and interacting with others. These early competencies lay the foundation for the development of more complex capabilities later in life. Also, the more individual competencies children develop, the more they will view themselves as globally competent people, which will give them the confidence to explore their world, try new things, take risks, and persist in the face of obstacles and setbacks. In other words, competence begets competence.

Second, you can be sure that they gain the most value from their experiences. You can help them to recognize their accomplishments ("You just swung on the monkey bars all by yourself."). You can direct their focus to the competencies that enabled those successes ("You really worked hard to hold on."). And you can praise their accomplishments ("It must feel so good to have done that yourself.").

But you shouldn't just focus on the successes, because, as every parent knows, as your children develop, they will experience far more failures than successes as they begin to gain competence; just think about the process of your children learning to walk. How you react often dictates how they will respond to those failures. If you show disappointment and frustration, they will judge their experience as negative, and it may cause them to be reluctant to try again in the future. Catie's avoidance of riding her bike after my unhealthy reaction to her struggles illustrates this point powerfully. But if you are positive and supportive, your children will get the message that failure is okay and just a part of life.

Allowing their children to be wrong or do something poorly is very difficult for parents who hold the mistaken belief that these experiences will hurt their children's sense of competence and scar their little psyches. But children, like everyone else, will probably fail the first few times they try anything new. Plus, they're little kids, so you wouldn't expect them to do much of anything very well at first. Whether they do it well isn't important, because success isn't really the goal. Instead the goal is to develop their willingness to keep trying. And you can have faith that if your children continue to try at something, they will, sooner or later, achieve some degree of competence and success.

Another mistake that parents make is that, after their children are unsuccessful when they first try something, they try to correct their children so they will succeed the next time they try (otherwise, their children will be further scarred by the repeated failures). But put yourself in your children's shoes. How would you feel if you tried really hard at something and your parents jumped right in to show you that you did it the wrong way and how to do it the right way? Wouldn't it irritate the heck out of you? Well, that's how your children probably feel. And what message are you sending with your rapid-fire intervention? That you don't believe your children are competent enough to figure it out on their own. You may ask, but how are they going to learn to do it the right way? I assure you that they will most likely figure it out themselves over time, through practice or observation. When they do finally get it, they will own it and will make a big deposit in their competence "bank." That's not to say that you can't lend a hand when they are struggling. But let them take the lead; if they really want your help, they'll ask for it.

PRAISE

Praise is a powerful tool for developing competence in your children. Yet praise is an incredibly misused strategy for building competence and self-esteem. Without realizing it, many parents use praise in a way that, at best, does nothing to build competence, and at worst, actually undermines their children's ability to cultivate a true sense of competence.

What is the most common praise you hear parents (and teachers and coaches) give kids at home, on the playground, in class, and on the sports fields? Well, the one I hear most frequently is "Good job!" and it is like fingernails on a chalkboard to me. "Good job" (and other variants such as "Way to go," "Nice job," and "That's great") have become knee-jerk reactions from parents whenever their kids do something worthy of acknowledgment. If I had a dollar for every time I've heard "Good job!" I would be a rich man today.

What's the problem with "Good job"? Well, it's lazy praise; it's worthless praise; it's actually harmful praise. It has no value to children, yet parents have been brainwashed into thinking that it will build their children's self-esteem. Plus, it's the expedient thing to say; parents don't have to think about what their children actually achieved specifically, what enabled them to gain that accomplishment, or what might be the most beneficial way to praise them.

Here's why "Good job!" is of such little value. Let's start with the purpose of praise: to encourage children to continue to engage in behaviors that produce positive outcomes. Now you can start to see the problems with "Good job!" First, it lacks specificity; it doesn't tell children what precisely they did well, and without that information they can't know exactly what they should do in the future to get the same outcome. Second, "Good job!" focuses on the outcome rather than the process, which, as I have discussed previously, actually interferes with children achieving that desired outcome. If you're going to be lazy with your praise, at least say, "Good effort!" because that phrase focuses on a controllable attribute—effort—that your children use to do a good job.

The reality is that children don't need to be told "Good job!" when they have done something well; it's self-evident. Whether they are learning to walk, swim, do a forward roll, or read or write, children are able to experience firsthand that they were successful. At the same time, children probably don't know what exactly they did to produce that great result. They need to be told *why* they did well so they can do it again and experience the same sense of competence; for example, "You were really focused walking on the balance beam."

Research has shown that how you praise your children has a powerful influence on their development. For example, studies found that children who were praised for their intelligence, as compared to their effort, became overly focused on results. Following a failure, these same children persisted less, showed less enjoyment, attributed their failure to a lack of ability (which they believed they could not change), and performed poorly in future achievement efforts. Too much praise of any sort can also be unhealthy. Research has found that students who were lavished with praise were more cautious in their responses to questions, had less confidence in their answers, were less persistent in difficult assignments, and less willing to share their ideas.

Children develop a sense of competence by seeing the consequences of their actions, not by being told about the consequences of their actions. Other research reported that children who were praised for their effort showed more interest in learning, demonstrated greater persistence and more enjoyment, attributed their failure to lack of effort (which they believed they could change), and performed well in subsequent achievement activities. Rewarding effort also encouraged them to work harder and to seek new challenges.

Based on these findings, you should avoid praising your children about areas over which they have no control. These include any innate and unalterable abilities and attributes such as intelligence, physical attractiveness, or athletic or artistic gifts. You should direct your praise to areas over which your children have control—attitude, effort, responsibility, commitment, discipline, focus, time management, decision making, compassion, generosity, respect, love . . . the list goes on. You should look at exactly why your children did something well and specifically praise those areas. For example, "You worked so hard preparing for this test," "You were so focused during the chess match," or "You were so generous about sharing with your sister."

Here's a revolutionary idea: You don't need to praise children at all. The best thing you can do is simply highlight what they did. For example, if your toddler just climbed a playground ladder for the first time, just say, "You climbed that ladder by yourself!" with enthusiasm and a smile on your face. Their own smile of pride for accomplishing what was for them an Everest-like challenge lets you know loud and clear that they got the message you wanted them to get, namely, "You did it!" Nothing more needs to be said.

As another alternative to praise, just ask your children questions. You can find out what your children thought and felt about their achievement; for example, "What enabled you to hit the T-ball?" and "What was most fun about your soccer game?" When you allow your children to decide for themselves how they feel about their accomplishments and enable them to reward themselves for their own good actions, you help them to understand how they were successful and encourage them to own those successes. The result: Your children send and receive their own messages of competence which carries a huge "wallop" when it comes to instilling a sense of competence.

Or really go out on a limb and don't say anything at all to your children. As I just mentioned, kids usually know when they "done good." By letting them come to this realization on their own, they learn to reinforce themselves, and they don't become praise junkies dependent on you for how they feel about their efforts and accomplishments.

Here are my challenges to you. First, next time you're at a playground or a youth sports competition, take note of what parents say to their children. I'll bet you hear "Good job!" (or some variation) constantly. Next, monitor what you say to your children in the same situations. Then, erase "Good job!" from your vocabulary; we've already established how useless it is. Finally, start to praise your children in the healthy ways I just described. When you have broken yourself of the "Good job!" habit, you can then pat yourself on the back and tell yourself, "Good job!"

LET YOUR CHILDREN DO WHAT YOU DO

Children love to contribute, and they love to do adult things. Why? Perhaps they are hardwired to want to do what adults do, the value of which is that it teaches them the skills they will need to survive as adults. Regardless of the reasons, even if they aren't actually doing anything of consequence, just "being in the game" gives them a great sense of accomplishment and competence. For example, whenever I am carrying or moving something around the house, Catie and Gracie want to help, even if that means just placing their hand on the side of a box I am carrying. From an adult perspective, they aren't doing anything of consequence because they aren't bearing any of the weight. But through their eyes, they are doing the same thing as I and they are helping. For young children, that is a very big deal!

Perhaps the greatest obstacle to providing these naturally occurring opportunities to develop competence is time, or the lack thereof. It's just easier and quicker (and often less messy) for you to do it yourself. From your perspective, allowing your children to help you prepare dinner, repair something, clean up the living room, or do the laundry is often more trouble than it's worth; it takes time, it's harder, and it may not turn out as well as if you just did it yourself. But for your children, these experiences, and the sense of competence that emerges from them, open a world of possibilities from which they can learn and benefit. When you deprive your children of these opportunities, you are not only preventing them from gaining very positive messages about their competence, but, more detrimentally, you are sending them unhealthy messages and meta-messages. First, you don't think they are competent, and second, you don't have time to act in their best interests—both truly harmful messages to be sure.

RESIST THE "EDUCATIONAL-INDUSTRIAL COMPLEX"

There is such emphasis these days on fast-forwarding children's development to prepare them for the rigors of school. So parents buy all kinds of "educational" games and toys that are purported to enhance competence, build self-esteem, and accelerate children's capabilities. Yet these products have no real value, and research backs up my assertion. In fact, the research shows that children's development can't be accelerated; they can only do what they are developmentally prepared to do. When parents try to push their children ahead, they may actually be stunting their development because their children aren't being allowed to lay the necessary building blocks for later development. Studies show that all parents really need to do to ensure their children's normal development is to do what parents have always done (at least until the "educational-industrial complex" started controlling the parenting messages). Without even realizing it, when your children engage in the activities that kids have always been involved in, they will progress in developing a sense of competence. And, in case you haven't heard, under pressure from education and media groups, Baby Einstein, the leading maker of so-called educational products for children, has removed the word "educational" from their advertising and packaging and offered a refund for their products in an implicit admission that their products do not, in fact, have any developmental benefit.

MESSAGES OF COMPETENCE

Competence is an essential quality that children need to develop to become fully functioning adults. In fact, one thing that separates adults from children is the former's broad repertoire of capabilities that enable them to navigate the world, including physical, intellectual, emotional, social, and practical skills. Competencies are necessary but not sufficient to become a capable adult. Of equal importance is belief in those capabilities; people won't use the competencies that they have unless they believe that they have them and that using these skill sets will lead to success.

Early childhood is the time not only when the basic competencies are established but also when the fundamental belief that "I am a competent person" is instilled. The initial experiences that children have as they first engage in the world, from grasping your finger in infancy to sitting and standing to walking, eating, dressing, and talking, lay the foundation for their future beliefs about their ability to master the increasingly complex world in which they will live as they mature. Research has demonstrated that early experiences are vital to establishing competence beliefs. Negative competence beliefs are more resistant to change once those beliefs become ingrained. Conversely, positive competence beliefs that are established early on will be less likely to falter in the face of subsequent setbacks and failures.

Children crave opportunities to demonstrate their competence, almost as if they are hardwired for it. Catie and Gracie are constantly saying "Let me do it!" We often find ourselves "trying to help" when neither of them asked for our help, out of expediency, to make things easier for the girls, or because we see that they can't quite do the thing they are trying to do. And, to their credit, our efforts to help them are constantly rebuffed with "I can do it myself" (in a dramatically indignant tone). A powerful lesson is that your children are willing to work hard to develop their competence, and intervening too early or too often sends the message that you don't think they are competent.

Patience is the key here. Let them struggle for a while. If they realize that they aren't quite ready to do what they are trying to do, your children will ask you for help and you should then lend a hand only sufficient for them to surmount the immediate difficulty and then turn the task back over to them to finish. The rewards of overcoming what are for them monumental challenges are immediate and clear. Bright smiles of accomplishment spread across their faces, and they gush with pride.

Yet, many children have already internalized a sense of incompetence. You see them on playgrounds, in classrooms, and on sports fields. They are pessimistic ("I can't do it."), fearful ("I'm afraid."), and reluctant to even try ("No, Mommy, no."). Certainly, some of these children were born with cautious or fearful temperaments (all the more reason to provide them with the attitudes and tools necessary to gain that sense of competence). For others, you can see why they haven't developed a sense of competence by observing their parents, who are worried, anxious, overly protective, and intrusive. These parents don't allow their children to experience opportunities for competence either out of a lack of recognition of their importance or because it's just easier for the parents to do it themselves. They intercede at the first hint of difficulty, seemingly worried that struggles and possible failure will hurt their children's self-esteem. These parents also see danger everywhere and communicate that message to their children. They don't allow their children to take even benign risks and hover over their children to swoop in at the first sign of potential harm or distress. These parents are, of course, well intentioned and believe they are doing what is best for their children. Is there any more powerful instinct for parents than to protect their children from harm? But they are unwittingly sending messages that "You can't do that" and meta-messages that "You are not competent" to their children that will undermine their children's sense of competence as they progress through life.

Though almost all children will undoubtedly gain mastery over the basics of their world, only those who develop a strong and resilient sense of competence will truly gain dominion over their lives. The early messages that you send about your children's competence will play a vital role in its development.

CATCHPHRASES FOR COMPETENCE

Catie came up with our catchphrase for competence when she was only two and a half. She was walking unassisted along a three-foot-high stone wall in our front yard (with me spotting her) and when she got to the end, she yelled "I did it!" with great enthusiasm and pride. And the catchphrase stuck. To this day, whenever Catie or Gracie accomplishes something, they yell "I did it!" Sarah and I have latched onto it, too; when the girls do something well, we say "You did it!"

CATCHPHRASES FOR COMPETENCE

- "I did it!"
- "Try bird, fly bird!"
- "Yes, you can!"
- "Thumbs up!"

Debi, the mother of four-year-old Ethan, knew she was risk averse and saw how it had hurt her growing up. She was determined not to send that message to Ethan. Once when Ethan was about two years old, they saw a mother bird in a field with her baby trying to fly. At first, the baby bird would flap its wings and would just barely get off the ground, at which point its mother chirped incessantly, which Debi translated for Ethan to mean "Keep trying, you can fly, I know you can!" With each attempt, the baby bird rose higher and higher until, after much effort, it soared high and far on its maiden flight. The baby bird landed near its mom, and insofar as a bird can, gushed with pride and chirped with excitement. At that moment, Debi's catchphrase for competence dawned on her: "Try bird, fly bird." To this day, any time Ethan is reluctant to try something or Debi feels hesitant about something he wants to try, she says "Try bird, fly bird!" Ethan gives a big grin, and he, like that baby bird, takes off.

Mark, the father of two boys and a girl, wanted his children to fear nothing (within reason, of course). He was inspired by President Obama's attitude and successful run to the White House. So using our president as his inspiration, Mark made his family's catchphrase for competence a modified version of President Obama's campaign slogan, "Yes, we can!" When his kids were trying something for the first time, he would declare "Yes, you can!" And before any new challenge, he or his wife would also ask their children "Can you do it?" and they would say "Yes, I can!"

As I mentioned in my last chapter, catchphrases don't have to be just words. They can be physical movements, too (catchmoves?). At one point some time ago when Catie accomplished something, I spontaneously gave her a "thumbs-up." She loved that and now when she or Gracie do something, I either flash them the thumbs-up or I combine it with saying "Thumbs up!" with enthusiasm. In doing so, I send them a message praising their competence through three conduits: the physical action of the thumbs-up, my saying "Thumbs up!", and the emotional tone of my saying the catchphrase.

And now when I ask them how something is, they often don't say anything, they just flash me the thumbs-up. Catie and Gracie have even created a rating system with the thumbs-up. Double thumbs-up is "awesome." One thumbs-up is "great." A thumb parallel to the ground is "fine." And a thumbs-down is "bad."

ROUTINES AND RITUALS FOR COMPETENCE

Anything that takes effort to accomplish is an opportunity for your children to get the message of competence. And as I noted in chapter 2, the more repetition to which you can expose your children, the more likely that the specific competency and the general sense of competence will be instilled. Without realizing it, you likely already have

> **ROUTINES AND RITUALS FOR COMPETENCE**
>
> - Household chores.
> - Setting and clearing the dinner table.
> - Bedtime responsibilities.
> - Getting ready for school.

many daily routines that enhance your children's sense of competence. When you think deliberately about these opportunities, you're able to identify even more such opportunities and can really maximize the benefits of those to which your children are exposed.

You can build these "windows" of competence into your daily routines and combine them with other messages such as responsibility. For example, the chores that you assign your children, such as folding and putting their clothes away or piling their books on the table in the family room, are also great openings for them to gain that sense of competence.

Dinnertime is one of those windows. Since they were less than two years old, Catie and Gracie have set the table before dinner and have been required to bring their dishes, cups, and silverware to the sink after dinner. For some time as they mastered these skills, after-dinner cleanup was a pretty precarious and messy time, as the girls frequently dropped their (wood) plates and spilled food and milk. But before too long, they not only learned to clear the table with ease and skill, but they now like to serve dinner as well. They are also required to fold their napkins after dinner, no small feat of fine motor coordination for young children.

Darlene and Peter use their twin son and daughter's bedtime to instill competence. They have given them progressively more responsibility to clean up their rooms, get undressed and into their pajamas, brush and floss their teeth, and pick out their books. It has gotten to the point where their children don't want them to intrude on their bedtime preparations (even though they aren't quite ready to go it alone). Darlene and Peter combine these experiences with appropriate praise ("You brushed your teeth all by yourself!") to reinforce the children's belief in their own competence.

Edie sees competency windows in her boys' morning routines. From just after their fourth birthdays, Tommy and Greg were required to make their beds and get themselves dressed for preschool. Of course, Edie had to "ride herd" over them at first, coaxing and coaching them in how to pull the top sheet and blanket up on their beds, take their clothes out of their drawers, and put them on (as adults, we forget how incredibly difficult it once was to zip up pants and button shirts). But by age five, both boys were old hands at getting ready while their mother prepared breakfast and packed their school lunches. Edie readily admits that her efforts were partly selfish. Because her husband leaves for work well before the boys wake up, this early "training" has lightened her load in the morning and made life a whole lot easier for her.

ACTIVITIES FOR COMPETENCE

Your days are rife with activities, both mundane and fun, in which your children can gain that sense of competence. You just need to recognize them for what they are and look for ways to include your children in them.

ACTIVITIES FOR COMPETENCE

- Gardening.
- Grocery shopping.
- Meal preparation.
- Home fix-it projects.
- Games, puzzles, sports, pretend play, art.

Sarah has a garden in our backyard in which she grows all kinds of vegetables. It is a source of great pride to serve our family produce right from her own garden. And our girls love being "farmers," too. Sarah assigned Catie and Gracie a corner of the garden that is their own and even bought them children's gardening kits complete with a pink bucket, gloves, and gardening tools. Sarah helped our girls decide what vegetables to plant and then showed them how to prepare the soil, plant the vegetables, and harvest the fresh produce. When Catie and Gracie share the fruits (I mean vegetables) of their labor with me, they are two happy (and increasingly competent) little agriculturalists.

After returning from the supermarket, Jonah and Lucy require their two children to carry a bag of groceries into the kitchen. If the bag is too heavy, which most bags are for small children, Jonah or Lucy will take one handle and their kids will take the other. Similarly, when they visit extended family, each child packs their own little roller bags and carries it to and from the car. If their family is flying, their children are required to roll their bags through the airport.

Our girls love to "help" Sarah make dinner. I put help in quotes because, as you might have experienced yourself, two little girls trying to help their mother prepare dinner can actually make the process longer, more complicated, and messier. Despite these drawbacks, Sarah usually allows them to take part by pouring, mixing, and chopping (with a dull knife, of course) ingredients. Catie and Gracie are not only gaining a sense of culinary competence, but also mastering a wonderful skill that will offer them practical value and joy for a lifetime.

Karl is a real "do-it-yourself" guy; he just loves fixing things (his motto is: I usually fix the problem, but I don't guarantee my work). His three children love to be his "apprentices." When Karl goes to repair something, he allows them to carry a tool. During the repair itself, he gives each of them the opportunity to use a tool so they feel like they are making the repair, for example, they screw in a screw, tighten a bolt, or hold on to the drill while Karl is drilling a hole.

Darcy and Wayne weren't going to fall for all of the advertising for so-called educational games and toys. They grew up without all of that fancy rigmarole and turned out just fine. They believed that if they just stuck to the basics, their two children, Lars and Lena, would turn out just fine, too. So their time with their kids is filled with reading, playing games, doing puzzles, playing sports, engaging in pretend play, exploring nature, and creating art.

6

Message #3:
Security Is Your Child's Safe Harbor ("I'm Okay")

Your efforts to instill the messages of love and competence in your children are devoted to developing your children's fundamental sense of security in themselves and the world. There are three messages you want them to get for this budding sense of security. First, there are people in my world who will protect me when needed. Second, I am master of all that is me (body, mind, spirit) and am capable of taking care of myself. Third, the world is a safe place that I can explore with confidence and free from fear.

SECURE ATTACHMENT

The first message of security involves your children feeling securely attached to you. The operative word with attachment is "trust." Simply put, secure attachment develops in children who learn that they can trust their parents to meet their physical and emotional needs. When they are cold, hungry, or thirsty, they know you are there to provide them with warmth and sustenance. When they are scared, sad, or lonely they can turn to you for comfort.

This attachment isn't just important for you and your children to develop healthy relationships. You are their first exposure to the world. The experiences your children have, the emotions they feel, and the perceptions they assume about you and their relationship with you become the foundation for the experiences, emotions, and perceptions they will have with the world beyond you.

Imagine children who grow up without that attachment, trust, and sense of security. They learn that the world is a dangerous, unpredictable, and neglectful place that can't be relied on to care for them. Such a worldview would have a profoundly negative impact on every aspect of their future lives, including how they come to see themselves and their emotions, relationships, and ambitions. Who they ultimately become and what they eventually do would emerge from this dark place of doubt, fear, and need. Research has shown that children with insecure attachment experience significant separation anxiety when parents leave, yet find little comfort when they return. They are often described as needy and clingy by teachers and other caregivers. In adulthood, they fear intimacy, have difficulty expressing their emotions, lack trust in their intimate relationships, and take rejection badly.

Now consider children who are raised with a strong feeling of attachment, trust in their parents and the world, and that sense of security. They come to view the world as a safe, friendly, and predictable place that they can count on to meet their needs. The worldview that they subsequently develop would be one of comfort, interest, and opportunity. Studies on attachment have found that securely attached children separate from their parents with ease, welcome them back with enthusiasm, and are readily calmed by parents when frightened. In adulthood, these children generally have high self-esteem, are socially competent and able to establish and maintain intimate relationships, and are emotionally expressive.

Learn to Read Your Children

As I have noted earlier, children have distinctive temperaments, moods, emotional styles, and needs. They also send messages through different conduits to alert you to their specific requirements. You need to learn your children's personalities and the particular messages they send about their needs.

An essential way to build the trust that underlies secure attachment is to interact with your children in ways that are consistent with those unique attributes and messages. By doing so, you respond to their needs in ways that are most meaningful and comforting to them. This congruence between your children's needs and your responsiveness sends a powerful meta-message, namely, that you understand them and can give them what they need in the way that they need it. Their recognition of your understanding acts as the foundation for that trust and secure attachment. In contrast, when you respond to your children's needs in ways that are out of sync with who they are, their deepest needs are not met, and they feel misunderstood, disconnected, and unvalued.

Be Consistent

Consistency is especially important for establishing secure attachment because your children's trust in you is based on your creating a consistent and predictable world around them. The dangers of inconsistency in attachment behavior are evidenced by the type of attachment referred to in the research as "disorganized." Children with disorganized attachment demonstrate no clear pattern of attachment behavior, sometimes approaching, other times avoiding, and still other times resisting their parents. They often appear to be disoriented and anxious. Findings suggest that inconsistent responsiveness by parents may contribute to disorganized attachment; for example, parents may be quick to respond at one time, but neglectful the next, or loving and supportive at one turn and angry and critical at another. With these mixed messages, children can't predict if, when, or how their parents will respond, creating a state of mistrust, detachment, and insecurity.

SECURE SELF

The second message of security is the sense of security and safety that children develop about themselves. For children to feel truly secure, they must believe that they are safe and have mastery over themselves. The secure self initially emerges from the love you give your children as described in chapter 4; this love contributes to the secure sense of attachment that I just discussed. Your love provides your children with the knowledge that there are people in their lives who can and will protect them when necessary. The secure self also evolves from the sense of competence that I explained in chapter 5, because when children feel competent, they know that, even when their parents aren't around, they have the power to feel safe or make themselves safe when they encounter uncertain, risky, or dangerous situations.

In contrast, children with an insecure self feel as if they are in a constant state of danger. This insecure self arises due to the absence of all of the experiences, relationships, and qualities that produce a secure sense of self. These children don't feel loved and lack strong attachment to their parents. They also lack the sense of competence that would be especially necessary given the dearth of comfort and safety from others. As a result, they have no safe harbor, either external or internal, in which to reside or to which to return, so they are caught; they don't feel secure where they are, yet they are also afraid to venture outward because they don't feel capable of feeling safe "out there." The result is that they experience a persistent state of threat and engage their world with fear and reluctance.

An essential area in which this message of security has relevance is children's physical well-being. If you consider the developmental trajectory that children's lives take, you notice that control over their bodies is the first step (no pun intended) they take in gaining mastery over their lives. From their first finger grasp and head lift to sitting up, crawling, and walking, gaining control of their body is their first source of competence and sense of authority over their world.

This sense of security over their physical existence has broader implications for the creation of a secure self. The experiences that children garner from such a "primitive" aspect as their physicality establish early perceptions about themselves that will then be applied to their ever-expanding internal and external worlds. A secure self acts as the starting point from which children can engage their internal world, that is, their thoughts, emotions, physical feelings, needs, and wants, with comfort and confidence. Children can also use their secure self as the "home base" from which they can explore their growing outer world, including their surroundings and relationships, with assurance and ease.

The messages that you send and that your children receive about a secure self are particularly important when their being is threatened in some way. In times of urgency and emergency, when children are sharply attuned to their emotions and highly vigilant to your messages, your emotions and the reactions that your children see set the tone for the degree of security they feel in threatening situations.

Sarah and I experienced the power of this message in an unsettling way when Catie was about two and a half years old. While doing the dishes after dinner, I stupidly left an opened tin can on the floor to be put outside in the recycling bin. Catie picked it up and began playing with it. In doing so, she cut her finger severely enough to warrant a trip to the emergency room to get stitches. Sarah got to her first, and despite a significant amount of bleeding, Sarah was incredibly composed, and I did my best to follow suit. From that moment, Catie didn't shed a tear—not when we were waiting in the emergency room, not when I physically restrained her so that she could receive several shots of a local anesthetic, not when she got four stitches from the physician. Catie was calm and attentive throughout. The ER physician said most kids in this situation are hysterical because their parents are hysterical. I don't tell this story to congratulate ourselves for being so calm; we were wrecks inside. I tell it to demonstrate the importance of the messages we send to our children. The message we sent to Catie after she cut her finger was that it was pretty serious, but we had the situation—and ourselves—under control, so she could be confident that we would take care of her. With her trust in us, she was able to accept our message and use it to help her remain under control, too. In a nutshell, Catie got the message that, if Mommy and Daddy thought she was okay, then she could trust that she was okay.

SECURE WORLD

The third message of security gains increasing importance as your children achieve full mobility, move beyond the prescribed limits of their immediate family, and enter the physical and social world of nature, neighborhoods, playgrounds, childcare, preschool, and elementary school. A significant part of your children's development involves steadily increasing the range of their physical and social worlds. The perceptions that children develop about these worlds, whether they view them as safe or dangerous, will dictate the degree to which they are comfortable exploring and expanding these worlds.

Early experiences in which your children feel safe to discover the world beyond you enable them to develop the sense of a secure world and gain comfort and confidence in being "out there" on their own. This belief in a secure world is made up of three distinct perceptions. First, children know that, however far they may roam, their parents (and other significant others such as extended family, caregivers, and teachers) will provide them with a safe haven to which they can return when they reach the outer limits of their comfort zone. Second, as they explore the world around them, children who live in what they believe is a secure world know that, should they experience some threat, whether real or imagined, they have the capabilities to navigate the choppy waters. Third, children come to believe, through the messages they receive from their parents and direct engagement with the world, that the world is a fundamentally safe place (while also recognizing that risks and dangers are always present and that reasonable precautions need to be taken).

Children who develop a belief in an insecure world have vastly different experiences and perceptions. They may have received messages about a dangerous world from their parents. They may have had early experiences that caused or reinforced their perception of a dangerous world. Or they may have felt overwhelmed by the world and believed themselves to be incapable of responding to its inherent dangers. Regardless of its causes, children who have an insecure view of the world feel unsafe and scared, which can lead to lasting clinginess and an aversion to exploration and risk.

Protection Is an Instinct

Parents are naturally concerned for their children's safety. As I have noted earlier, parents' instinct to protect their children is paramount. Just as mama bears protect their cubs, so you protect your little brood. Unfortunately, this essential inborn concern can sometimes transform into irrational apprehension and extreme fear. Parents can communicate their own insecurities and fears about themselves and the world to their children through role modeling and out-of-proportion reactions to situations their children encounter. Objectively small risks by children, for example, climbing high on a ladder at the playground, can be viewed as a threat by parents who have a fear of heights or don't perceive themselves to be capable enough to successfully navigate the climb. With these reactions, parents communicate a message based on their own experiences and perceptions rather than one that is appropriate for their children and the present situation.

Parents are also vulnerable to the "if it bleeds, it leads" mentality of the 24/7 news cycle. If we are to believe the news these days, children live in a truly dangerous world in which they are being lost, abducted, molested, assaulted, and killed at an alarmingly high frequency. But the reality is that, based on the objective statistics, the world in which your children live has never been safer. Even threats of considerably less severity, for example, injuries and illnesses, have been reduced through improvements in product safety, hygiene, childproofing, and increased vigilance on the part of parents—creating a world that is a far cry from the "dangerous" environs in which children of previous generations lived.

Your children have sensitive radar that is tuned directly to your emotions and underlying perceptions about them and the world; they will pick up your anxiety on their emotional radar screen as soon as it emanates from you. They will sense your nervousness about their exploring beyond your comfort zone, and they will feel scared themselves because you are sending the message that there is reason to be scared of the world. This message will cause them to learn not only to fear the world, but also to mistrust themselves.

Let Your Children Find Their Limits

Your goal in instilling a sense of a secure world in your children is to allow them to find their own comfort zone and to encourage them to expand it steadily. Children seem to have a pre-wired comfort zone, based on their inborn temperament, that will initially dictate how far they are willing to roam; some are risk averse, some seem fearless, and others lie somewhere in between, depending on the nature of the "risk," for example, whether it is intellectual, physical, or social.

Of course, for your children's safety, before you allow them to explore their world, you need to judge their impulsivity and the degree to which you trust them to be safe when they venture forth.

If they tend to rush off and aren't responsive to your calls to stop, you'll want to keep a tighter rein on them for their own safety.

The key is to allow your children to set the pace of exploration. If you have timid children, you may feel compelled to push them to go further than they are comfortable with to help them overcome their apprehension. This tactic will probably fail because it will send the wrong messages. First, you send the message that you don't respect their comfort and limits. Second, you convey the message that you think there is something wrong with them. Third, your disappointment and frustration may convey unhealthy emotional messages to your children. Your strategy may backfire because when you push children who are not ready beyond their comfort zone, they may feel more discomfort and fear, which may cause them to be even more reluctant to venture forth in the future.

It's better to create opportunities in which they can still explore, but also ensure their perceived security and comfort in the process. For example, you can have them initially venture out with a sibling. Or have your children walk between you and another family member who is some distance from you, thus distracting them from who they are leaving and focusing them on who they are going to. You can also give them a specific goal to pursue, for example, climbing a boulder at the park, which takes their focus away from leaving you (thereby not triggering fear of separation) and directs it toward something positive that they want (thus producing positive emotions such as curiosity and excitement). Some children like to learn the lay of the land before they go off on their own, so you can go with them the first few times they embark on an adventure. You can also set an intermediary goal that is more manageable, such as having them climb only halfway up a hill and touch a rock while you wait at the bottom. As they become more comfortable with these "assisted" explorations and gain confidence in the security of their world, they will probably choose to expand their comfort zone on their own.

When you allow your children to become the first arbiters of their own sense of security for themselves and the world, you send them several messages and don't send several others. The first message is that they can trust you to be there when you are needed (secure attachment). The second message you send is that you trust your children to take care of themselves in most situations and to tell you when they need you (secure self). The third message is that you will respond to them in a manner that is consistent and proportional to the situation (secure world). The messages you don't send your children are those grounded in your own baggage, be it your well-intentioned, though misguided, desire to protect them, or your own fear and panic.

Push Your Own Limits

Awareness of your own perceptions about whether we live in a secure or insecure world is essential to ensuring that you send the right messages to your children. You know you have "baggage" related to security when your children go beyond your comfort zone and you feel that twinge of anxiety or spike of fear consume you (assuming that most people would agree that your comfort zone isn't very big and doesn't even remotely expose your children to any danger). If you can recognize those feelings for what they are, namely, your issues, you will be better prepared to resist your protective urges and send your children messages that will encourage them to find their own limits.

The challenge for you involves determining your own natural comfort zone for allowing your children to explore. That zone is dictated by your inborn temperament, your perceptions about how secure the world is based on your own experiences growing up, and where you lie on the continuum from risk taker to risk averse. And, if you allow yourself to, you will send messages to your children about where that comfort zone is. If your children's inborn comfort zones are smaller than yours, then you will probably just reinforce those limits and possibly prevent your children from extending those limits through experience. If their limits are farther than yours, then your comfort zone may act as a leash, restraining them from broadening their already more expansive comfort zones. In either case, you may inhibit your children from finding their own comfort zones, based on their own innate temperaments and experiences, and instead cause them to adopt yours because of the messages you are sending them.

To bolster your children's confidence, comfort, and willingness to take appropriate risks, I recommend that you first determine where your natural comfort zone lies. If yours is quite small and you typically react with anxiety and reluctance when your children approach the boundaries of your comfort zone, then it will be helpful for you to understand why you have such a reaction and see if you can keep those feelings in check. Then, for the benefit of your children, you should make an effort to extend your comfort zone just a little farther. But only do so if you can manage the anxiety you may feel as a result of allowing your children to go beyond that limit (otherwise, you will likely communicate that angst and they will not explore beyond it anyway). If you are unable to maintain such control, then you might just have to accept that there are some experiences that you should not engage in with your children and leave those to your spouse, who may have a larger comfort zone. Conversely, if you have an expansive comfort zone, in other words, you are a risk taker, you may need to rein in your propensity for risk, recognizing that your children lack the experience and wherewithal to manage the risk that your comfort zone allows. Of course, regardless of which way you shift the comfort zone you allow your children to have, you want to ensure that they are still generally safe.

Safe and Not Sorry

You want to strike a balance in building your children's sense of a secure world. You want them to roam as far and wide as they are comfortable doing, and thereby gain confidence that their world is, in fact, secure. At the same time, you of course don't want to expose them to inappropriate risk. You can start this process by allowing your children to test their limits in settings that are generally considered safe (no situation is completely risk free), for example, a large fenced-in playground or a field. Your children won't know that they are totally safe, so they will explore as far as their comfort propels them. At the same time, because you know it is a safe environment, you won't be anxious no matter how far they roam, and as a consequence, won't send any messages to the contrary. The result is that your children will get the message from the world itself and from you that they are secure. As your children gain more experience, maturity, and confidence that the world is secure, you can let them explore and seek out their limits in less secure environments.

CATCHPHRASES FOR SECURITY

We learned our catchphrase for security from Catie when she was learning to walk. As you know, learning to walk is a very challenging experience for children, perhaps their biggest to date, and there are a lot of trips and falls, scraped knees, and tears along the way. When Catie would fall down, like every parent out there, we would immediately run to her to be sure she was okay and comfort her if she was hurt (which she usually wasn't). We intervened even before there were any messages from her that she needed help! Then, one day Sarah and I observed a similar situation at a playground in which a little girl fell down and her mother came racing

CATCHPHRASES FOR SECURITY

- "I'm okay!"
- "I'm here for you."
- "Safe and sound."
- Scale of "bonkness."
- "Hold it!"
- "Family forever."

to her screaming as if her daughter had been run over by a truck. We looked at each other and realized that could easily be us.

The next time we were out for a walk with Catie, she, as usual, fell down. But instead of rushing to her, we just waited a few seconds. And in those brief moments, our catchphrase was born. Catie got to her knees and announced to us, "I'm okay!" From that day forward, whenever Catie or Gracie did something that could hurt them, for example, tripping or falling off a chair, we let them tell us if they were hurt and whether they needed us. More often than not, no damage was done, and they would let us know with an "I'm okay!" On the occasions when bruises were sustained or blood was spilled, our girls let us know, usually with a cry for help or tears, and we would go to them and calmly and supportively provide the comfort that they asked for. If they didn't say anything at first, we took this as an essential moment when they were figuring out if they were okay. Children are, after all, the best judges of their own well-being, but they need these sorts of experiences, and time to assess their own condition, to hone these capabilities. By rushing to them, especially in a panicked state, you deprive your children of the opportunity to figure out their state of well-being on their own.

Even in situations where there was potential risk, we empowered our girls to decide for themselves when they had left their comfort zone and wanted our support. For example, Catie and Gracie love to walk on a stone wall in our front yard (with a four-foot drop to the street!). We made a rule that they couldn't walk on it unless we were there to spot them. But we never offered or told them that they had to hold our hand for safety. It was always up to them to decide when they got uncomfortable and wanted our hand for added safety. We now use our catchphrase ("I'm okay!") and the approach that we have taught our girls about exploration and risk taking for more complex and potentially dangerous situations such as skiing and biking.

Admittedly, this approach didn't always work out that well. When Catie was four years old, she wanted to walk along another stone wall in our backyard with a three-foot drop to a concrete path.

As I tend to allow our girls to take more risks than Sarah does, I said Catie could. I hadn't noticed that there were some flowery vines that obscured the edge of part of the wall, and Catie lost her footing and fell to the path below. Fortunately, she somehow missed hitting her head on the lower wall on the other side of the path (that would have been really bad!) and the only damage Catie sustained was a big bruise and a small cut on her forehead. Of course, I suffered a near heart attack and a deserved glare from Sarah, and to this day the image of Catie falling still haunts me.

Dirk and Emily had an idea for their catchphrase for their son Harry from day one. From the time he was born, whenever they came to him, they would say, "I'm here for you." Whether Harry's cries were due to a wet diaper or hunger as an infant, his inevitable bumps and bruises as a toddler, or his failures and frustrations as a preschooler, Dirk and Emily sent Harry the message that when he needed them, they were there for him. By the time Harry got to be two years old, he had gotten the message. When Harry would, for example, climb high on a play structure, he would ask, "Are you here for me?" And one of his parents, while spotting him, would say, "Yes, Harry, I'm here for you."

Yuki and Mitch adopted Gregor and Vera from an Eastern European orphanage when they were three and one years old, respectively. Though Yuki and Mitch learned that the orphanage was, by the country's standards, quite nurturing, they had read that adopted children often have difficulty attaching to their new parents and feeling secure after a life that was anything but. So from the time Gregor and Vera arrived in their new home, the catchphrase Yuki and Mitch used (they referred to it as their mantra) was "safe and sound." From those simple words, they sent a message to their two children that communicated security, comfort, and stability.

Erin, the mother of three-year-old Ross, loved the catchphrase idea, but decided to take it one step further. She had read somewhere that having a rating system to judge risk helps children make better choices in their risk taking. The article suggested a numbered system of one for low risk to five for high risk. Around the time that she saw the article, Ross fell off his tricycle, came to his mother crying, and said, "Mommy, I had a bonk." It was then that Erin had the idea of a "catchphrase rating system" with which Ross could rate the potential risk of doing something or the severity of an injury on a scale of "bonkness." For example, Ross loves using the curb on their street as a balance beam. The problem is that if he falls off the curb along some parts of the street, he could fall down a steep embankment. Erin and Ross decided that this risk would result in a "mondo bonk" and he would have to hold his mother's hand while walking on the curb on those sections of the street. Moderately risky stuff, such as bouncing on his parents' bed, would rate a "medium bonk," and less risky stuff, like tripping while running on their backyard lawn, only warrants a rating of "baby bonk."

Rita and Sam believed in teaching their two-year-old daughter Emmy the skills she needed to feel safe. So they thought of the most common ways in which Emmy could get hurt at their house and developed routines to give her the means to prevent these situations from arising. For example, they had a steep stone stairway from their garage to their flat. So they created a catchphrase, "Hold it!" which had a double meaning: Stop before walking up or down the stairs, and hold onto the railing when using the stairs.

Tanya has a different take on security. She emphasizes that her children can rely on the security that comes from being a part of a family. Her catchphrase, "family forever," sends the message that her son and daughter can always count on their family to love and support them.

ROUTINES AND RITUALS FOR SECURITY

Getting lost may be the most disturbing experience that precipitates feelings of insecure attachment, self, and world in your children. It encompasses every bad message about insecurity: I can't trust my parents, I'm not capable, and the world is a dangerous place. As a consequence, we prepared Catie and Gracie for their first forays into the world beyond Sarah and me with several routines and rituals.

We set reasonable boundaries far beyond any that we expected them to exceed. These boundaries, for example, the sidewalk across the field or the top of a hill on a hiking trail, sent them the message that we were aware of and ultimately in control of their journey. We also told them that they always had to be in our sight, sending the message that we could respond to their needs immediately. Finally, as they moved away from us, we made sure that, when they looked back at us, we made eye contact with them and offered a smile, reassuring nod, or wave, communicating the message that we were attentive to their security.

Bob and Maria loved taking their three children to carnivals, amusement parks, concerts, and the like. But because they were "playing a man down" (i.e., outnumbered by their children), they were always worried about losing one of them. During one visit to a county fair, their worst nightmare was briefly realized; their middle boy wandered off and was lost for about fifteen minutes, the worst quarter hour of their lives. Fortunately, a concerned parent, who noticed him lost and crying, comforted and waited with him until Bob found them. After they concluded that keeping their children on leashes wasn't realistic, Bob and Maria decided to figure out a way to make getting lost less scary for their children. Maria's initial reaction was to tell their children to ask the nearest adult for help. But, while searching online for more information, she came across an article that warned against this approach because not all adults could be trusted. The writer recommended that children should ask for help from an adult with children or an adult in uniform, for example, a police officer or an employee with a badge. From that point forward, when they arrived at an event, Bob and Maria established the routine of pointing out people their children could turn to if they got lost. Bob even had the idea of writing his and

Maria's names and mobile-phone numbers on cards and putting them in their children's pockets. Then, if they got lost, they could hand the information to an adult who could call Bob or Maria and tell them how to find their lost child. These strategies not only gave their children a greater sense of security, but allowed Bob and Maria to relax a bit more, too. Of course, their first goal was not to lose their children at all!

Debbie wanted to ensure that her two sons, Kenny and Jed, felt secure enough in themselves to be proactive if they got lost. She started a bedtime routine when they were each around three years old that involved singing songs to help them memorize their address and her phone number: "My name is Kenny (Jed) Smith. This is my address. 421 West Hill Road. Green Valley, California." and "My name is Kenny (Jed) Smith. This is my telephone. XXX-XXX-XXXX." (I changed the address to protect their privacy). Within six months, both boys knew the ditty by heart, and Debbie felt confident that if her sons got lost, they could tell someone how to find her.

Rita and Sam associate the catchphrase "Hold it!" with the routine of their daughter Emmy always having to hold onto either the railing or their hand when ascending or descending the stairs. In fact, Rita and Sam have made it a family routine in which they, too, have to use the catchphrase and abide by the rule. So Emmy gets this message of security through many conduits including the

CATCHPHRASES FOR RITUALS FOR SECURITY

- Set reasonable limits for exploration.
- Keep your children in sight.
- Be available for eye contact.
- If lost, have your children ask for help from a parent or person in uniform.
- Give your children a card with your contact information.
- Have your children memorize their name, address, and phone number.
- Create safety rituals, e.g., holding a stair railing.
- Sing songs with messages of security.
- Use hugs and physical contact to foster a sense of safety.

catchphrase, the routine, seeing her parents do both, and her own experience of navigating the stairs safely.

Tanya, whom I mentioned above and whose catchphrase is "family forever," also has a ritual she uses with her children to further emphasize that message. After dinner, they sit down on her lap, and they all sing "I don't need anything but you" from the musical *Annie*. Tanya is getting this message to her children through several powerful conduits. They are getting the message through both the lyrics and the music (she read somewhere that singing taps into another part of the brain than just saying words). And by holding them while she is singing, Tanya communicates the message of safety and security to her children through physical contact and emotions.

ACTIVITIES FOR SECURITY

Security may be the most subtle message you communicate to your children. Though you can talk to them about what security means, your children will feel a deeper sense of security if it is woven into the fabric of their interactions with you and the world. They receive this message through the conduits that are implicit in your daily lives, whether role modeling, expressions of love, daily routines, or outings.

Secure Attachment Activities

The basics of instilling a sense of secure attachment in children are pretty simple and obvious; just do what parents are supposed to do. Yet when you make the connection between what should be normal parenting and its profound importance to security, this may heighten your awareness of its value and ensure that you take extra steps to provide these fundamental ingredients for healthy attachment.

Be there. Jonah grew up with a father who wasn't "there" much literally or figuratively. His father traveled constantly, and even when his father was home, he didn't show a lot of interest in his three children. When Jonah learned that he was going to be a father, he was determined not to be *his* father. He believed that nothing sends a more powerful message to children than their parents simply being present. And, by gosh, he was going to be very present in the lives of his two children. Jonah didn't just mean being physically there; he didn't want to be in the room as just a warm body with a cold mind (meaning distracted and otherwise occupied). That, he knew firsthand, was worse than not being there at all, because it sends the message that even when you're physically in the room, your children aren't important enough for you to be all there. And in the hectic and connected world in which his family lives, it is so easy to focus on the million and one things he and his wife Lucy could be doing instead of being with their children. Jonah's goal is to really be there for his children—attentive, engaged, and interactive; present in mind, body, and spirit. And he believes that they feel his presence in the deepest way.

Respond to your children's needs quickly and appropriately. Myra grew up feeling neglected. It's not that her mother meant to neglect Myra and her three brothers, it's just that she was a single mother who worked two jobs. When Myra was about to become a mother herself, she read about attachment and realized it was one

---

ACTIVITIES FOR SECURITY

- Spend time with your children.
- Respond to their needs quickly and appropriately.
- Be loving.
- Be close.
- Decision making.
- Environment: parks, beaches, museums, trails.
- Social: parties, camps, playdates, school, concerts, sporting events.
- Physical: play structures, riding bikes, hikes, sports, performing arts.

thing that she didn't get from her own mother. Because Myra's mother was so overwhelmed, she simply couldn't respond to her children when they needed her.

Myra was committed to building that trust and attachment by responding to her two children's needs quickly and appropriately. She wanted to make sure that when Erik and Melanie need her, she would be there to protect them, particularly when they experienced what Myra calls primitive needs, that is, the needs that are most relevant to their survival (even in the twenty-first century), including physical ones, such as hunger or pain, and emotional ones, such as fear, frustration, or sadness.

At the same time, Myra didn't want to spoil her children by being too responsive. She has taught them that not all of their "needs" are real needs ("But Mom, I really *need* that book on my shelf!") and she tries to make the speed of her response appropriate to the urgency of their need. When it is not a crisis, then she wants to send the message that she isn't always at her kids' beck and call and that some of their so-called needs can wait. Myra realizes that when she responds to her children in ways that are out of proportion to their needs, she ends up sending them very different messages (e.g., messages of fear or that they always come first) that can undermine rather than bolster their attachment to her.

Be loving. Before their daughter Kaylie was born, Ike and Lisa heard a great lecture about attachment, the central message of which was that love is children's most basic emotional need and lies at the heart of secure attachment. So Ike and Lisa were going to make sure that they gave Kaylie plenty of love to attach to. When they express their love to their daughter through their words and emotions, they believe they are giving her something to which she can metaphorically "attach." When they express that love through their hugs, kisses, and touches, Ike and Lisa give Kaylie something to which she can literally attach. And when they not only meet some other need, be it fear or hunger, but do so with love, they give her a double dose of the magical elixir that creates secure attachment.

Be close. Rene and Todd made close physical contact a part of their family life. They both worked full time and Rene only took two months of maternity leave, so they worried from day one that their three daughters, now ages nine, five, and three, wouldn't bond with them because they were in childcare so much. Therefore, when they were together, Rene and Todd "wore" their children constantly (with the Baby Björn and Ergo baby carriers, early on, and then in backpacks, in their arms, and on their shoulders as they got older). Rene and Todd were big fans of attachment parenting, and all three girls have slept with them for most of their lives (they even bought a California king bed so everyone could be comfortable).

Secure-Self Activities

Activities that encourage children's development of a secure self involve anything that reinforces their sense of competence and control over themselves and their lives. Such pursuits can be organized, such as sports or arts classes, or informal, such as puzzles and games at home. They can also include household activities, such as chores, cooking and baking, and yard work. You can also incorporate secure-self experiences into your children's routines by allowing them to make decisions about when and how they fulfill their daily tasks. For example, they can decide in what order they want to complete their bedtime routine, what they want for lunch, or what they want to wear to school.

One of the most important secure-self activities in which we got both of our girls involved early on was swimming. By having Catie and Gracie learn to swim as early as possible, not only have we sent a powerful message about their competence and control over themselves in a relatively unnatural setting, namely, the water, but we also have taught them an essential skill that may save their lives (drowning is the second leading cause of death among children twelve and under). Plus, swimming is just plain fun for children.

Dave is an absolute sports fanatic. He loves playing and watching sports. And he wanted his daughter, Patrice, to feel the same way. So from the time she was in a crib, he surrounded her with every kind of ball imaginable (okay, not a rugby or cricket ball, but most other kinds of balls). As soon as she could walk, Dave had her kicking soccer balls, throwing baseballs, and swinging at golf and tennis balls. When Patrice turned three, she took her first soccer class and now, at seven, is playing in a soccer league coached by, you guessed it, her dad. And, happily for Dave, Patrice absolutely loves sports (go figure).

Secure World Activities

Any activity that enables children to explore their world and expand their comfort zone geographically, socially, physically, and emotionally will help instill their sense of a secure world. Open spaces—parks, beaches, museums, or mountain trails—give children the opportunity to expand their geographical comfort zone. Camps, playdates, and school allow children to experience and master social discomfort. And physical pursuits, such as playing on play structures, climbing boulders on a mountain, riding bikes, and going on hikes, can extend their physical comfort zones. All of these activities help children to explore their emotional comfort zone, allowing them to experience, for example, fear, frustration, and disappointment. These activities send the additional message of a secure self because they enhance children's feelings of competence and control over their bodies and the world.

We love taking our girls to parks and watching them explore away from us. Catie, from when she first became mobile, would go quite a distance from us, but always kept in frequent eye contact. She also seemed to intuitively know when she had gone far enough, and often, just when we felt she was getting too far away for our comfort, she'd come to the same conclusion and begin her return journey back to us. Gracie, in turn, was more cautious, often asking us to go with her the first few times she ventured out. But once she gained familiarity with a particular setting, for example, a park or playground, there was no holding her back.

Barb had always been shy and uncomfortable with people, and it had caused her a lot of problems in her life. She figured this was so because both of her parents were introverts with few friends. But she didn't want her son, Richie, to be held back socially. Barb had read that, though shyness was genetic, life experiences could moderate the impact of this aspect of a child's temperament; in other words, Richie wasn't doomed to a life of shyness and social discomfort. So she began to expand his social comfort zone within months of his birth. It started with playdates and childcare at the gym at which she exercised. As Richie developed, Barb took him to parties, concerts, and sports events just so he could be around a lot of people. She also taught him to smile and say hello and good-bye to everyone he met. When Richie was ready for preschool, she enrolled him in one with a small class size his first year so he wouldn't be overwhelmed, but then transferred him to another preschool with a larger class, so he would become comfortable in large groups in preparation for kindergarten. Now in first grade, Richie shows initial signs of shyness when he joins a group (the apple doesn't fall that far from the tree), but in a short time he is right in the mix with the other children—thanks, Barb believes, to her early efforts to enlarge his social comfort zone.

PART III

I Like Others

7

Message #4:
Compassion Is Your Child's Hands ("Sharing Is Caring")

Think of all of the qualities that you admire most in others and that you would most like to instill in your children. My guess is that compassion is high on your list. Why is that? Perhaps because compassion is such a rare gem—a diamond that stands out in our society, where selfishness and disregard for others are as common as rhinestones.

Consider what compassion is. Most fundamentally, it is "not about me." Compassion involves being aware of and caring about the needs of others. It means wanting to help others who are less fortunate than you. Compassion has so many other wonderful attributes associated with it, for example, benevolence, goodwill, selflessness, and empathy, just to name a few. If these qualities were ingredients to be mixed and baked, you would have the recipe for about as fine a person as you could imagine.

We are assured by experts that compassion is hardwired into all human beings because such qualities help us to become functioning members of society. But, if you're like Sarah and me, you would swear that children are born without an ounce of compassion in them; when children are young, they only seem to care about themselves. We are also told by development experts that egocentrism is a stage through which all children pass, but which they will inevitably outgrow. But for parents, that knowledge is little solace when they see their children seemingly incapable even of concern for others, much less compassion in any form. How often have you had this exchange with your children? You: "Please be kind to your brother." Child: "No, I won't" (he says stubbornly). You: "Please be kind to your brother" (said with increasing frustration). Child: "I won't, I won't, I won't" (said with angry finality). You: "You will be kind to your brother or else." Definitely not the best way to send a message of compassion to your children, I'm sure you would agree.

If you follow the science of genetics, you know that just because a trait is genetically transmitted from parent to child doesn't mean that it will naturally emerge in the child. Rather, the new understanding of genetics, contrary to the old argument of nature *versus* nurture, is nature *via* nurture. In other words, genes (nature) are like light switches that are flipped on or left off based on children's experiences (nurture). As a result, the problem is that, even if children are genetically predisposed to compassion, what begins as an egocentric stage can turn into an entrenched attribute if that genetic switch isn't turned on. And the way parents ensure that the switch is flipped is by sending children messages that discourage selfishness and encourage compassion.

It's never too early to get your children out of their "the world revolves around me," "I want it now," and "I don't care about anyone" world. In fact, you must send messages of compassion early and often because once they enter the world of popular culture and peers, your children will be getting messages that actually confirm their egocentric predisposition. As your children first resist your admonitions to "be kind to your little sister" and then slowly but surely absorb your clear and persistent messages of compassion through many conduits, the emergence of this essential attribute in your children will be a wonderful thing to behold. But it definitely won't happen unless you make it so.

POPULAR CULTURE'S MESSAGES ABOUT COMPASSION

Despite its beauty and value, compassion is not held in high esteem by our popular culture. To the contrary, if our popular media (e.g., television, film, music) are any measure, people worship at the altar of "me." This creates a perception that self-love, egotism, vanity, pride, entitlement, and disinterest toward others are attributes to which we should aspire. Video games aggrandize violence and misogyny. Reality TV encourages greed, deception, and humiliation. Our culture of celebrity makes important the trivial and trivializes the important. Professional sports foster an attitude of "win at all costs." Popular culture sends messages to your children that it's cool to be cold, and even worse, that compassion is for weaklings, wimps, and losers.

Popular culture doesn't want your children to be compassionate. To the contrary, it wants your children to be self-centered and totally focused on having their own needs met. When children are acculturated into "Generation Me," they become easy prey for popular culture because its messages about self-indulgence go directly to their egocentric need for immediate gratification—"You can have it all, now, and without any effort." There is no more powerful example of this message of selfishness than the widespread popularity of the expression, "It's all about me." This expression teaches children that everyone and everything in their lives should be directed toward satisfying their needs. It also tells children that the needs and wishes of others are irrelevant.

HOW THE OTHER HALF LIVES

Our world, with its rapid advancements in communication, appears to be shrinking, and the influence that people can have on others, both good and bad, has never been greater. Yet so many children are being taught to look no further than the narrow world in which they live. In earlier generations, most children had greater contact with others different from themselves—people of different races, ethnicities, and socioeconomic status—and this contact fostered an awareness of and appreciation for life on "the other side of the tracks," and by extension, compassion for those who might be different from them.

In contrast, many children today, because of private education, homogenous neighborhoods, and gated communities, have little exposure to people and cultures different from their own. Without a broader perspective on how others in the world live, children are not given the opportunity to develop compassion and empathy for those less fortunate than they.

THE VALUE OF COMPASSION

Developing compassion starts with the recognition that we are not isolated creatures, but rather individuals who are each a part of many groups—families, communities, races, religions, nationalities, and citizens of planet Earth—that not only must coexist, but actually need each other to survive. This realization leads to an awareness of others: who they are, the culture in which they live, what they believe, how they live their lives, and the challenges that they face. Compassion provides us with a context in which we can place ourselves in relation to others. In doing so, we realize that people are more alike than they are different. We all want to be healthy and happy, safe and secure, and feel connected; we work, we play, we raise families. In recognizing the similarities among the most disparate people and cultures, we gain our first sense of compassion through empathy, the realization that we all feel the same things: love, sadness, joy, pain, hope, despair, inspiration, frustration.

From empathy, we develop a concern for others and a wish to put others' needs ahead of our own when necessary. What makes compassion so important is not just that it elicits thoughts and feelings of concern for others, but that it also spurs people to respond to the needs of those for whom they feel empathy.

Compassion can enable your children to understand others who are different from themselves and will allow them to see perspectives different from their own. Compassion will enable your children to contemplate ideas and experiences that will enrich their lives and expand their worldview. It shows children the joy of reaching out to others and helping to make the world a better place. Compassion gives children care and appreciation for others and a deep connection to the world in which they live. Children learn that acting compassionately is also in their best interest. Compassion encourages others to act compassionately toward them, providing them with support and assistance when they are in need. Children learn that compassion can bring them meaning, satisfaction, and joy that they could never experience in the egocentric world in which many children now live. Compassionate children learn the important lesson that compassion begets compassion and that everyone benefits from its expression.

Compassion has been shown to be beneficial to people in other ways. Research has found that compassion acts as armor against popular culture. People who value compassion, helping, and contributing to the world are less likely to be seduced by popular culture's values related to wealth, materialism, superficiality, and popularity. Compassionate people have also been found to be happier and more well adjusted than those who hold values common in popular culture. They also have more energy, fewer behavioral problems, and a lower incidence of depression and anxiety than people who have bought into popular culture's values. The bottom line is that compassion is a very good message for children to receive and integrate into their worldview.

MESSAGES OF COMPASSION

Compassion starts with a thought ("I am a part of this world.") and an emotion ("I care for others and others care for me."), and it is only fully realized and valued when it is expressed through action ("I want to help others."). Your challenge is to send messages to your children that encourage the value of compassion and that provoke in your children those thoughts, emotions, and actions that bring compassion into their lives. Only when children are engulfed by messages of compassion will they come to see its value and embrace it as their own.

MESSAGES OF COMPASSION

- Live a compassionate life.
- Surround yourself with compassionate people.
- Talk to your children about compassion.
- Explore compassion.
- Engage your children in compassionate activities.
- Teach interdependence.

Generosity is the most powerful way to communicate messages of compassion because, unlike thoughts and emotions, it can be observed; generosity involves acting on compassion. At the heart of generosity lies generosity of spirit, which can be thought of as a willingness, in fact, a strong desire, to give of oneself without expectation of anything in return. There are some notable qualities that help to define generosity of spirit. It is voluntary and given freely without strings attached. It has the power to produce meaningful change. It is so effective because people who are instilled with a generosity of spirit are driven to take action. Generosity of spirit is also contagious, causing others to catch and transmit this "affliction of goodness." Finally, generosity of spirit can be expressed in many ways, based on each individual's abilities and opportunities.

Because of the egocentrism of children's early years combined with the increasingly prevalent messages of selfishness and disregard for others that popular culture communicates to children, they're not likely to readily learn compassion on their own. You must nurture your children's ability to care about others in their early years and weave compassion into the very fabric of your family's life, so that your children receive the messages of compassion through many conduits.

The wonderful thing about compassion is that there are so many conduits through which you can communicate messages about compassion to your children. When you immerse your children in a sea of messages about compassion, they are all but assured of getting the messages loud and clear.

Live a Compassionate Life

A common theme throughout *Your Children Are Listening* is that you send the most powerful messages to your children by living and expressing those messages in your own life. This unconscious influence is even more important than consciously sending messages of compassion to them. If you lead a compassionate life, your children will get this message frequently and consistently, and will likely internalize it in their own lives.

Expressions of compassion in your life are communicated to your children in several ways, both obvious and subtle. Your children, particularly when they're young, will most notice the larger compassionate acts you engage in, for example, volunteering your time for a worthy cause or traveling a long distance to support a family member in need. As your children get older and begin to grasp the subtleties of compassion, they will also see the smaller expressions of compassion you make, such as comforting them when they scrape their knee, assuming dinner duties when your spouse is stressed out from work, or helping a neighbor with a house project. Even smaller acts of compassion, such as being kind to a waiter at a restaurant, offer your children subtler lessons about the depth and breadth of living a compassionate life.

Also, as I mentioned earlier, emotions are a powerful means of conveying important messages about compassion. When you express emotions related to living a compassionate life, you show your children how they will feel when they act compassionately. You can begin to make this emotional connection for your children by letting them see the emotions that motivate you to act compassionately (e.g., empathy, kindness) and the emotions you feel when you have acted compassionately (e.g., satisfaction, pride). At first, you may need to tell your children about the emotions you feel, but as they learn and absorb the emotional connection, they will be able to sense them directly from your actions.

Surround Yourself with Compassionate People

Early in your children's lives, you have the most influence over the messages that your children receive. However, as they expand their social world, your messages become less influential and those of others gain sway over them. Unfortunately, many of those messages (e.g. from peers and popular culture) will not be ones that you necessarily want your children to get. But you can create a critical mass of people and institutions who will support and reinforce your messages of compassion. The neighborhoods in which you live, the other families with whom you socialize, the schools your children attend, and the activities in which your children participate are all a part of your children's "message environment" over which you can exert an influence. When you surround your children with like-minded people, those people not only ensure that your children get supportive messages from many different sources, but also act as a shield against unwanted messages directed toward your children.

Talk to Your Children About Compassion

As your children mature, you can begin to talk to them directly about compassion. This conduit enables them to develop an intellectual understanding of what compassion is and the role it can play in their lives. Explain what compassion is and why it is important to them, your family, and the world as a whole. Because compassion is, at its core, an emotion, you should describe what it is like to feel compassion (an urge to do good for someone else) and how it feels to act compassionately (satisfying, joyful, inspiring). To help show your children why it is so important, you can talk to them about the consequences of compassion (connectedness and meaning) and those of indifference (alienation and insignificance). The way to really reinforce this message is to offer your children examples of compassion. Point out ways in which your children can express compassion in your family, for example, by being kind to their siblings. You can also highlight ways they can show compassion toward their community, such as donating old clothes to charity. Finally, you can establish clear expectations about compassion in your family and attach appropriate consequences for violations of those expectations.

Explore Compassion

Raising your children's awareness and understanding of compassion is not going to be accomplished in one or even a few conversations. Instead, this process is an ongoing dialogue in which you regularly engage your children in discussions and experiences related to compassion. You can search for examples of compassion— or its opposites, indifference and hatred—in various forms of media: newspapers, magazines, and the Web will offer daily examples occurring in your own backyard and around the world.

As your children gain a deeper appreciation for and understanding of compassion, you can further engage them with other resources, for example, books, television shows, films, and lectures that describe acts of compassion, indifference, and hatred in greater depth and give your children the opportunity to more fully delve into all aspects of compassion. The goal of these many and diverse forms of messaging is to evoke in your children the thoughts, emotions, and calls to action that will make compassion a part of who they are and the way they live.

Engage Your Children in Compassionate Activities

There is no more powerful way to send messages of compassion to your children than through their actions, by having them directly experience compassionate activities. You can start these undertakings within your family by encouraging acts of compassion toward siblings and toward you, such as consoling a sibling who is upset or being extra loving when you have the flu.

You can then expand the circle of compassion by having your children participate in activities that help others outside the home. The easiest way to express compassion outside of your family is to give money or goods to a worthy cause; we saw this outpouring of compassion and generosity following the hurricanes on the Gulf Coast and the earthquake in Haiti. These messages, though worthy, are less effective with children because the act of giving is at a great distance from the recipients of the generosity, so it is more difficult for children to see, experience, and connect with their acts of compassion.

The most effective way to communicate messages of compassion to your children is through hands-on acts of compassion that give your children direct contact with those they are helping. Making these activities family affairs further strengthens the message of compassion. You can then talk about the experience over dinner to share stories, discuss who and how everyone helped, and share the feelings that the experience evoked.

There are many benefits to this direct experience. Your children see the connection between their efforts and their results, in other words, they put a human face to the beneficiaries of their generosity and see the impact of their compassion firsthand. Your children also experience the emotions associated with compassion, including empathy, caring, and satisfaction, with immediacy and intensity. And they meet and interact with others who value compassion, thus providing an additional conduit for your messages of compassion.

Teach Interdependence

The conventional wisdom is that the transition from childhood to adulthood is marked by a shift from dependence on parents to self-reliance, and that when independence is achieved, children have reached adulthood. But they are, in fact, still one step away from being truly mature adults. Children gain independence by disconnecting from their parents and learning to satisfy their own needs. The problem with stopping at this stage of development is that children maintain the egocentrism that characterized their childhoods. The only difference is that they are now able to satisfy their self-centeredness on their own.

There is actually one more shift that is required for children to become value-driven and contributing adults. This final, essential step for raising children to be compassionate people is teaching them to be interdependent. Children who achieve this final stage of maturity get the message that they must find a middle ground between being self-reliant, being dependent on other people, and others being dependent on them. When children learn the lesson of interdependence, they gain an appreciation for the connectedness between people, which in turn lays the foundation for valuing compassion in their lives.

WHO COMPASSIONATE CHILDREN BECOME

Compassion is a powerful attribute because it is the wellspring of so many other special qualities—such as kindness, love, generosity, and charity—that not only help your children become just plain decent people, but also will serve them well in many aspects of their lives.

Compassionate children are gentle, considerate, and sympathetic. They are responsive to others' needs, helpful, and motivated to do good. Compassionate children are also generous and willing to give of themselves to others. Children who are able to express compassion are loved, valued, and respected, and when they grow up, they become extraordinary friends, coworkers, spouses, and parents. What makes compassion so wonderful for children is that it is a win-win for those involved. The giver feels the satisfaction of giving, and the receiver expresses appreciation and will likely reciprocate in some way, both with the giver and with others.

CATCHPHRASES FOR COMPASSION

The catchphrase that we use to encourage compassion in Catie and Gracie is "sharing is caring." I must admit that I didn't make this one up. Rather, I stole it from my good friend, Dr. Glen Galaich, who was using it with his daughter (I did get his permission to steal the phrase from him). When our girls were very young and were sharing with each other or someone else (or when they weren't!), we would tell them that "sharing is caring." As they got older, when they shared (or should have shared), I asked them, "Why do we share?" and they would respond, "Because sharing is caring." We even heard them tell their friends who weren't sharing that sharing is caring. Catie and Gracie have also taken ownership of our catchphrase by being playful with it. When I ask them why we share, they will now say something like "Garing is laring" or "Haring is maring" and get a real kick

CATCHPHRASES FOR COMPASSION

- "Sharing is caring."
- "Sorry is kind."
- "Feel what they feel."
- "Walk in their shoes."

out of it. But the important thing is that they know what it means. Now "sharing is caring" has become a part of our family's vocabulary and a constant reminder of the importance of compassion and generosity.

Sonya and Ned have always felt that the most important time to be compassionate is when people (children and adults) do something wrong or hurt someone. That is obviously a frequent occurrence with children, whether they are hitting, saying something mean, or not sharing. Their catchphrase for compassion is "Sorry is kind." Whenever one of their three children hurts a sibling or takes something from them, they have to say "I'm sorry for [add offense here], I wasn't being kind." If the child physically hurt someone, they have to give that person a gentle touch as well.

Rose believes that compassion arises from empathy, so she created a catchphrase, "Feel what they feel," to help her son understand how others may feel when he isn't kind. Whenever he did something that was unkind, for example, not sharing, she would say the catchphrase and then ask him "How would you feel if you wanted to play with a friend's toy, but he didn't want to share with you?" and "How would your friend feel if you shared with her?"

Ellen and Kristo also believe that empathy is the key to compassion and use a catchphrase with the same meaning as Rose's. When their two daughters start blaming each other for something, Ellen and Kristo tell them to "Walk in their shoes." The idea is that if each of them can put on her sister's shoes, each can see her sister's perspective and understand why she is reacting as she is. One of the funniest things that emerged out of this catchphrase is that, on several occasions, the two sisters actually exchanged shoes and the conflict was resolved.

ROUTINES AND RITUALS FOR COMPASSION

Your family life is rife with rituals that can send messages of compassion, kindness, and generosity to your children. When you sit down for a meal, you are sharing your food and each other's company. When you hug and kiss your children good night, you are sharing your love. When you play games together, you are sharing your time. When you tell your children stories, you are sharing your knowledge and your imagination.

ROUTINES AND RITUALS FOR COMPASSION

- Recount daily acts of kindness.
- Donate money to charity.
- Give away old clothes, books, and toys to those in need.
- Participate in food drives.

Catie has a job chart on which she places little magnets signifying that she has fulfilled her responsibilities each day (more on the job chart in chapter 11). One of her responsibilities is to "be kind." Every evening while completing her job chart, she has to recount how she was kind that day and to whom.

Catie also has a piggy bank in which she deposits her weekly allowance (more on allowances in chapter 11). We ask her to donate 25 percent of her allowance to charity. Every two months, she donates her charitable savings to a cause of her choice. In the past, she has given her money to earthquake victims in Haiti, a local nonprofit organization that takes care of injured animals, and a nearby homeless shelter. In all cases, Catie takes the money out of her piggy bank, puts it in a little purse of hers, and delivers it personally to the charity.

Some friends of ours, Dirk and Emily, have a ritual with their son that involves giving away, rather than selling, his old clothes, books, and toys. They've told him that they choose to give away things that they could sell because there are many less fortunate families who can't afford to buy everything they need. Every time their son gets something new, he has to give away an old item. (This also reduces clutter in their home.)

Ron and Georgia participate in a local program called Homeward Bound in which they and other families take turns buying, packing, and delivering groceries to a family living at a homeless shelter.

Every other month, they and their three children complete a ritual to support Homeward Bound. The family sits down at the kitchen table and compiles a list of groceries they want to buy, paying special attention to the time of year and the upcoming holidays. The kids paint the shopping bags that will hold the food in bright colors and make cards for the family. Each of their children also selects a small toy from their room for the children in the recipient family. The entire family then goes to the supermarket, and the children are responsible for finding and checking off the items on the grocery list. When they get home, they all pack the groceries and then deliver them to the family at the shelter. Ron and Georgia's children introduce themselves to the family and hand the shopping bags full of food to them. After the delivery, over dinner, everyone shares what the experience meant to them, what they learned from meeting the family, and one other thing that they might do to express their compassion.

ACTIVITIES FOR COMPASSION

Sharing is a huge challenge for young children. Because they are still in an egocentric stage of development, they lack the compassion and empathy necessary to see how not sharing affects those around them. Yet, sharing, as an expression of compassion, is a message that your children must get. We try to strike a balance in which we establish the expectation of sharing (i.e., we encourage and

---

ACTIVITIES FOR COMPASSION

- Create expectation of sharing.
- Allow your children to designate "special" items that they don't have to share.
- Expose your children to diverse people and cultures.
- Expand compassion outward from family to friends and neighbors and beyond.
- Live a life that is about compassion.

sometimes require sharing), yet we also give Catie and Gracie permission not to share some things. We allow them to designate some
of their possessions as "special" things that they don't have to share
with others. Of course, we encourage them to share everything, but
the "special" category lets them feel that they have some things that
are truly theirs. Also, at times when they don't want to share, we
make a point of telling them that the best kind of generosity occurs
when they don't want to share.

Eve and Darren believe that compassion arises from the realization that there are people in the world different from you. So from
their two children's earliest years, they exposed their kids to as
much diversity—racial, religious, age, and socioeconomic—as possible. They live in a neighborhood of mixed ethnicity in a large and
diverse city and explore every nook and cranny of the urban landscape, even poor areas in which they are a bit uncomfortable. Eve
and Darren expose their children to every kind of international cui-
sine they can find (though, admittedly, not every taste is welcomed). They read books to their children that teach them about
other peoples, cultures, and religions. Once the children were old
enough, the family took trips to India, China, Russia, and Africa.

Carly and Jake see compassion as starting close to home and expanding outward. They emphasize to their son and daughter that
caring for each other is the foundation of their family and of compassion, kindness, and generosity toward others. They establish
clear expectations of how they want their family to treat each other
and focus on activities that require cooperation. For example, they
play games, work on puzzles, and do household projects that can't
be accomplished alone.

From this foundation of compassion within their family, Carly
and Jake expanded their message to include their friends and neighbors. They built a strong network of like-minded people who shared
the value of compassion. They and other parents in their network
organized social activities and charitable work aimed at helping not
only those outside their circle, but also those within. In recent

months, Carly and Jake organized a Tom Sawyer–style house-painting party for elderly neighbors who couldn't afford a new paint job. They, along with other parents in their group, arranged a condolence-card-writing event for a member of the group whose father had recently died. And Carly and the other moms in the group, with their children, prepared several weeks of meals for a family whose mother had become seriously ill, requiring surgery and a lengthy convalescence.

One of the most interesting and courageous acts of compassion I have learned about firsthand occurred during my recent visit to a Southern city with a large African-American population, high levels of poverty, and almost uniform geographic racial segregation. Randy, the chaplain at the school at which I was speaking, did considerable charitable work in one of the poorest neighborhoods in the city. Five years ago, he had decided that, for him to have the greatest impact on this struggling community, he, his wife Christina, and their three young children needed to move into the neighborhood, where they would be one of only a few white families. At first, his wife was resistant and worried for the safety of her family. But seeing her husband's passion and determination, she steeled herself and agreed to the move. To their surprise, their family was welcomed into the neighborhood. In the five years since their move, they have never had any problems being a white family in the area. The chaplain's ability to effect positive change in the community has grown exponentially. And their children are not only seeing and hearing messages of compassion, but also living a life immersed in compassion.

8

Message #5:
Gratitude Is Your Child's Heart ("Mo' Grat'")

One of the most neglected messages that you'll want your children to get early and often is the power of gratitude. Consider a simple "thank you." Those two words offer a win-win benefit for the sender and the receiver of the message. A surprising and robust finding of the growing body of research into what makes us happy is that gratitude increases our happiness. For example, when people express genuine, heartfelt gratitude to others, the senders say that they feel happier for several days. And how does the receiver of that gratitude feel? Darned good, of course, because they feel appreciated.

Yet, teaching children to be grateful seems like an impossible task sometimes. How many times have you done something for your children and received no "thank you" in return? More times than you can count, in all likelihood. And how did you feel? Unappreciated? Perhaps a bit angry and resentful because your children have not acknowledged your efforts on their behalf? Less willing to help in the future? All very reasonable reactions to an absence of gratitude. And how many times, after you or someone else helps your children, have you asked them to say "thank you"? I'm sure that if you had a dime for every time, you would be wealthy today.

Though there is some evidence that gratitude, like other "prosocial" behaviors, is inborn, you wouldn't know it from the struggle that just about every parent has in getting their children to express gratitude.

And parents don't get any help from society. We live in a culture where a sense of entitlement is ubiquitous. There are daily media accounts of celebrities, professional athletes, CEOs, and politicians who believe that they deserve everything they receive and who react to their riches, status, and fame with smugness and disdain rather than gratitude. Advertising aimed at children tells them that it is their right to have what they want, how they want it, when they want it, and not be asked for anything in return. And research suggests that we are collectively moving further away from, rather than closer to, gratitude: Narcissism has risen significantly among college students in the past three decades, and a 2006 study of 200 celebrity actors, musicians, and comedians found that they were significantly more narcissistic than the average person, with reality-TV stars scoring the highest on narcissism.

THE POWER OF GRATITUDE

It's easy to overlook gratitude because, for most people, its expressions are often knee-jerk reactions; most adults say "thank you" without even thinking about it. Perhaps because there isn't typically much thought behind gratitude, we take it for granted both as senders and as receivers. Yet, over the last decade, an expansive body of research has emerged demonstrating the extraordinary power that gratitude has in all aspects of our lives. For example, people who express gratitude have been found to be happier, to experience more positive emotions, to have lower levels of depression and stress, and to rate their relationships and lives as more fulfilling. They are more accepting of themselves and others, say they have more purpose and control in their lives, and are able to deal with life transitions better. Grateful people also deal with challenges better because they maintain a positive attitude, reach out for support from others, and focus on finding solutions rather than dwelling on problems. There are social benefits as well: People who are grateful are generous, more empathic, better able to hear others' perspectives, and more likely to help or support others. They also have stronger bonds to others. Most relevant here, children who regularly express gratitude are more optimistic about their families and schools.

There is also an emerging body of literature that has found that gratitude isn't just psychological, but rather affects us physiologically and neurologically. Gratitude appears to produce beneficial hormonal changes and boost the immune system. And these benefits aren't just short-term. Ongoing practice at gratitude produces the repetition needed to wire the neural pathways that make it easier for children to override unhealthy thinking, emotions, and behaviors and to experience positive physiology, thoughts, emotions, and behaviors in the future.

MESSAGES OF GRATITUDE

Gratitude is a message that can be communicated to children through many conduits. That's a good thing because, maybe more than any other message, you're going to have to send the message of gratitude frequently and seemingly for ages before your children finally get it. Though it's easy to blame your children for not expressing appropriate gratitude, their apparent unwillingness to absorb the message of gratitude isn't really your children's fault. Young children are often not developmentally ready to move beyond their egocentrism and recognize the role that others play in their lives. In turn, older children are probably being bombarded by messages from popular culture and peers that stand in sharp contrast to your messages of gratitude.

The experience of gratitude can be thought of in three ways. First, you can send messages to your children about the awareness of what they should be grateful for. When you ask your children simply to recognize all that they have in their lives for which they can be thankful, you send the message of gratitude through several conduits. You send it simply by discussing gratitude with them and allowing them to process your words. They also think about and verbalize what they are grateful for. In this process, they will also experience emotions of empathy and caring that emerge from feeling gratitude. This internally directed experience with gratitude enables children to feel the full force of considering and appreciating everyone and everything for which they are grateful.

Second, you can send messages to your children about expressing gratitude to others who have helped them. This form of gratitude is even more powerful because it involves your children actually engaging in, rather than just thinking about, gratitude. When children express gratitude toward someone, they create a relationship with gratitude that offers both themselves and the recipients tremendous benefits. This externally directed experience with gratitude has an additional impact of exposing your children to reinforcing messages from the beneficiaries of their gratitude. Children will not only generate their own emotions associated with gratitude but also receive verbal and emotional messages about gratitude from the recipients that further bolster the meaning and value of gratitude in their lives.

The most common way that children can express gratitude is to simply say "thank you" to those who help them. But there are other, more powerful ways they can convey and experience gratitude. The idea of "paying it forward" is an active way in which children can, through their actions, honor the help they have received from others. Children who, for example, were consoled by a friend when they were sad can show gratitude toward that friend by, in turn, caring for another friend who is feeling blue. Additionally, one of the best ways for children to express gratitude to adults who give them enriching opportunities, for example, parents who provide them with sports or music lessons, is to take full advantage of those opportunities.

Third, children receive powerful messages about gratitude when they are the recipients of gratitude. When they help other people and receive thanks in return, they experience firsthand the positive influence they can have on others. Children can bask in the emotional reactions of those they help. When children respond to gratitude with a "You're very welcome," they affirm the value of the assistance they provided and the gratitude that was expressed. They can also experience the wonderful feelings of satisfaction, joy, and pride in having helped others.

Fourth, you can reinforce the importance of gratitude and make your children feel darned proud of themselves by acknowledging their actions to others. For example, if a neighbor stops by just after your daughter helped you clean out the garage, you might say, "I really appreciated her help because it would have taken so much longer without her." Of course, you don't want to brag about your children's good deeds (e.g., "My son spent the weekend saving the world!," said with self-congratulation), but a heartfelt and appropriately expressed acknowledgment to others of what your children have done can go a long way in teaching your children about gratitude.

Finally, an underappreciated way to teach your children gratitude is to teach them to express gratitude toward themselves. If your children can appreciate for themselves the value of what they have to offer ("I did a nice thing sending that card to my grandma"), then they will be in a better position to understand others' appreciation for what they do and to appreciate what others do for them. This "self-gratitude" can also contribute to your children's development of self-esteem and self-respect because it requires that they recognize and hold in high regard who they are and what they are capable of giving.

CATCHPHRASES FOR GRATITUDE

Our catchphrase for gratitude is "mo' grat'," short for "more gratitude." When Sarah or I don't feel like we are being adequately
appreciated, we simply say,

CATCHPHRASES FOR GRATITUDE

- "Mo' grat'."
- "You get what you get and you don't get upset."
- "_____, thank you for _____"
- "Have a grateful heart."
- "Gratitude back and forth"

"mo' grat'" and a "thank you"
soon follows. Catie and Gracie will even catch us with a
"mo' grat'" when we don't say
our thank-yous.

Before Myra and Gene had
children, they cringed at the
sense of entitlement in so
many children they met. It
seemed like kids these days
feel they deserve everything they want, when they want it. When
Myra and Gene had children, they sure weren't going to allow that
attitude to creep into their family. And one day after preschool,
their four-year-old son, Erik, gave them their catchphrase for gratitude. Their two-and-a-half-year-old daughter, Melanie, was whining
loudly about not getting the snack she wanted, and Erik spouted
out, "You get what you get and don't get upset." Myra and Gene
looked at each other in shock at the clarity of Erik's message. They
asked him where he learned that, and he said that it was part of a
song that one of his teachers had sung that morning. Then they
asked him what it meant. He said that kids need to learn that a lot
of kids don't have much, and they should be grateful for what they
get and not get angry for not getting everything they want. So the
family decided to adopt it as their message for gratitude. Admittedly, when their children really, really want something, the catchphrase doesn't always settle them down, but Myra and Gene believe
that just putting it out there will enable the message to sink in
sooner or later.

Henry and Anna like to keep things simple. Their catchphrase is "_____, thank you for _____." I add the "_____" because they expect their three children not only to say thank you to those who help them, but also to be specific in what the expression of gratitude is for and to name the person who is the recipient of gratitude; for example, "Mom, thank you for dinner," or "Mrs. Camby, thank you for helping me with my math problems today."

Gloria believes that all good actions must come from the heart. So her catchphrase for gratitude is "Have a grateful heart." Whenever her two children take what they have for granted, she invokes "Have a grateful heart." Plus, she reminds them that there are many children who are less fortunate than they. As she admits, these reminders don't always placate them (and often irritate them), but when the phrase is combined with other messages of gratitude, her children slowly come around to appreciating and expressing gratitude for what they have.

Alma believes that gratitude is actually an exchange between the helper and the helpee. Her catchphrase for her family is "Gratitude back and forth." Alma expects her son, Rex, to solicit help by beginning every request with "Would you please . . ." before he specifies the assistance he is asking for. When it is provided, Henry and Anna urge Rex to then give thanks to the specific person for the particular act of helping (e.g., "Daddy, thank you for getting me more milk.") The recipient of the gratitude then concludes the exchange with "You are very welcome. I'm happy to help." Of course, Alma can't ensure that every person who helps her son will respond this way, but she makes sure she does.

ROUTINES AND RITUALS FOR GRATITUDE

Our family also has a "mo' grat'" ritual every evening when we sit down for dinner. In this case, it means a "moment of gratitude" during which we hold hands around the table, take a deep breath, close our eyes, and for a few seconds reflect on who and what we are grateful for. This ritual has several wonderful benefits. It allows us to put the busy day behind us and relax and be present at the dinner table. "Mo' grat'" enables us to really focus on the good things in our lives. Also, at least once a week, Sarah or I ask Catie and Gracie what they are grateful for and we share with them what we were grateful for. To our pleasant surprise, they almost always are able to readily come up with the names of people they appreciative.

ROUTINES AND RITUALS FOR GRATITUDE

- Moment of gratitude.
- Prayer.
- Require "please," "thank you," and "you're welcome."
- Requests, not demands.
- Gratitude for meals.

Patrick and Denise are devout Christians and use prayer at dinner and bedtime to teach their four children about gratitude. As a part of their dinnertime prayer, the family thanks the Lord for all that He has given them. At bedtime, their children express gratitude toward three people who helped them that day.

To encourage their son Arnie to want to help, Ted and Betsy use his chores as opportunities not only to model gratitude but also to turn the tables on him so he experiences and gains the benefits of being the recipient of gratitude. When Arnie does a chore such as making his bed, Ted and Betsy say, "Arnie, thank you for making your bed. We really appreciate it." In turn, they have taught him to respond with "You're welcome."

Renny is a no-nonsense father who was raised by a no-nonsense father with certain expectations of civility. He wanted his two sons to learn good manners just the way he did. Their family has a simple rule: You don't get anything until you ask for it rather than demanding it, ask specifically for what you want, and then express thanks after receiving it. You know how kids are when they want something, for example, "I want more strawberries!" Demands like that just don't fly in Renny's house. If his boys utter such commands,

Renny gives them a look and says, "If you want something, what do you need to say?" His sons know the answer to their father's question: "Daddy, may I please have more strawberries?" Then, after receiving them, they must say, "Daddy, thank you for the strawberries" (or some variation on that theme). If his boys don't express thanks after they receive what they asked for, Renny takes it away until they do. As his sons have gotten older, they have gotten the message, and he is regularly complimented on their manners.

Terry knows how hard his wife Jaime works to prepare interesting and healthy dinners for their two children, Casey (age four) and Ivy (age two). From five to six o'clock every day, Jaime is in the kitchen, reading cookbooks and following recipes so her family can have a tasty and enjoyable meal together. Unfortunately, their children's response to what appears on their plates was sometimes a resounding—and hurtful—"Yuck!" And even when their kids liked the meal, they were finished in five minutes and their mother received no thanks for her efforts. And Terry had to admit that he didn't always thank Jaime either. After a while, Jaime told him that she felt unappreciated for all of the time and effort she put into making dinner.

Terry decided it was time to take action. At first, he said, "Thank you, Jaime, for a wonderful meal," making sure his kids heard him. But even after several weeks of consistent gratitude, the children still hadn't gotten the message. He could have gotten heavy handed and demanded that they thank their mother for the meal, but he decided to see if he could make it fun instead. At the end of each dinner, Terry would lean toward each of his kids and, covering his mouth from Jaime's sight (giving his children the impression that Jaime wouldn't be able to hear him and this was their secret), whisper "Would you please thank Mama for dinner?" Casey, being older, would get the message and thank her mama immediately, often in a goofy voice and with a funny expression on her face. Ivy was a little more reluctant and would resist Terry's whispered exhortations. But she soon found her own way of expressing gratitude toward her mother. Ivy began to mimic her dad by leaning toward her mom, putting her hand on the side of her mouth, and whispering thanks to her mother. Then, a few weeks later, Ivy said thanks with sign language.

ACTIVITIES FOR GRATITUDE

Sarah is a bit "old school" in her approach to gratitude. In an age of e-mails and text messages, she likes our family to express gratitude the old-fashioned way. When Catie and Gracie receive birthday or Christmas gifts or are given some special opportunity or experience, they are required to send handwritten (or scrawled, in Gracie's case) and decorated notes of thanks to everyone. Their grandparents and others have commented on how much they appreciate the time and effort Catie and Gracie put into the thank-you notes.

ACTIVITIES FOR GRATITUDE

- Write handwritten thank-you notes.
- Play the "wish game."
- Keep a helping chart.
- Read about others who express gratitude.

Frank and Lila play the "wish game" with their three children, often when they are getting bored during a long drive. The game involves identifying someone they care about and making a wish for that person that would make them happy. For example, when Lila's father, "Granddad Earl," left after a recent visit, their three children each chose something they wished for him. Their eldest, Roger, wished for Earl to have a safe trip home. The middle child, Eva, wished for better health because Earl had been ill lately. And their youngest child, Freddie, wished for Earl to make another visit so he could give his grandfather more hugs and kisses. Each child then wrote and mailed a card to their grandfather expressing their wish for him. When Granddad Earl received the cards, he almost burst with joy.

Dede had read that a great way to send the message of gratitude to her three children was to learn about other people who expressed gratitude. If children hear about the experience of gratitude in others, it causes them to think about gratitude and the good things in their own lives. So on her visits to the local library, Darlene selects books to read to her children that focus on helping others and on gratitude. She also searches online for stories of gratitude that she can share with her children at the dinner table.

Anthony and Blair approach gratitude from another angle. In addition to encouraging their two sons to be givers of gratitude, they also want them to be receivers. This means making it part of their daily lives to help others. Blair created a "helping chart" on which the boys record the acts of kindness and generosity they engage in each day and the number of thanks they receive. The two boys are so into the "grat game" that they compete to see who will get the most gratitude points each week.

9

Message #6:
Earth Is Your Child's Home
("We're a Green Family")

Children love the Earth. They really do hug trees. Kids care in the purest and sweetest way for birds, flowers, plants, and animals. Smelling a flower, marvelling at a bee buzzing around them, and jumping with joy at seeing a deer are just a few of the ways that children express their connection, love, and awe for Mother Nature. They wouldn't want to do anything to harm nature. And they would be really mad at their parents if they learned what was being done to their Earth.

I hope there is no argument that, environmentally speaking, we simply can't sustain our current habits for much longer: Air pollution caused by the growing number of automobiles on the road and coal-burning power plants worldwide. Our oceans and seas being fished out. Massive deforestation. Globally, billions of people rising to the middle classes and demanding more of everything. The list goes on. And who will suffer from our disregard for the health of planet Earth? The answer is our children. This chapter is about our children and the Earth that they will inherit. My plea is that we hand our planet over to our children in reasonable condition so that Earth will have many more miles around the sun ahead of it, and our children and their children can enjoy its many wonders as we have.

The sad reality is that our children will be inheriting an environmental mess. Even more sadly, by the time they grow up, most of them will become a part of the problem rather than a part of the solution. In our voraciously consumptive culture, many if not most children are receiving messages that will perpetuate the environmentally destructive legacy of their parents.

Our planet's only hope is for parents to send very different messages and raise "green children" as a result. Parents can connect the wonderful feeling that young children have for nature with a sensitivity to the impact they can have on the Earth and a sense of environmental stewardship for how they can help protect it in the future. We all love our children and want them to have a bright future. A part of that bright future should be the condition of the planet that we pass on to them. If parents can send the right "green" messages to their children, then perhaps they will care enough about Mother Earth to work to undo the damage their parents caused to it.

CONNECTION TO EARTH

A wonderful series of books, *Teaching Green* by Tim Grant and Gail Littlejohn, offers parents many ideas on how to help children develop a deep connection to Earth that can result in a commitment to and sense of stewardship for the future health of our planet.

Develop a Personal Relationship with Nature

At the heart of children's connection with nature is the love that I just discussed. Children will want to take care of Mother Earth because they care for nature. And children will care more about nature if they have a relationship with it. And the only way to develop such a relationship is for children to experience nature fully: they must walk in, play in, explore, see, touch, and smell it. Experiences that are rich in sensory stimulation, intellectually and emotionally engaging, and directly related to the natural world act as the "hook" that makes children feel not only connected to but also an integral part of nature.

Emphasize the Connection Between People and Nature

Because children don't have much life experience, they can't readily see the connections that we have with nature and other people. We are far more connected than children (and many adults) realize, through what we eat, wear, and use in our daily lives, and how we move around. Recognition of this interdependence between ourselves, nature, and others shows children how their everyday actions affect Earth and its inhabitants.

From Awareness to Action

Understanding and stewardship of Mother Earth begins when children gain an awareness of the natural world in which they live through hands-on experience. That awareness should then pique their curiosity and inspire them to gain knowledge about how nature works. This knowledge then gives children the desire and capacity to act to protect Earth.

Past, Present, and Future

Because children have little experience, they tend to view the world in the present. When children study nature, they are able to expand their perspective to include the past, present, and future. They can learn about how the Earth used to be and how nature has evolved over the eons. Children can see how the evolution of both nature and humanity has resulted in the current state of the environment. They can then project Earth into the future and consider possible futures based on where we are now and whether we make environmentally beneficial changes. Then, as children gain both love and understanding for nature, they can project themselves into the future and contemplate how their actions might help foster the brighter future that they envision.

MESSAGES ABOUT THE EARTH

You have a powerful influence on your children's attitudes toward Mother Earth because just about everything you do has an impact on the environment. From the moment you wake up, you use water and electricity (e.g. when you adjust the heat, turn on the lights, brush your teeth, and flush the toilet). For your breakfast, you select, store, and prepare certain foods and drink (your appliances use energy, you absorb the carbon foorprint of the food, and you use water for cleaning dishes). You choose the means by which you get to work and your children get to school (walk, bike, car, or public transportation) and where you shop for groceries (e.g., supermarket or farmers' market). This constant use of our natural resources continues until you turn off your light and go to sleep (and, even then, it continues to a lesser extent all through the night).

Of course, you can communicate messages about the value of being green to your children by talking to them about it, but, particularly when they are young, they won't understand many of your messages. The best messages you send are through role modeling and action. But I should point out that the messages you send will depend to some extent on where you live and the kind of life you lead. For example, in the city, you can send messages about taking the bus or subway rather than driving your car. In the suburbs, your messages might emphasize shopping at farmers' markets and recycling. For those who live in the country, green messages might include growing your own food and heating your house with solar energy instead of oil, natural gas, or electricity.

Regardless of the specific messages you send your children, their initiation into being green will involve allowing them to connect directly with Mother Earth and gain a real love for nature. As that feeling develops, you can teach them practical steps they can take, such as turning off lights and recycling, to honor and protect their planet. In doing so, you give your children several essential gifts. You connect them deeply with the most basic source of their lives. You educate them about the impact that they have on the Earth. And most importantly, you give them the power to ensure that Mother Earth continues to live a long and healthy life.

A useful exercise to help you figure out how you can model a green life for your children is to look at your life and see all of the ways that you have an impact on our planet. Questions to consider include where you live, what and how much you drive, the types of food you eat and where you shop for groceries, what kind of waste you generate and where it goes, and how much time you spend in nature. Your answers to these questions will clarify the messages that you send your children about the environment. They can also provide you with direction on changes you might want to make to convey greener messages to your children.

CATCHPHRASES FOR EARTH

Our catchphrase for sending positive messages about the environment to Catie and Gracie is "We're a green family." Whenever a situation arises where a lesson about conservation or nature can be taught, we point it out and say "We're a green family." Whenever the girls are doing something wasteful, such as leaving the bathroom faucet running, we remind them that "we're a green family" and that "the Earth wouldn't be happy." At around two and a half, Catie surprised us once while we were recycling by saying, "Are the trees happier now?" Our girls understand that our admonitions to, for example, turn off the lights, are tied to a larger message about the Earth—for which they care deeply.

CATCHPHRASES FOR EARTH

- "We're a green family."
- "Mother Earth takes care of us, and we take care of Mother Earth."
- "Reduce, Reuse, Recycle."
- "Green is keen."
- "Save, don't waste."
- "I love nature!"

Not surprisingly, given its nurturing quality, "Mother Earth" is common among catchphrases for the environment. Steve and Caitlyn use "Mother Earth takes care of us, and we take care of Mother Earth" as a reminder to their twins when an opportunity arises to act green. Similarly, Jake's catchphrase for his two sons is "Let's help Mother Earth." He likes his catchphrase because it is collaborative and active; there are things he and his sons can do together to assist Mother Earth.

Jonah and Lucy want their two children to focus on what they can do to help Earth stay healthy, so their catchphrase is the popular three R's of waste, "Reduce, Reuse, Recycle." They feel that the strength of their catchphrase is that it tells their children what they can actually do to support their planet.

Blake says that he tends to come up with corny ideas, and he admits that his catchphrase for Earth is as corny as it gets: "Green is keen." But his three children always get a kick out of his saying it with a funny voice and goofy expression on his face. His children love the rhyme and add a tune to it when they use it. Though Blake has fun with the catchphrase, he also makes sure that his kids get the message by connecting it with the green activities in which they participate.

Marcy is an organizational efficiency consultant, so she is hyperattuned to waste both at work and at home. She and her husband Cameron try to make their home as efficient and waste free as possible, for the sake of the Earth and their wallets. And they want to send this message to their children, Sami and Jessie. Their catchphrase is "Save, not waste." Whenever Marcy or Cameron see waste occurring around the house, for example, lights left on or water running for too long, the children simply tell their children "Save, not waste" and the children get the message and stop the waste.

Tanya wants to instill the same love she has for nature in her son and daughter. So her catchphrase is simply "I love nature!" (said with enthusiasm, of course). When she is outside with her children, whether they are walking, skiing, gardening, or playing, she spontaneously announces "I love nature!" Before long, her kids learned to yell out the catchphrase after she did. Clearly, the message was getting through.

ROUTINES AND RITUALS FOR EARTH

When Catie and Gracie were very young, Sarah and I created routines that taught them about environmental stewardship. For example, they are expected to throw their waste into one of three recycling bins in our kitchen (compost, paper, and plastic) after meals. On Monday evenings, they help me take the recycling from the kitchen and deposit it in the big bins outside, which we then roll out to the curb for Tuesday morning pickup. One of our longest-standing rituals involves eating an orange together after dinner. It is my job to peel the orange, and it is Catie and Gracie's job to take turns bringing the rinds to the compost.

ROUTINES AND RITUALS FOR EARTH

- Participate in recycling.
- Pick up trash while walking and hiking.
- Walk or ride bikes when running errands.
- Celebrate "Green Day" every week.

Tanya created two rituals for her son and daughter about picking up trash they come across. Once a month, they walk the length of their street with trash bags and collect the many bottles, cans, and assorted trash that accumulate on the side of the road. She thinks of it as a kind of "adopt-a-highway" without the official imprimatur. Their neighbors often come out to greet and thank them, providing another conduit to reinforce her message of environmental stewardship. She and her children have been big hikers ever since her kids could walk, and Tanya saw a great opportunity to have a spontaneous "adopt-a-trail" experience. While out on a hike, Tanya will see some trash, pick it up, and announce her catchphrase, "I love Earth!" Within a short time, without any explanation or discussion, her children have begun to follow her lead by picking up trash that they see and then declaring "I love Earth!"

Even though her family lives in the suburbs, Nancy is committed to driving as little as possible. Fortunately, they live in a town where there are many stores not far from their home. She makes biking to the grocery store and on other errands a weekly ritual with her son, Andy. Andy loves the different ways he gets to go biking with his momma. At first, it was on one of those handlebar seats where he had a front-and-center view. He then progressed to a bike trailer where he was able to read and play with his stuffed animals. From there, he moved to a trailer bike that enabled him to pedal. Now Andy, at age six, rides his own bike when they go shopping. Nancy has found this ritual to be one of those special times when she can really connect and have fun with Andy. Plus, in addition to the environmental message, she's able to send positive messages about physical health and enjoying the outdoors.

Mark and Rachel decided to celebrate "Green Day" every week with their three children, the goal of which is to use as little energy as possible. On Saturdays, they walk or bike instead of driving their cars, use candles for light and the fireplace for heat, use only the smallest possible amount of water, and don't use any large appliances, such as the washer/dryer, stove, and oven (they do keep their fridge plugged in though). The family also chooses an activity that will make the Earth happy; for example, they pick up trash in the neighborhood or ride their bikes to town.

ACTIVITIES FOR EARTH

As I mentioned in chapter 5, Sarah has a wonderfully productive vegetable garden that has been a great "classroom" for teaching Catie and Gracie about nature. They are Sarah's little farmers who participate in all aspects of the growing process, from soil preparation to sowing to reaping. Of course, their favorite part is getting to eat the vegetables right off the plants.

ACTIVITIES FOR EARTH

- Grow a garden.
- Use environmentally safe products made from recycled materials.
- Minimize use of energy and resources.
- Educate your children about conservation.
- Explore the outdoors (e.g., hike, fish, camp).
- Pack your children a waste-free lunch.
- Patronize local farms and farmers' markets.
- Eat organic food.
- Reduce your clutter.
- Have a garage sale.

Darlene and Peter believe that, in addition to developing a deep love for Mother Earth, their three children need to learn specifically what they can do to care for their planet. When they're shopping, Darlene and Peter buy only products that are made from recycled materials and aren't toxic to the environment. They also explain what recycled products are, how they are made, and how they benefit the environment. By the time their children entered kindergarten, they were green "pros" who could talk the talk and walk the walk in taking care of Mother Earth.

Along with their catchphrase, "Save, not waste," Marcy and Cameron make an effort to model saving energy and resources at home for their children. They always turn off the lights when they leave the room and keep their water usage to a minimum when showering or brushing their teeth. They also only use the clothes washer or dishwasher for full loads. Marcy and Cameron have taught Sami and Jessie these Earth-friendly habits from an early age and now find that they rarely have to tell their children, ages five and eight, to turn off lights or the like.

Karl grew up in a family of outdoorsy people; hiking, biking, camping, fishing, rock climbing—he did it all. He has a great love for nature, and he assumes it is because his parents showed him their love for the outdoors and then allowed him, through experience, to find his own. While growing up, Karl rarely spent time inside; he always preferred being outside over playing or watching TV indoors. When he became a father, he was determined to instill that same love in his three children. For example, before his kids were one year old, they were old hands at overnight camping (though, admittedly, there were many nights of little sleep). If he finds his children lying around the house, he kicks them outside (in a fun-loving way). All three learned to ride their bikes before they were four years old. Now that they are all in elementary school, his kids are experienced veterans of all things outdoors, and they love nature. As you might expect, Karl is one proud, Mother Earth–loving father.

Dirk and Emily have done everything they can to be both environmentally conscious and active with their son, Isaac. They send him to school with a waste-free lunch, which means no plastic bags and that anything he doesn't eat has to be brought home for composting. They also buy only organic food, such as produce and meats, from local growers. Dirk and Emily make shopping an environmental adventure for the family. For example, they visit a ranch not far from their house where they choose cuts of organic meat, chicken, and pork. The ranch also raises chickens, and Isaac is able to go into the henhouse and handpick their eggs. And Isaac loves playing with the piglets, goats, and calves!

Bob and Maria read a newspaper article about "simplicity parenting," the premise of which was that, by simplifying a family's environment, parents could raise happier and less stressed children. As they read the article, they realized that this approach could also help Mother Nature. They looked around their house and saw, really for the first time, a lot of junk: toys that their children never used, games that they never played, and enough clothing in their children's drawers and closets to outfit an army of little people. For example, they looked in their four-year-old daughter's short-sleeved-shirt drawer and found, much to their shock, that she had thirty-eight shirts (and that didn't include her long-sleeved shirts!). Bob and Maria decided to simplify, and they recruited their kids to help. Each of their three children were allowed to keep fifteen of everything they owned, including toys, games, shirts, pants, dresses, underwear, and socks (they could keep all the books they wanted). Bob and Maria had to follow suit, cleaning out their own closets. Their children were happy to get rid of some stuff, but vociferously resisted discarding other things (kids can get attached to their stuff!). But with some coaxing and surreptitious removal, the entire family successfully filled more than a dozen garbage bags with stuff.

But the cleansing process didn't end there. To throw everything out would have been against their green ethic. So to make this an exercise in environmental stewardship as well as simplification, their family held a garage sale. The sale was a huge success and a great testament to the saying, "One person's trash is another person's treasure." Over the weekend-long sale, they unburdened themselves of most of the items.

Bob and Maria wanted to communicate several other messages to their children through this experience. They donated the remaining items to a local charitable thrift shop, sending the message of compassion. To reward their children's efforts, Bob and Maria gave each of them five dollars to spend or save as they wished, conveying a message of gratitude. (To their parents' pleasant surprise, two of the children decided to save the money.) The rest of the money earned from the garage sale was divided among the three children to each give to their favorite charity. By the end of the weekend, there were five exhausted, yet satisfied and simplified, souls in their home. Now the family repeats this purifying experience yearly.

PART IV

Others Like Me

10

Message #7:
Respect Is Your Child's Measure ("The Look")

The value of respect is one of the most powerful messages that children need to get. It acts as the foundation for others liking your children (no one likes disrespectful people) and for your children establishing healthy relationships. Yet, despite its obvious importance to your children's development, it is a difficult attribute to define. We all know what it feels like to be treated with respect and how it feels to be "dissed." But what exactly does respect entail? A common dictionary definition refers to respect as an appreciation, admiration, esteem, or deference toward another person. But I don't find that characterization thoroughly satisfying. So I came up with this: Valuing someone enough to treat them with kindness, consideration, honesty, fairness, politeness, and trust. And your children should learn that respect applies to you, other people they encounter, and, very importantly, themselves.

Unfortunately, teaching respect to your children can feel like an uphill battle in today's popular culture. NFL star Terrell Owens does his outrageous touchdown dances. *American Idol's* Simon Cowell humiliates well-intentioned—if untalented—singers. Hip-hop artists demean women in their music. There is no shortage of forces in popular culture that counter your efforts to send your children healthy messages about respect. It can sometimes feel as if you're being overwhelmed by an onslaught of messages of disrespect.

RESPECT FOR YOU

The reality is that you have an immense impact on your children, particularly in those early years before they become fully immersed in the social world. That influence initially comes from their absolute dependence on you for all of their needs. But as your children develop, they are increasingly able to rely on themselves to get their needs met without you—so your influence on them is based less on need and more on love and respect. And even when other influences such as peers and popular culture gain a foothold in your children's psyches, you can still have a significant influence on them, but only if you maintain their respect for you.

The challenge, of course, is figuring out how you can earn that respect from your children. The operative word here is "earn." Respect can't be forced, cajoled, or bribed. Respect that is forced is called fear, and all you get for it is obedience and anger. But once your children gain sufficient power to no longer fear you, you lose control of them. Plus, your relationship with them will probably be over. Respect that is cajoled out of children is not respect at all because, by cajoling, you hand your power over to your children. They realize that you need their respect more than they want to give it, so they are now in the position to use their respect as a tool to manipulate and control you. Respect that is gained through bribery isn't respect at all, but obedience for a price. The problem is that, again, because your children gain the power in the relationship, they can up the ante on their incentives whenever they want.

The only way to establish respect in your relationship with your children is for them to value the role you play in their lives by meeting their many and diverse needs. This requires that your children sees that you are willing and able to meet their needs and that their best interests are your priority. If they sense that you are acting in their best interests, even if they don't like it, your children are going to respect your actions and likely follow accordingly. In contrast, if they decide that your actions are in your own best interests and that you relegate their concerns to a lower priority, they are not going to respect you and will likely resist your wishes.

ROLE-MODEL RESPECT

The old adage "Do unto others as you would have them do unto you" never grows old and is an essential tool for communicating messages of respect to your children. You can role-model respect in several ways. Because "do as I say, not as I do" just doesn't work, you should treat your children in the respectful way that you would like them to treat you and others, but being respectful of children is sometimes easier said than done. They can really "push your buttons" and bring out the worst in you; you're sometimes going to get frustrated and angry with them.

As parents, you must at times be tough on your children—for example, requiring that they complete a chore to which they are resistant or holding them responsible for their bad behavior. But being tough doesn't mean being cruel, angry, and demeaning. Rather, it involves holding your children to expectations of appropriate behavior. And that can be done in a respectful way, though it is easy to go to the "dark side" of disrespect, particularly when you are tired, stressed, or rushed, or when your children are being really disrespectful or uncooperative.

This is the juncture that should separate you from your children. When they are being obstinate and disrespectful, you should continue to treat them with both respect and firmness. As difficult as it sometimes is, this means continuing to be loving and calm, and listening and responding to their messages to you so that they get the message of respect that you are communicating to them. At the same time, by holding your ground and providing appropriate consequences for their ill-mannered conduct, you send another message of respect, namely that their disrespectful behavior will not be tolerated, and you expect respect from them. Though you are not likely to be rewarded for your heroically respectful behavior at the time—chances are that they will continue to be stubborn and rude toward you for the moment—the long-term rewards of this messaging are substantial. Specifically, they will also get the message that you are not going to accept their bad behavior. Your calm demeanor will send the message that you are standing firm because it is in their best interests. And they will learn that there is a better way to react when they don't get what they want.

Children are vigilant little beings; even when you don't think they are listening or watching, they are attuned to your every word and action. As a result, your children get messages about respect not just from your interactions with them, but also from their observations of how you treat others. Think about all of the people you come across every day while you are with your children. And think about how you treat them. Are you kind, courteous, and considerate, whether toward your spouse, friends, colleagues, store clerks, or waiters? The bottom line is that if you want to really bombard your children with messages of respect, you have to be respectful of everyone when your children are around. That's not to say, of course, that it's okay to be mean to people when your children aren't around!

RESPECT STARTS WITH MANNERS

Both with your children and with other people in your world, perhaps the most simple and clear way to model respect is through good manners. In the rush and hubbub of daily family life, it's easy to forget the basic "P's & Q's" that every mother tries to instill in her children: Asking instead of demanding. "Excuse me" instead of interrupting. Please and thank-you. Hello and goodbye. Good morning and good evening. "How are you?" and "I'm well, thank you." What is great about good manners is that they are skills that children can practice and develop. A meta-message is that good manners are rewarded with respect from the recipients of the civility and extended back to the giver for a win-win exchange of respect.

BE THE PARENT

Another powerful message about respect you can communicate to your children is that you are their parent. Unfortunately, this isn't an easy message to convey these days because popular culture sends a very different message to parents, namely, that to be a good parent you should be friends with your children. The idea is that children are more likely to listen to their friends than their parents because peers have more of an influence on children than do parents. Admittedly, peer influence grows and parental influence declines with each passing year. But, and this is a very big but, parents can and must maintain their influence for their children's long-term health and well-being, and the way to do that is to continue to be their parents, not their friends. Think of it this way: If your children don't respect you and don't believe that you respect them, they are going to turn to another source for respect, and popular culture is only too happy to show them "respect." But what popular culture is really doing is manipulating children to buy stuff that makes it more money.

The survey of 1,600 parents that I introduced in chapter 1 describes a category of parents who are "Best Buddies" (8 percent of the sample) and who unanimously agreed with the following statements: "I try to be a very different parent than my own parents were," "I sometimes feel more like my child's best friend than their parent," "I sometimes do too much explaining," and "I sometimes praise too much." The message from parents who are Best Buddies is that they are doing everything they can to not be their own parents, regardless of whether their approach is actually good for their children.

When you are friends with your children, you give up your unique relationship with them because they have many friends, but they have only two parents (or sometimes just one). However fun it may seem to be friends with your children, you will actually lose their respect and surrender your influence over them. Let me make this very clear: You cannot and should not be friends with your children. That's not to say that you can't have a friendly, loving, and fun relationship with them. And you are certainly free to become friends with your children when they grow up. But, for now, your children want and need you to be their parents.

Why shouldn't you be friends with your children? Children have equal power with their peers, yet parents and children should not share power. Parents have to do things that friends wouldn't do; friends don't tell friends to bring their dishes to the sink, and friends don't tell friends to take out the garbage. Yet parents need to do precisely that.

Despite their frequent protestations, your children don't want you to be their friends. When I ask children how they feel about being friends with their parents, they look at me as if I'm from another planet. Your children don't want to be friends with you. Why? Because you're not hip (and if you use the word "hip," you're definitely not hip!). It's just not in their mind-set to be friends with their parents. You're their *parents*!

Your children also need you to be their parents. These days, kids as young as seven, six, and even five look, dress, act, and talk like little adults, but the reality is that they are still children without the experience, maturity, or skills to feel safe in their world. Your children need to know that there is someone in their lives who will protect them from the big, scary world in which they live (of course, they would never admit that to you!). When children are friends with their parents, they have equal status and power. Because there is no one in their family who is more powerful than they, children live in a state of fear because they're not ready to take on the world alone. When you're a parent, you show your children that you're there to protect them when needed. This position affords them the security and comfort to explore freely as they navigate their world. Also, when you maintain an authoritative parent-child relationship, you send them meta-messages about respect in other nonequitable relationships they will encounter as they progress through life, including teacher-student and boss-employee.

And amazingly, when you are their parents you send another meta-message, that you love them and are willing to do whatever it takes to keep them safe, happy, and flourishing. And, contrary to the messages that popular culture may be sending you, your children will actually love and respect you more for putting their needs first. They may not thank you now, but I'm confident that they will thank you later.

MAINTAIN POWER

"Maintain power" sounds like such a draconian phrase, as if I were suggesting that you lock your children in their rooms at night or put them on leashes when you leave the house. To the contrary, when applied in the way I describe, maintaining power is all about respect. When you maintain power over your children, you communicate the message to them that you're in charge and it is a good thing for them. You communicate messages of respect to your children by making your children's best interests your number-one priority and by doing what you need to do to ensure their safety and well-being. And you convey to your children that you deserve and expect respect from them.

When you maintain power you aren't utterly dictatorial, but rather strike a balance between setting reasonable expectations for your children and giving them the appropriate freedom they need to develop on their own. You must establish unambiguous expectations and make the consequences of transgressions clear to your children. You need to follow through firmly and consistently when your children demonstrate disrespect to you, others, or themselves. You express respect for your children when you are flexible in your use of power by allowing them to participate in family decisions. In turn, they show you respect by ultimately allowing you to make the final decision on what is best for them.

You also exhibit respect for your children by giving them opportunities to earn more respect and trust. However, if they violate the respect you've given them, they must be held accountable. Your children must get the message that with earned respect comes responsibility and that if they are not responsible, your respect—and their independence—will be lost. Inevitably, your children will periodically abuse the respect you show them; that's just part of being young. What's important is that they get the message from these experiences that respect takes time to earn, but can be lost with one bad act.

BATTLES OF WILL

Whether your children learn the value of respect also depends on how you handle the inevitable conflicts that the two of you will have as they move through childhood. Conflict is a natural part of the parent-child relationship and is essential to your children's separation from you into independent beings. The challenge is not to avoid having occasional conflicts with your children, because conflicts are inevitable and healthy. Rather, it is to keep conflicts from devolving into full-scale wars that fuel disrespect and enmity and drive you and your children apart, so that you lose your ability to send positive messages to them.

Battles of will always involve two messages. The first message relates to the specific area of contention. For example, not long ago, Catie was quite adamant about wanting to wear white tights on a hike, clearly not a good choice for an experience that will inevitably result in dirty clothing. Sarah told her that she couldn't and stood firm in the face of quite strong opposition to her decision (otherwise known as a tantrum!). There were several messages that Catie needed to get from this almost-confrontation. First, clothes have degrees of appropriateness for different situations. Second, she can't expect to get what she wants when she is disrespectful of her mother and throws a tantrum. And third, a meta-message that there are some decisions we will make that she simply must abide by.

Early in your children's lives, you may enter these battles of will unwittingly. It's sometimes easier to surrender and allow your children to win out of embarrassment or fatigue. In public, your children will try to win by embarrassing you in front of others. For example, when you and your children are in a store and they want a balloon that is conspicuously displayed, you say no several times, but they start screaming. Just to quiet them down as others look on disapprovingly, you give in and give them the balloon. Without realizing it, you are sending your children several unhealthy messages. First, that they can be disrespectful of you and get their way. Second, that they can get what they want simply by being loud and persistent.

There will also be days when you are thoroughly exhausted and just don't have the energy to "put your foot down." So you give in to their demands. The meta-message here is that all your children need to do is keep an eye out for when you are tired, and then they can get whatever they want.

Though losing these battles of will may be easiest for you at the time, the messages such incidents convey to your children are definitely not in their best interests in the long run. If they learn that they can get what they want by nagging you, they will learn a painful lesson when they grow up—namely, that stubbornness and tantrums don't work for adults. Instead, if you handle these battles of will well, your children will receive important messages about respect for your authority, self-control, and consideration of others that will serve them well in adulthood.

You have the power to avoid or control battles of will with your children. Battles of will require two participants. If you don't join the fray, battles can't be fought. So pick your battles wisely. Many battles can seem really important at the time and motivate you to dig in your heels and fight to the finish, but, in retrospect, aren't worth the fight and do more harm than good. When you're faced with the opportunity to get into a battle of wills, ask yourself how important it really is, considering the specific issue at hand and the meta-message that might underlie the battle. A benefit to not engaging in some battles of will with your children is that the occasional victory lets them know that you respect them and that they have some control over their lives. When you cede victory before the battle has begun, you send them the message that you respect them enough to allow them to win sometimes. Of course, they don't realize that you have let them win. And you shouldn't tell them!

But when you do decide to take a stand, remain steadfast. Send the message clearly that your children won't get what they want no matter what they do ("No means no!"), and especially if they continue to be disrespectful. If you're in a public place, remember that every parent faces these challenges, and when you stand your ground, those watching will actually envy your resolve.

Respect also takes a hit when you get pulled into battles of will and lower yourself to your children's level. When you react to their provocations by losing control (in other words, by acting like a child), you hand them a ready-made strategy for winning future battles of will. And you communicate the double message that you don't respect them (because you're shouting at them) and that you don't deserve their respect (because you're acting just like they are). Your children learn that if they push hard enough for long enough, they'll ultimately tear down the veneer of maturity that earns you respect and reduce you to their equal. As soon as you stoop to their level, for example, by yelling at your children when you get angry with them, they see that they're now in a battle of wills with another child, and that is a battle they know they can win (because they are better at being a child than you). What gives you the power to win these battles of will, and your children's respect for you, is your ability to maintain control over your emotions when your children lose control of theirs.

The ideal way to deal with battles of will is to create a win-win situation in which both you and your children feel like the winner. This approach to battles of will is best because there is no loser, so no one feels disrespected, and everyone walks away with their heads held high. For example, sometimes after dinner, Gracie doesn't like to bring her dishes to the sink, and despite (or because of) our urgings, she digs her heels in. In our family, both girls are required to clear the table after dinner, so there is no other option. At the same time, we've learned that Gracie, who can be pretty darned stubborn, sometimes just needs a little space so she can feel more in control. So in this situation, we will allow her to do something that she wants to do, such as play for a few minutes with Catie, before asking her to return to the kitchen to clear her dishes from the table. It works every time. In a win-win scenario, you communicate several important messages to your children. They get the message that they are respected enough to have gained a victory. Because you were the one who formulated the win-win, your children see that you are being fair with them, thus earning their respect. Finally, you send the message that compromises can work out better than battles of will.

SELF-RESPECT

When children learn to respect you and others, they get the meta-message that all people should be respected, including themselves. Yet, so many of the messages children get these days from popular culture don't engender respect at all. The messages that children get from popular culture, for example, about junk food and drugs, are decidedly not respectful because they are not healthy.

Certainly, self-respect in children arises from self-esteem; the love, security, and competence that I discussed in chapters 4–6 form the foundation for children being respectful of themselves. If children have self-esteem, they will, by definition, value themselves. Additionally, the messages that children get from their parents and other important people in their lives, for example, extended family, teachers, and friends, reinforce the feelings of being valued that lie at the heart of self-respect. This healthy self-respect can act as armor against the bludgeons of popular culture aimed at pounding down children's self-esteem until they are willing to believe and do anything regardless of how bad it is for them.

You can send messages about three areas of self-respect to your children. First, they should learn to respect themselves physically because without a healthy body, not much else is possible. This is easier said than done in a culture that encourages children to treat their bodies like garbage dumps rather than temples. In a society where obesity is epidemic among young people, junk food and sugary drinks are the rule rather than the exception, children sit on a couch in front of a screen more than they play outside, and inexplicably, physical education and recess are being cut from school curricula (despite the clear evidence that physical activity improves attention, behavior, learning, and grades). You can send simple and practical messages to your children about healthy eating by eating healthy food yourselves and offering your children a balanced and healthful diet. You can convey messages about the importance of exercise by being active and fit yourself and getting your children off the sofa and outside where they can be physically active. You can also sign your kids up for sports and exercise activities.

Research has also shown that children today are not getting enough sleep to function at their best. The blame for this persistent state of fatigue is placed on the consumption of caffeinated or energy drinks, even among young children (25 percent of children over three years of age average more than one caffeinated beverage a day), and the presence of televisions in children's bedrooms (40 percent of children have one). You can communicate a message about the importance of sleep by limiting (or prohibiting!) your children's consumption of beverages with stimulants, and by not allowing TVs in their bedrooms. You can also be sure they get to bed at a reasonable hour.

Perhaps the most dangerous expression of physical disrespect in our culture is the prevalence and promotion of drug use and sexuality, even among children. The sad truth is that your children are entering a world in which they will be bombarded by messages about both that are truly destructive. The only chance your children have is if you inundate them early and often through multiple conduits with messages that bolster their self-respect. These healthy messages will provide them with honest and accurate information to help them make good decisions and support them in withstanding harmful messages.

Your children's attitude and approach to their achievement activities is the second area in which you can help instill self-respect in them. The message of achievement is important within the context of self-respect because positive achievement experiences can have a dramatic impact on your children's sense of competence and self-esteem. If they value their achievement efforts, they will want to devote the necessary commitment and time to perform their best and experience pride in their efforts. How well your children buy into this message may also dictate how successful they are in their academic, athletic, and artistic pursuits because research shows that the greatest predictor of success is the number of hours people put in. Children who derive self-respect from their achievement activities will be motivated to give their best effort.

You can send your children messages about self-respect in their achievement activities by working hard for and taking pride in your own successes. You can also convey positive messages of hard work by showing your children examples of people who have become successful and how they reached their goals. You can reward your children's efforts with appropriate praise, thereby helping them make the connection between those efforts and their successes. Following those successes, you can highlight the wonderful emotions they experience, including satisfaction , pride, and inspiration.

The third area in which self-respect has an influence is children's conduct toward others. Children with self-respect will feel confident and secure in their own personhood, and as a result, will express their attitude about respect to others through kindness, consideration, and compassion. They truly get the message of "doing unto others." Your children will learn about being respectful of others through your messages of respect as I described earlier in this chapter.

In contrast, children who don't have self-respect will probably be unhappy, frustrated, and angry, and as a result, will convey those unpleasant feelings through disrespectful behavior toward others. The issue of children being disrespectful of others has gained prominence in recent years, as the frequency and intensity of bullying among children (even as early as kindergarten) has been on the rise with some tragic results. Analyses of these events generally boil down to two primary causes: Parents who don't set limits or don't hold their children accountable for their behavior, and a culture of wanton disregard in which those who are disrespectful (e.g., the "mean girls") are deemed worthy of admiration.

Cyberbullying has been receiving increased attention in the media and from researchers. In the last few years, there have been several high-profile cases of cyberbullying that led to teen suicide. Research exploring the impact of cyberbullying on young people has found that victims of cyberbullying report higher rates of depression than victims of traditional bullying. Additionally, cyberbullying seems to be particularly harmful because there is no refuge: Information proliferates quickly and widely, cyberbullies can easily hide their identities, and direct engagement isn't possible.

Children with self-respect don't bully others because they have no need to dominate or demean others to feel good about themselves.

Nor do they allow themselves to be bullied because they value themselves enough to stand up to the bullies (who usually back down when challenged) or walk away from their antagonists. Conversely, those lacking self-respect are often either the perpetrators or the victims of bullying. Some children who don't feel good about themselves lash out at others to gain a sense of control or power, and thus validation of their self-worth. Other children who don't value themselves communicate their vulnerability to their peers, thus making themselves easy targets for bullies.

CATCHPHRASES FOR RESPECT

The Taylor family doesn't have a catchphrase for respect, but rather a "catch-expression," which Catie dubbed "The Look." Let me explain. When Catie was about two and a half and started to behave disruptively or disrespectfully, I would, without realizing it, give her an expression in which I would tilt my head, raise an eyebrow, and convey the message, "You are being disrespectful, and if you continue down this road there will be consequences." Then, one evening at dinner when she was about to throw her food, she saw my expression and yelled, "Daddy, don't give me The Look!" I was completely unaware of what she was talking about, and Catie had to explain it to me. From that point on, whenever the girls (Gracie also got the message when she was old enough) were disrespectful, I would either slightly raise an eyebrow or ask them, "Do you want

CATCHPHRASES FOR RESPECT

- "The Look."
- "The easy way or the hard way."
- "Use your kind words and voice."
- "It's not what you say; it's how you say it."
- "Respect your body."
- "Your body is a temple."

The Look?" and they would usually stop their bad behavior because they knew what was coming next. Catie and Gracie had fun with The Look, too; when either Sarah or I did something that the girls deemed disrespectful, for example, if Sarah ordered the girls to do something (we try to ask rather than demand) or I forgot to thank Sarah for dinner (an after-dinner ritual), they would give us their version of The Look. And they often asked me to give them the "fake Look" and would giggle uncontrollably when I complied. But the message of The Look was clear to them: Disrespect will have consequences.

Susannah emphasizes the importance of respect by getting her children to cooperate during their bedtime rituals. They often get rambunctious during their preparations or drag their feet when they are, for example, brushing their teeth or putting on their pajamas. At that point, Susannah invokes their catchphrase, "We can do this the easy way or the hard way." The message here is that her children are going to complete their bedtime rituals whether they like it or not, and it is their choice whether they are cooperative and the process goes quickly and smoothly or they are obstinate and getting ready for bed becomes a struggle. And, in the latter case, there are consequences for their lack of respect. More often than not, Susannah's children choose the easy way.

Yuki and Mitch believe that respect is best expressed through the words and tone of voice that are used. Their two children, Gregor and Vera, often make demands in a most unpleasant tone of voice. Needless to say, that strategy doesn't get them very far. At that point, Yuki or Mitch invokes their catchphrase, "Use your kind words and voice," and Gregor and Vera restate their wishes, and, not surprisingly, often get what they want.

Ty has a similar attitude with his two daughters, but their catchphrase is "It's not what you say; it's how you say it." If either of his girls wants something, they must pose a question that starts with the name of the person to whom they are speaking, followed by a "please" and then the request. When they get what they want, they have to say "thank you" followed by the name of the person who fulfilled the request.

Martha, a massage therapist and yoga instructor, is obviously highly attuned to people's bodies. She has found that the respect her clients show for their bodies is a reflection of their self-respect. And Martha has seen the messages that girls are getting about their bodies from popular culture and is determined to send her daughter Amanda very different messages. Her catchphrase is "Respect your body," which has many different connotations. It means treating her body with respect by eating healthily and being active. "Respect your body" also conveys the message that Amanda has control over what is done to her body. For example, Martha and Amanda have "tickle fights," but if the fun gets uncomfortable for either of them, she can declare "Respect my body" and the other has to stop. Martha believes this is good early training for teaching Amanda to stand up for herself if an adult makes inappropriate advances on her, or if someone is too forward with her when she starts dating.

Terry and Jaime met at a running race and were immediately attracted to each other for their attitudes toward health and fitness. They exercise almost every day and eat a healthy diet, and want to share these beliefs with their children, Casey and Ivy. Their catchphrase is "Your body is a temple," meaning that it is something to be treated with respect. Before every meal, each member of their family says the catchphrase and gives an example of a way in which they treated their body well that day.

ROUTINES AND RITUALS FOR RESPECT

The timeout (we actually call it a "time-off") is a key ritual that we use for sending the message of respect to Catie and Gracie. Time-outs are one of the most commonly used forms of punishment or consequences these days for children who are disrespectful or misbehave (we see it as a teachable moment), but also one of the most controversial. Some parenting experts suggest that timeouts aren't healthy because they cause children to feel rejected, isolated, and dehumanized. We, however, have found

ROUTINES AND RITUALS FOR RESPECT

- Time-off.
- Make eye contact.
- "Meet and greet."
- Share fitness activities.
- Prepare healthy meals together.

them to be an effective tool in teaching respect and responsibility when applied consistently, judiciously, and combined with an explanation and an "I love you" (and considerable research supports its value when used appropriately).

Timeouts communicate three important messages: The adults are in charge, there are some things children must do and other things they are not allowed to do, and actions have consequences. Despite the protestations of critics, timeouts are hardly harsh; they are boring, they prevent kids from doing things they want to do, and kids may feel bad during timeouts. The benefits are that they give children time to calm down, to think about what they did, and to realize that their actions have consequences.

If Catie or Gracie is disrespectful, we first give her a chance to make amends. If she refuses, we pick her up and place her in a corner of a nearby room. We explain why she is getting a time-off (e.g., you hit your sister, wouldn't do your job, or threw your food) and how she can end the time-off on her own (e.g., by apologizing, doing her job, or cleaning up her mess, respectively). After she has made amends, we once again explain why she got a time-off, thank her for being so respectful, give her a hug, and tell her "I love you."

Eve and Darren believe that paying attention is an important sign of respect. It was incredibly frustrating for them to speak to their two children and routinely be ignored. They would ask their children to do something repeatedly with no results. They sometimes got angry because they thought their kids were being disrespectful. Then they learned an important lesson: their children weren't necessarily being disrespectful, but rather got so absorbed in their world that they just didn't hear their parents. To combat this disconnect, when they want something from their kids, Eve and Darren first ask them to look them in the eye. When they do this, Eve and Darren know their children are paying attention and are ready to hear what they want to say. Their children learn that eye contact is respectful, and Eve and Darren are sure that their children are focused on them so they don't need to repeat themselves (or at least not as many times!).

Rene and Todd want their three girls to make a respectful first impression when they meet people. From an early age, they expected Danika, Jenny, and Annie to shake a person's hand, look him or her in the eye, and say hello. This ritual wasn't easy to teach their girls, especially Jenny, who was very shy, but Rene and Todd were determined. They practiced shaking hands with their girls, looking them in the eye, and saying hello. They made a game, called Meet and Greet, that their daughters loved. In the game, they created elaborate stories in which their daughters would play (and even dress up as) characters, for example, princesses at a ball, where they would approach "strangers" (their parents) and introduce themselves. Rene and Todd probably played Meet and Greet a thousand times with their girls, but the payoff was huge: By age five, each of the girls was comfortable and confident enough to, when meeting a new person, extend her hand, look the new person in the eye, and greet him or her with a "hello."

Terry and Jaime wanted to make sure Casey and Ivy got the message of respecting their bodies from an early age. Along with their catchphrase, "Your body is a temple," they shared their exercise routines with their girls. Terry alternated taking their kids on runs with him in the baby jogger. Jaime gave both of them toy dumbbells so they could follow along with the strength routine that she did in the family room three times each week. Casey and Ivy participate in family bike rides, progressing from riding in bike trailers to riding their own bikes. Terry and Jaime also include their children in cooking dinner so they can learn about the different healthy foods that are being prepared.

ACTIVITIES FOR RESPECT

Like most young children, Catie and Gracie have a disrespectful (and annoying) habit of stating their wants as statements (e.g., "I want some more oatmeal."), or even worse, as demands (e.g., "Go get my doll" in a loud voice). When either happens, we simply look them in the eye and wait till they ask a question. If they don't come up with a respectful request, we say, "So you want some more oatmeal. If you want more oatmeal what do you need to do?" If they still don't ask respectfully, we say, "We only accept questions with please." When Catie and Gracie finally make a respectful request, we say something like, "I would be happy to get you some more oatmeal. Isn't it amazing what you can get when you ask in a respectful way?" We then wait for them to say "thank you." If that isn't forthcoming, we say "Isn't there something you should say after someone helps you?" Once they express their gratitude for our assistance, we conclude with "You are most welcome."

> **ACTIVITIES FOR RESPECT**
> - Requests, not demands.
> - Say "excuse me" rather than interrupting.
> - Ask to be excused from dinner table.
> - Call adults by honorific and last name.
> - Be role models of respect.
> - Apologize after bad behavior.

Having been raised by parents who were sticklers for manners and seen how politeness had served her so well in life, Debi was committed to instilling that same courtesy in her son Ethan. She had three requirements related to respect for him. Rather than interrupting her when he wanted to say something, Ethan had to say "excuse me." He also wasn't allowed to leave the dinner table without asking to be excused. Lastly, Debi had noticed that all of Ethan's friends called adults by their first names. When she was growing up, that wasn't even an option, and she felt that such familiarity created a casual atmosphere lacking in respect. So Ethan was required to refer to the adults he met by their honorific and last name. Debi believes that this decorum is a reminder that grown-ups are not like peers and deserve respect from children.

Sonya and Ned noticed that their three children were becoming less and less respectful in their tone toward each other. They had always tried to encourage civility in their kids, but the message didn't seem to be getting through. Before dinner after a stressful day, Sonya and Ned had a real wake-up call; they realized that they were being terrible role models when it came to the way they were talking to each other and to their children. They were speaking with harsh voices and demanding rather than asking; there were no pleases and thank-yous. No wonder their kids weren't very respectful! So Sonya and Ned made a commitment to each other to change their ways for the sake of their children (and perhaps their marriage). With a great deal of awareness and effort, they shifted their tone toward each other to one of calm and civility (most of the time anyway; no one's perfect!) and added those essential little tools of politeness: excuse me, please, thank you, and you're welcome. And lo and behold, after just a few months, they noticed a change in the way their children spoke to them and each other.

Ty and Alicia believe that one of the greatest signs of respect, for both the giver and the recipient, is the ability to apologize after acting badly. Apologies are powerful because they demonstrate that the people who give them have the self-esteem and self-respect to admit they were wrong, something that is pretty uncomfortable for most people. They also show that the giver of the apology values the receiver enough to want to make amends. Ty and Alicia also realize that apologies are relatively rare occurrences in our culture; they often come only after someone has been caught "with their hand in the cookie jar," and they usually lack conviction.

To ensure that their daughters learned the "art of the apology," Ty and Alicia did their homework and learned what the best kind of apologies are made of. They found out that an effective apology has several components: saying you're sorry and being specific about what you are apologizing for, sounding like you mean it, making immediate amends, and changing your behavior for the better in the future. So as soon as their girls were old enough to understand, they were required to apologize for their misbehaviors. Ty and Alicia coached them in the proper way to apologize. For example, if their elder daughter Leigh hit her younger sister Ellie, she was asked to say "I'm sorry for hitting you" (as convincingly as possible), make amends by giving Ellie a gentle touch or a hug, and tell her sister that she would try to not hit her in the future. Of course, the two girls, being sisters, continue to get on each other's nerves with some regularity, so there is plenty of practice in the art of the apology!

11

Message #8:
Responsibility Is Your Child's Shoulders ("That's the Job")

Responsibility is another one of those attributes, along with respect, that is so essential to developing healthy relationships. Consider the phrase, "He (or she) is such a responsible person." What does that message convey about someone? They can be trusted. They are honest and can be counted on to do the right thing. And if they mess up, they'll, well, take responsibility for their mistakes. That's the kind of person we want to befriend, work with, or just generally have in our lives. And that is the kind of person you want your child to become.

Our country was built on responsibility and self-determination. The American Dream was about people pulling themselves up by their bootstraps to create a better life for themselves and their families. People didn't wait for others to give them what they wanted; rather, they "cowboyed up" and did what they needed to do for themselves. If people made mistakes, they accepted culpability and did what they had to do to correct the situation. Americans of early generations knew that the value of responsibility lay in controlling their own destinies and that getting ahead was up to them rather than up to chance or in the hands of others.

Unfortunately, children these days don't often get positive messages about responsibility. We live in a culture where people are led to believe that they can get what they want without effort, struggle, or sacrifice (think reality TV and self-help books). Our culture is also one of victimization in which no one, from politicians to athletes to celebrities, seems willing to accept responsibility for their actions and where "the buck" always stops elsewhere. But someone is to blame, and we're going to sue them to see that "justice" is done.

Parents don't always help either. Many parents believe that holding children responsible for their actions will hurt their self-esteem. Instead, parents blame everyone but their children for their bad behavior or poor performance. If Susie isn't doing well in school, it must be the teacher's fault. If Joey isn't winning games, blame the coach. These parents have spoiled their children by giving them everything they want with no strings, such as responsibility, respect, or hard work, attached. The problem is that these children miss out on the benefits of responsibility. Children can't take responsibility for their good deeds and successes unless they're willing to accept responsibility for their mistakes and failures. Plus, if they don't accept responsibility for their lives, they are unable to do anything to change their lives, so they are true victims, at the mercy of parents, teachers, coaches, popular culture, and other random forces in their lives.

You want to raise your children to take responsibility for themselves. Sure, they'll experience the downsides of responsibility—disappointment, frustration, and sadness—that's just a part of life. But they will also experience all of the upsides—excitement, pride, and joy—because their successes and failures are truly their own. Your challenge is to communicate messages about responsibility that show your children its fundamental value in their lives. Much of your parenting should be devoted to helping your children develop this sense of responsibility, to make the connection that they have control of their lives. This ownership means that you must reject our culture's messages of entitlement and victimization and send your children messages to take responsibility for their lives.

EVERYONE HAS A JOB TO DO

Popular culture communicates unhealthy messages about responsibility to your children. Through its focus on the pampered lifestyles of the rich and famous and advertising that suggests that life should always be a party, popular culture tells your children that if it's not fun, easy, or interesting, or if it's tiring, boring, or uncomfortable, they shouldn't have to do it. The messages of rebellion in pop and hip-hop music, the sense of entitlement shown by professional athletes, and the disdain spoiled movie stars express toward what most people would see as normal responsibilities tell your children that being responsible is just not cool.

Sooner or later, though, your children are going to learn that life for most people just doesn't work that way. To prepare your children for the real world, perhaps the most basic message of responsibility you must convey to them is that everyone in your family has a job to do, and everyone must do their job; that's what makes a family a family and what makes families work. Part of being a responsible person is accepting that there are a lot of things in life that we don't care to do, but we do them anyway because we have to. How often do you do things for your children that you would really rather not do? I'll bet there are plenty of days when you don't feel like preparing dinner, doing the laundry, or putting your children to bed. But you do because that was in the job description that you accepted when you became a parent. Your children need to learn that they, too, have a job to do and that life, now and in adulthood, often involves doing things that they don't want to do.

The obvious benefits of having your children get your messages of responsibility are readily apparent in a family and home that functions well. Additionally, your children will receive several important meta-messages related to responsibility. First, they will get powerful messages about gaining specific competence in useful tasks that will serve them well later in life (e.g., cooking, cleaning, laundry) and a broader sense of competence in their general capabilities that will pay dividends into their self-esteem. Second, by having family responsibilities, your children will feel like needed and valued members of your family. Because they fulfill necessary family functions, they perceive themselves as being important to the operation of family life. This sense of being necessary to the family makes them feel like they are an integral and vital part of it.

FIRM, BUT FLEXIBLE

As you send messages of responsibility to your children, you will walk a fine line between imposing those responsibilities on them when they often do not want to accept them and allowing them to take ownership of those responsibilities and to fulfill them for their own sake. This balancing act will require that you be firm but flexible as you increase the responsibilities you place on your children as they mature.

You must be firm and consistent in ensuring that your children carry out their responsibilities. They must understand that they have no choice but to do their "jobs." When you take this stand, you must be prepared for battles of will. For any number of reasons, being too tired, wishing to assert their independence, not feeling like it, or just sheer stubbornness, there will likely be times when your children, in the most vociferous ways, resist your demands that they complete their responsibilities. And these are battles that you must win if you are to clearly communicate messages of responsibility to your children. This hard-line stance can be frustrating and exhausting at times because children can be obstinate, and they generally don't tire as easily as parents do. They figure they can win these battles simply by attrition. But if you allow them to win these battles, they will get the message that responsibility is not that important and that they only have to be responsible when it is easy and convenient, or when they feel like it (and that is definitely not the way things work in the adult world). You must be resolute; simply don't give in, even if it means a lot of nagging, tears, and time. If you can remain firm and send those messages of responsibility consistently, your children will, in time, get the message and accept the responsibilities as their own.

At the same time, you should be flexible in letting your children choose (within limits) when they can do some of their jobs. For example, you can ask your children in what order they would like to do their bedtime routine. Or you can allow them to clean up their bedroom after they've had a chance to play for a little while. This strategy can reduce resistance (and tantrums!) because your children feel like they just won a battle (when, in fact, you handed them the victory) and had a choice with the job. In a way, you're tricking them into doing the job, but that's what happens when you pit a clever parent against naïve children. Hey, all's fair in love and family!

There are also going to be times when your children are just too tired or just not in a place where they can fulfill their responsibilities. When this happens, you can either help them do their jobs or actually do their jobs for them. You can send several meta-messages of responsibility by being flexible in these situations. One meta-message is that families support each other and can work together to get their jobs done. Another meta-message is that being rigid is a bad thing and being flexible is a good thing. Still another meta-message is that you are sensitive and responsive to your children's needs.

DON'T MICROMANAGE

You have to micromanage your children's lives when they are young for the simple reason that they are entirely incapable of taking responsibility for themselves. As babies, they can't get around, feed themselves, or change their diapers on their own. But, by two years old, children are remarkably capable of taking responsibility for

206 | Your Children Are Listening

much of their lives, and that ability increases exponentially as they mature. The problem is that you may have a difficult time making the shift from micromanager to manager for several reasons. If you dwell on how little your children could do in the past, you may not recognize all that they are capable of in the present. You just become accustomed to doing things for your children and continue doing so out of habit. It is also usually easier for you to take care of things yourself; you can do what needs to be done faster and more easily— for example when getting your children dressed in the morning. But when you retain responsibility for your children past that point when it is necessary, you send them several meta-messages, including that they aren't capable of taking responsibility and that they don't need to take responsibility for themselves.

As your children mature, they become increasingly competent at micromanaging themselves, but aren't yet fully capable of managing their own lives. That is the point at which you must gradually move from micromanaging to managing, in which you oversee the big-picture parts of their lives, for example, establishing boundaries and assisting in decision making. If you continue to usurp your children's responsibilities past the point at which it is beneficial to them, you may hurt their ability in the long term to manage their lives in several ways. Your children won't gain the experience necessary to become more skilled at managing their own lives. They may come to see your micromanaging as an intrusion on their lives and begin to resent you for your efforts. And the longer you micromanage their lives, the more you stunt their development and make it less likely they will be prepared for the responsibilities of adulthood.

GIVE RESPONSIBILITY

The only way for your children to get the message of responsibility is for you to give them responsibility. These messages can focus on responsibility for themselves, for example, taking care of their physical health and well-being, putting effort into their studies, and taking care of their belongings. The messages can emphasize your children's responsibilities as contributing members of your family through chores you assign them, for example, clearing the dinner table and keeping their rooms clean.

Your messages can communicate your children's responsibilities as citizens of the local community and the world at large; examples include participating in school activities, doing charitable work, and demonstrating environmental stewardship. Think about all of the different aspects of your children's lives that they will need to take responsibility for in the coming years and into adulthood. You can begin to prepare them for the rigors of adult life by giving them age-appropriate responsibilities and expanding their "quiver" of responsibilities as their maturity and capabilities warrant.

EXPECTATIONS AND CONSEQUENCES

The best way to send messages of responsibility to your children is through expectations and consequences. When you establish expectations and consequences for responsibility, you convey the message that responsibility is important and that you are counting on your children to live up to that standard. By holding your children to these expectations, you are communicating the meta-message that meeting expectations is also of essential value. For example, when you establish an expectation that your children will make their chores a priority over play, you are sending a message on the importance of responsibility. They can choose to meet the expectations and reap the benefits (e.g., your approval, the good feelings associated with accomplishing responsibilities, increased responsibility and freedom) or fail to fulfill the expectation and accept the consequences (e.g., your disapproval, feeling bad for neglecting their responsibilities, reduced responsibility and freedom).

To maximize the strength of your messages on responsibility for your children:

- Explain to them what responsibility is and why it is important
- Be specific in your expectations of responsibility (e.g., "We expect you to clean up your room before bedtime)
- Encourage them to give their input on your expectations and consider modifying the expectations based on their feedback. The more involvement, buy-in, and ownership they have, the more likely it is that they will take responsibility and satisfy the expectations.

Early in your children's lives, they won't understand the inherent value of fulfilling their responsibilities and meeting your expectations. Rather, they will or won't follow them based on the consequences that you attach, most commonly your approval or disapproval. As they mature and come to understand the meaning of responsibility, they will internalize your messages and follow them because they accept them as their own. Two mistakes that many parents make are:

- Not attaching reasonable consequences to the expectations they place on their children
- Not following through consistently on the consequences they do put in place.

The consequences can be implicit in your expectations (e.g., "If you don't clear the table, we will be very disappointed in you") or explicit (e.g., "If you don't make your bed, you'll have to do a time-out"). These consequences provide your children with the initial impetus to meet your expectations and complete their responsibilities. Though I can't give you specific consequences that you should have for your children—consequences can be idiosyncratic to your family and each of your children—they should be aversive enough for your children to want to adhere to your expectations, but not so severe as to cause them to become angry and resistant because they view them as unfair. Consequences that induce boredom are motivating because children don't like being bored. You can take away something that is valuable to them, for example, a favorite toy, and then allow them to earn it back by doing their job. This opportunity further instills a sense of ownership of their actions because, just as they chose to violate the expectation, they also have the power to meet the expectation—and gain its benefits—in the future. Naturally occurring consequences are the most effective because they connect directly to the expectations; for example, if your children procrastinate when getting ready for bed, there won't be time to read books. Knowing your children and creatively putting yourself in their shoes are the best ways to come up with effective consequences.

Tangible rewards for fulfilling expectations should be avoided because they can turn your children into "reward junkies" who require you to continually raise the reward before they adhere to your expectations. A key step to instilling expectations in your children is to help them find the positive consequences within themselves. The best consequences for when your children meet your expectations are the positive emotions and social feedback that come from doing the right thing. You can help your children make this connection by pointing out the good feelings and positive feedback and by connecting them with the good deed.

Inconsistent or nonexistent consequences are obstacles to your children living up to your expectations. Due to time pressure, stress, fatigue, or expediency—in other words, life!—the best-laid plans of parents to enforce consequences can slip through the cracks. But without consequences, your children have little incentive to meet the expectations you have established. Without the early impetus from consistently applied consequences, your children will never learn or internalize the underlying messages about responsibility that you are trying to communicate through your expectations.

Inconsistent consequences also send conflicting meta-messages about the importance you place on responsibility. One meta-message is that responsibility is not as important as you say it is. If it was, you would enforce the consequences consistently. Another meta-message is that, even if the responsibilities are important, your children need not adhere to them because they won't get into trouble if they don't.

There is no magic formula for following through with consequences. You must make a commitment to the consequences before you establish any expectations (expectations without consequences have no "teeth"). When a situation arises where consequences are required, you must remind yourself of how important they are and, despite fatigue, stress, and other excuses, you must act on them because the consequences are in your children's best interests.

CATCHPHRASES FOR RESPONSIBILITY

As soon as Catie and Gracie had the language skills to understand us, we introduced them to our catchphrase, "That's the job." We told them that we all have jobs to do and we don't always like or want to do them, but we do them because they are our responsibility. Sarah doesn't always like cooking or getting stains out of their clothes, but she does them because "that's the job." I don't like doing dishes or going to work some days, but I do both because "that's the job." And our girls have learned that they have jobs to do, and though the jobs are not usually fun, the girls must do them because, well, "that's the job." Any

---

CATCHPHRASES FOR RESPONSIBILITY

- "That's the job."
- "Take it out, put it back."
- "Families work together."
- "Do it now, do it well."
- "Work first, play later."
- "Listen to your conscience."

time they don't feel like doing a chore, Sarah or I say, "that's the job" as a reminder of their responsibility to do it.

With two high-energy boys and a house full of kid stuff, Edie isn't about to let her home devolve into a chaotic mess. Plus, being a single, working mom with no help, she doesn't have time to pick up after her sons. So they have a simple catchphrase and rule, "Take it out, put it back." Whenever Tommy or Greg finish playing with a toy or game, they have to put it back where they found it before moving on to the next thing. If they forget (which they do frequently), Edie requires that they stop what they are doing and return the previous toy to its rightful place before they continue with their current activity.

Ron and Georgia have very busy lives. They have three children and both have careers, so everyone pulling an oar is a requirement for their family to make it through each day. They believe cooperation is an essential responsibility for families, so their catchphrase is "Families work together." Of course, cooperation is not an easy sell to children who want what they want when they want it and can dig in their heels and resist with all their might anything they don't want to do. As soon as their three children could understand them, Ron and Georgia explained what cooperation was and gave them many examples, such as everyone working together to get dinner ready or pack up for a weekend away. They even found a "secret strategy" that seemed to work with their three kids. When they wanted their children's cooperation, for instance, in getting them ready for bed, Ron and Georgia would "prime" them by asking beforehand if they will cooperate. Their children almost always say yes, after which Ron and Georgia ask if they promise to cooperate. Again, they say yes. Ron and Georgia find that, when they prime the pump, their kids are usually cooperative. It's almost as if, because they promised to cooperate before being actually faced with the prospect of cooperation, the children feel more compelled to follow through.

Ellen and Kristo want to send their two girls, Angie and Allie, two messages: the message that there are responsibilities they have to do in a timely manner, and also the message to do them well. Ellen and Kristo hope that this message will carry over to their school and work lives when Angie and Allie got older. Their catchphrase, "Do it now, do it well," is intended to instill pride in their daughters for fulfilling their responsibilities when they are supposed to and to the best of their ability. Ellen and Kristo are realistic enough to realize that their girls will not always do their chores promptly and well, but they find that with the constant messaging, Angie and Allie are not only mostly doing their chores when told, but also doing them as well as can be expected. After the girls do their jobs, Ellen and Kristo always say, "You did it and you did it well!" (with a lot of enthusiasm and with big smiles on their faces).

Carly and Jake saw it happening after almost every dinner. Their son and daughter would finish eating and immediately run off to play, even though they had jobs to do. So to prevent this behavior from becoming a habit, they created the catchphrase, "Work first, play later." When dinner was about to conclude, they would say the catchphrase to remind their kids that they had jobs to do before they were free to play. Carly and Jake also used "Work first, play later" during their children's bedtime routine to keep them focused when they wanted to engage in horseplay and jump on their beds.

ROUTINES AND RITUALS FOR RESPONSIBILITY

- Make a job chart.
- Have structured bedtime routine.
- Assign ready-for-school jobs.
- Give responsibility for school lunch.
- Create "family rhythm" with assigned jobs.

Erin believes that part of being responsible is making good decisions, so her catchphrase for her son Ross is "Listen to your conscience." She explained to him that his conscience is that little voice in his head that helps him choose the right thing to do. Whenever

Ross didn't feel like doing his chores, Erin would ask him what his conscience was telling him to do. He would stand quietly as if really listening to a voice in his head, and more often than not, make the right decision and fulfill his responsibilities.

ROUTINES AND RITUALS FOR RESPONSIBILITY

Catie and Gracie, like most children, love stickers, beads, and assorted other tchotchkes, and they love being rewarded for their efforts at just about anything. Over the years, we've used all kinds of "incentive" systems to motivate our girls to fulfill their responsibilities. When Catie turned four years old, we bought her a magnetic job chart to help her keep track of her daily responsibilities (you can also get creative and make a job chart by hand and use stickers as rewards). The job chart provided many different options for responsibilities from which to choose, for example, Say Please and Thank You, Take Out Trash, Brush Teeth, and Share. One of Catie's responsibilities has been to select the jobs that she wants to tackle. Recently, her choices have included Be Kind, Put Toys Away, Get Dressed and Make Bed (before breakfast), Stop Whining, Show Respect, Put Clothes Away (before bed). Every night as part of her bedtime routine, she has to place a magnet next to each job that she completed that day. For each responsibility, we ask her to recall a specific way that she did that job. For example, one of her responsibilities is to be kind, so she has to remember when and to whom she had been kind that day. We don't expect her to satisfy every responsibility every day (though she takes great pride in "running the table," a billiards phrase I taught her), but we do impose a consequence, loss of part of her allowance, if she really gets off her game. We also believe that the process of completing her job chart sends Catie messages of responsibility through several conduits: seeing the job chart, thinking about and describing how she fulfilled her responsibilities, placing the magnet on the completed job, and receiving her allowance for doing her jobs well.

Admittedly, completing the job chart every evening can be pretty tiresome, so we have given Catie the opportunity to earn temporary respites. As a reward for her great efforts at adhering to the job chart, we gave her weekends off. Then, when she ran the table two weeks in a row, we allowed her to take an undefined break from her job chart with the understanding that if she fell off the responsibility wagon, her job chart would be reinstated.

With four children, Patrick and Denise have to run a tight ship each night and morning to have any chance of getting the kids to bed in the evening and then getting them off to school and getting themselves off to work on time in the morning. They have clearly defined routines for bedtime and wake-up time. Given that they are outnumbered two to one, the only chance they have is to get their kids to take responsibility for their nighttime and morning activities as soon as possible. After age two, all of their children were required as part of their bedtime routine to brush and floss their teeth (with their parents' help), brush their hair, put away their toys, books, and clothes, and lay out their school clothes for the following day. Patrick and Denise found out the hard way that trying to rush or force their kids usually backfired, so they allow their four children to decide in what order to fulfill their responsibilities. Their morning routine includes getting dressed, making their beds before they head down to breakfast, brushing their teeth after they eat, and having their shoes on by 7:30, when they head out the door. Though there were initial battles with all four of the children, by the time they were all six or older, the family routines ran like well-oiled machines.

Every morning before leaving for school, Barb's eight-year-old son Richie is responsible for packing his lunch (which his mom has prepared) in his lunchbox. As they do their best to be environmentally conscious, he is also expected to keep and bring home, rather than throw away, everything he doesn't eat at lunch. When Richie returns home from school, he is required to wash and dry his lunch containers and utensils and place them on the counter for use the next school day.

Myra and Gene are big believers in "family rhythm," which they define as the natural flow that a family assumes in its daily life. They use responsibility routines to help shape and maintain the rhythm of their family in the face of an otherwise inconsistent and unpredictable life. They find these routines to be particularly beneficial in helping their family regain a calming rhythm after a hectic day of school, work, and afterschool activities.

Once everyone has arrived home in the late afternoon, each member of their family knows the jobs they have to do. Myra begins dinner with help from their five-year-old daughter Melanie. Gene and Erik, their seven-year-old, are responsible for getting the house in order and doing daily household chores such as taking out the trash. As dinner approaches, Erik and Melanie set the table, with Erik in charge of dishes and glasses and Melanie responsible for place mats, napkins, and silverware. After dinner, Erik and Melanie clear the table, then put away their toys, Gene washes the dishes and cleans up the kitchen, and Myra prepares the kids' rooms for bedtime. Their evening concludes with the children's bedtime routines and reading books.

ACTIVITIES FOR RESPONSIBILITY

ACTIVITIES FOR RESPONSIBILITY

- Teach fiscal responsibility.
- Give an allowance.
- Be responsible for time.
- Have pets.
- Teach decision making.

Given how the recent economic crisis is still affecting so many people, the powerful messages sent by our culture of "consumption beyond one's means," and the profligate spending and debt that is rampant in America, Sarah and I are determined to teach our Catie and Gracie to be fiscally responsible. We agree with

Charles Dickens's well-known adage, "Annual income twenty pounds, annual expenditure nineteen and six, result happiness. Annual income twenty pounds, annual expenditure twenty pounds ought and six, result misery." To that end, when Catie turned four, we began giving her an allowance so she could start to learn how money works and grasp the reality of spending and saving.

Our first question was how much allowance Catie should earn. Though the precise amount depends on your family's financial situation, the cost of living, and your children's needs, the experts I spoke to offered a few suggestions. Start with a weekly allowance that is the equivalent of half their age (so $2 for a four-year-old). An increase of $1 per week for each year of your children's lives is realistic until they reach their mid-teens. At that point, when they begin to drive and date, you can calculate their expenses and establish a reasonable allowance that covers their needs. Overall, better to start low and build than to give your children the big bucks now; kids shouldn't start in the corner office either!

Sarah and I decided that Catie would earn her allowance not for fulfilling specific responsibilities, such as making her bed or keeping her room clean, but rather for the totality of her contributions to the family. At the same time, as I mentioned before, Catie would get her pay "docked" if she didn't do the jobs she was assigned. This approach introduced her to the notions of work and exchange of goods and services for money and showed her that if she didn't do her job, she wouldn't get paid, just like in the adult world.

We found a great piggy bank that had four compartments labeled Save, Spend, Donate, and Invest. She is required to deposit 25 percent of her allowance into each slot. Helping her to decide whether to buy something right away with her spending money or to save up for something more expensive sends meta-messages of long-term planning, patience, and delayed gratification. Our hope is that learning to save will make Catie more resistant to the messages of "Gotta have it now!" with which popular culture will soon be bombarding her, and will help her grow up to be a financially responsible adult. Another meta-message, that of compassion and generosity, is conveyed by having her donate a quarter of her weekly allowance to her favorite charity. And we promised her that as soon as she fills up her Invest compartment, she can open up a savings account at our local bank just like her mom and dad.

An important meta-message we want Catie to get is that, as the saying goes, money doesn't grow on trees (at least not in our family). If she ever spends her allowance before the next "payday" (it hasn't happened yet), we won't be giving out any payday loans to tide her over. A related meta-message of fiscal responsibility is learning the hard lesson of living within one's means.

Eliana thinks that one of the most important lessons about responsibility her two daughters need to learn is to be responsible for how they spend their time. When she was young, her parents pretty much left her and her brother to their own devices on how to spend their time. If they were bored, her parents would say, "Well, find something to entertain yourselves." But, these days, she sees so many children whose lives are so programmed that they never seem to have ownership of their time. Between organized sports, music lessons, and study hours, most kids she sees rarely even have free time. And when they are bored, they simply entertain themselves with television or video games.

Eliana doesn't want that to happen to her children. So she keeps her daughter's extracurricular activities to a minimum and makes sure that her girls have plenty of free time. When either of them say they are bored, Eliana tells them that they are responsible for their time and it is up to them to find ways to fill it (and because they aren't allowed to watch much TV and don't own a video-game console, those aren't options). She provides them with plenty of art materials, musical instruments, and games. And on occasion, she will give them ideas about what they can do with their time. Both girls are pretty good at taking ownership of their time, and when they have no plans or are bored, they take it upon themselves to find something to do.

Both Henry and Anna grew up with pets in their families. From cats and dogs to turtles and guinea pigs, they had all kinds of animals in their respective households and loved each and every one of them. They not only wanted their three children to share that love of animals, but to learn about responsibility from them. So from the time their three children could walk, Henry and Anna began to work their family up the animal-kingdom food chain, first with fish, then turtles, then a parakeet, and then one, and finally two dogs.

The one rule that they instituted before they got every new pet was that it was up to the children to care for them, and all three of their kids had to make that commitment. With each pet, each of their children is assigned an age-appropriate responsibility. For example, when they got their first puppy, Dex, a mutt from the Humane Society (which sends a meta-message of compassion and caring for those less fortunate), three-year-old Jackie's job was to fill his water bowl each day. Six-year-old Cara had to keep his food bowl topped off. And nine-year-old Jace had the dirty job of cleaning up after Dex. Plus, the three had to take turns walking him every day.

As with most children who want pets, the three initially over-promised and under-delivered on their responsibilities, but Henry and Anna were firm in providing their kids with reasonable rewards and consequences for fulfilling or failing at their responsibilities. They are also persistent and patient in sending their children the necessary messages of responsibility. Over time, their three children have learned to do their jobs most of the time, and given the joy that their menagerie brings their family, Henry and Anna are happy to take up the slack when needed.

Aaron hadn't always made the best decisions in his life, but adopting May was the best decision he had ever made. In his meandering journey through life, he had come to appreciate the profound importance of decision making in becoming a responsible person. So he was intent on teaching May how to make good decisions early in her young life. He believes that the way to become a good decision maker is to experience the good, bad, and somewhat ugly of decision making firsthand. So from before May could even speak, he gave her opportunities to make decisions, about what to wear, what book to read, or what toy to play with. As May matured and her language skills developed, Aaron began to talk to her about why children make bad decisions; for example, they don't stop to think, they are bored, or they think something will be fun. He also made sure that May experienced the consequences of her decisions and has required her to take responsibility for whatever decisions she makes. Whenever May is faced with a decision, he asks her several questions: Why do you want to do this? What are your options? What are the consequences of your decision? And, finally, is this the best decision for you? Aaron also works at earning May's trust so that when she has an important decision to make (at least by her standards), she will turn to him, and he can coach her through. Aaron's real hope is that when May hits her teen years, she'll still hits out to him when the decisions she will be making are really important!

12

Message #9:
Emotion Is Your Child's Palette ("Feel Bad, Feel Good")

Although I place emotion as my ninth and last essential message, it is not because it's the least important. To the contrary, I conclude *Your Children Are Listening* with emotion because it is the most vital, yet most neglected, aspect of children's development. There is nothing more important to your children's future well-being than the development of what I call emotional mastery. The initial messages your children get about emotions will determine the degree to which their early experiences (nurture) shape their inborn temperament (nature). And the habits that result may very well determine the direction that their emotional lives will take. Despite the importance of emotion, children are typically left to their own devices to figure out the maelstrom of emotions they experience every day. Parents rarely provide their children with deliberate means of understanding their emotional lives, and few if any schools offer classes on emotion. Emotions are also my last message because they transcend and influence the previous eight messages that I've described.

The reality is that emotion is an uncomfortable and difficult topic for many parents (and, in fact, for most people). Previous generations sent their own messages about emotions that conveyed that emotions were something to either be suppressed (in the 1950s) or expressed in any way that feels good (in the 1960s and 1970s). The current generation of parents may not have had positive role models in their own lives (emotions just weren't part of the zeitgeist of their parents' generation), so they have only their own emotional experiences, not all healthy to be sure, to rely on in helping their children to shape their emotional lives.

Popular culture certainly doesn't help children to gain mastery over their emotions. On television, in movies and video games, and on the Internet, children rarely see realistic or healthy depictions of emotions; most often, they see people who are either totally repressed or completely out of control. The extreme expressions of emotion that we commonly see in the media make for great entertainment, but they aren't useful as learning tools for children who are trying to come to grips with emotions that are often overwhelming, difficult to understand, and even more difficult to control.

EMOTIONAL OVERPROTECTION

In recent years, parents have gotten messages from parenting experts that they need to be extra responsive to their children's emotions, the thinking being that negative emotions will somehow scar their children. In doing so, many parents have overreacted to this advice and have gone out of their way to protect their children from so-called bad emotions by placating, distracting, or assuaging these emotions rather than allowing their children to experience and learn from their own emotional ups and downs. For example, too often, I hear parents tell their scared child, "There's nothing to be afraid of," or say to their angry toddler, "It's not worth getting upset about." These parental messages are dismissive of the very real feelings that their children experience and ignore the profound complexity and meaning behind those emotions. They also deny the legitimacy of having these emotions (which the children feel acutely). And, to add insult to injury, these unhelpful messages offer children no way to better understand and manage their emotions.

Contrary to popular belief, when children are not allowed to feel so-called bad emotions, they are hurt in two ways. First, emotions are like two sides of the same coin; children can't feel good emotions, such as excitement, joy, and inspiration, unless they also have the opportunity to feel the bad emotions. Second, without feeling bad emotions, children never learn to deal with those emotions. Thus, overprotection leaves children wholly unprepared for the "real world," where bad emotions are just a part of life.

EMOTIONAL DEFAULTS

In chapter 1, I introduced the concept of defaults, namely, automatic responses to situations in which your children will find themselves. The idea of defaults holds particular significance for emotions because the emotional defaults that your children develop when they are very young will dictate how they experience and express their emotions in the future. The early messages you send them about emotions determine what those defaults will be. For example, when your children get angry, do they lash out at others or go off by themselves to cool down? When they get frustrated, do they give up or take a break and return to the task for another try? When they are scared, do they run away or ask for support and confront their fear? Your messages about emotions can influence the defaults children develop in response to these and other emotional situations.

ARE YOU AN EMOTIONAL MASTER?

Your children learn their most basic emotional habits from you through observation and modeling. Not surprisingly then, given that you are your children's most powerful role model for the first years of their lives, their development of emotional mastery is greatly facilitated when you possess the qualities that your children need to cultivate.

As a colleague of mine once noted insightfully, "A parent's unconscious is their child's reality." Whenever I say that, a chill goes up my spine because of the succinct, yet unsettling, message it conveys to parents. The reality is that, as I have discussed previously, most parents carry with them unhealthy emotional baggage and habits (e.g, low self-esteem, perfectionism, a need for control) from their childhoods that, if left unchecked, will be messages sent to their children. If you are, for example, an emotional victim, it is likely that you will send your children messages that they aren't capable of managing their emotions well, thus passing your emotional victimhood onto them.

Conversely, if you are an emotional master, you are likely to communicate messages that your children can be in command of their emotional lives, and as a result, pass your emotional mastery on to them. You will not only "talk the talk" of emotional mastery, but also "walk the walk"—you will act as a positive role model of the emotional habits and skills your children must learn to become emotional masters. Considerable research supports this link between parents' mental health and their children's, and the value of parents addressing their own baggage for their children's well-being. One of the strongest recommendations I can make to you is to explore your emotional life and ensure that most of the messages you are sending your children about emotions are beneficial for them.

There are a variety of ways in which you can examine your emotional life. You can seek out a trained professional, such as a psychiatrist, psychologist, or counselor, who can provide objective perspectives and insights into your emotional life. Workshops that provide instructional, social, and experiential components can be beneficial. You can also look at your emotional world by reading some of the plethora of self-help books that are available on every issue and neurosis out there. Meditation or other religious and secular forms of introspection can help you access and let go of your perhaps-hidden emotional life. Regardless of the method you choose, your ability to understand and gain control over your emotional baggage is the "gift that keeps on giving," because one of the greatest gifts you can give your children is not to hand over your baggage (like everyone else, they'll accumulate their own as they develop!).

EMOTIONAL COACHING

Emotional mastery doesn't mean eliminating or suppressing emotion. Instead, it involves children being able to recognize what emotion they are experiencing, understanding what is causing the emotion, and being able to express the emotion in a healthy way.

You can facilitate your children's understanding by engaging in "emotional coaching," in which you guide your children in the exploration of their emotional world. Research has shown that emotional coaching can act as a buffer against a variety of psychological problems and that children who are coached emotionally focus more effectively, are better learners, and do better in school.

Children can get so wrapped up in the negative emotions of the moment that they are unable to step back and see that their reactions are not serving them well. It's best not to try to engage children in an analysis of their emotions at this point; they are probably too overwhelmed to think clearly. The best thing you can do while they are in the "heat" of their emotions is to simply be there for them as a safe harbor in their emotional storm. Offer them quiet comfort with the security of physical contact ("hugs heal all wounds"), a calm air they can draw from, and some gentle words of observation and assurance (e.g., "You are really sad now. It's okay to feel bad. You'll feel better soon. Until then, I'm here for you."). Your children will settle down in their own good time, and they will have had the opportunity to fully experience their emotions with you there to support them.

When your children have moved beyond their upset and returned to a basic level of emotional equilibrium, you can then begin to coach them on their emotional experience. Children can easily separate negative from positive emotions, but only with experience can they learn the differences between different negative emotions. When your children feel bad, they may need help distinguishing whether they are, for example, fearful, angry, frustrated, sad, or hurt. Ask them what they were feeling. If they have difficulty identifying what they felt, suggest several possibilities. Then ask if they know why they had gotten upset (e.g., their sibling wouldn't share with them). If, again, they don't know, you can consider the situation and offer several possibilities. It is also useful to have them describe what they felt physically (e.g., "I felt like there was a monster in my tummy."); this exercise makes the emotion more tangible and manageable. Then, ask them if there might be another way to react to that situation that would not make them feel as bad. For example, with a sibling who won't share, they can ask again, ask their parents for help, or find something else to play with. You should, of course, consider your children's age in posing these questions and adjust them to your children's level of development. For example, a four-year-old can understand questions about who made them upset, but may not be able to say what the precise emotion is. In contrast, a seven-year-old will probably be able to say that they feel frustrated, angry, or sad. But even if children don't grasp their emotions fully at first, emotions provide you with the opportunity to begin to send messages about emotional mastery that will have more meaning and value for your children as they mature. They also provide your children with a basic opportunity to learn to coach themselves as they develop the capabilities and maturity to do so.

With your help both as a role model and an emotional coach, your children can learn to recognize and identify their emotions. They can then search themselves and their environment for possible causes of their emotional reactions. When they see the reasons for their feelings, they gain valuable information about emotional experiences that gives them greater understanding and control over what they feel. This process encourages your children to "step back" from their emotions, which lessens the intensity and impact of the emotions. It also provides your children with the opportunity to express what they feel in a healthy way that serves them best.

BE PATIENT

How you respond to your children's often intense and uncontrollable emotional reactions to the seemingly chaotic world in which they live may be your greatest challenge as a parent. Let's be honest. Their emotional lives can be a source of tremendous irritation, frustration, and despair—to the point that you want to throw up your arms and surrender. The development of emotional mastery is a lifelong journey, which your children are just starting. Your power as a parent lies in your ability to send positive daily messages about emotions and look for teachable moments in which to instill emotional mastery. The great thing about emotional mastery is that it is self-rewarding. When your children make a poor emotional choice, they feel bad. Conversely, when they make a healthy emotional choice, they feel better. And each time your children make the right choice, they are making it easier to choose the next time. A meta-message they receive from you is that if you are patient with them, they can be patient with themselves. The ultimate goal of emotional mastery is for your children to be able to fully experience the entire spectrum of emotions, embrace the positive emotions, and resolve the negative emotions in a healthy way.

CATCHPHRASES FOR EMOTION

Sarah and I believe that one of the most important lessons that children can learn is that life has its ups and downs and our emotions reflect those fluctuations.

CATCHPHRASES FOR EMOTION

- "Feel bad, feel good."
- "No yelling, no hitting, no kicking, no biting, no scratching, no pushing."
- "Be loving, be kind, be gentle."
- "Feelin' it big time!"
- "Cool and calm."
- "There is no joy in Whoville."
- "Your emotions, your choice."

There will be great times when we feel wonderful and there will be times when life doesn't go so well and we feel pretty darned bad. There will be highs of happiness, joy, and excitement, and there will be lows of frustration, anger, and sadness. And a related lesson is that neither the highest of highs nor the lowest of lows lasts forever.

Our catchphrase for emotions with our girls is "Feel bad, feel good," which sends the message that there are times when they will experience negative emotions and other times when they will feel positive emotions; that's just the nature of life. When Catie or Gracie (or both) are feeling bad, we don't jump in and try to ease their pain; we just say "Feel bad, feel good" empathically and are there for them. We have found that this catchphrase offers them much-needed perspective when they are engulfed in, and perhaps overwhelmed by, their very strong and immediate emotions. Periodically, when Catie is upset, she will say (between sobs) that she wants to stop crying, but she just can't and that she will never be able to; that is a pretty scary belief on the part of a child. "Feel good, feel bad" reminds her that, in fact, as bad as she is feeling at the moment, those feelings will pass, and she will feel better. And usually within minutes, she is happy again and her upset is a distant memory.

Rita and Sam's daughter, Emmy, has been an emotional little be-ing since birth; she can throw a tantrum with the best of them. Rita and Sam attempt to strike a balance between being empathic toward the intense feelings Emmy is experiencing and setting limits on what is an appropriate way to express her strong emotions. They believe it's okay to be sad, frustrated, or angry, and to express those feelings openly (and even loudly), but Emmy isn't allowed to be dis-respectful or hurtful. Rita created a little jingle that became their catchphrase: "No yelling, no hitting, no kicking, no biting, no scratching, no pushing." Whenever Emmy loses it, Rita or Sam will recite this little ditty in a singsong voice. Though Emmy may still continue to blow off steam, she has learned to express herself within the limits set by her parents. Rita and Sam believe that Emmy's small step toward controlling her emotions is an important step toward emotional mastery.

Rose has a similar, though slightly different, take on setting lim-its with her son, Mickey. One thing that constantly frustrates her is that her most common catchphrase seems to be "NO!" It seems as if she is always telling Mickey what he can't do rather than what he can do. So Rose created an emotional catchphrase that had a posi-tive slant to it: "Be loving, be kind, be gentle." This litany tells Mickey what he can do when he is upset, which Rose can then re-inforce with love and praise.

Frank and Lila are both very emotional people who see no problem with expressing their emotions in an uninhibited way; they fight hard and they love hard. They believe that experiencing emotions fully and intensely is what life is all about. They figure that without being able to express powerful negative emotions, people can't express power-ful positive emotions. Frank and Lila also believe that such intense emotional experiences provide their three children with more opportunities to learn about and gain control of their emotions.

Their catchphrase is "Feelin' it big time!," which is intended to convey to their children that if they are going to feel an emotion, they should experience it as completely and deeply as they can.

Admittedly, their house can be a boiling emotional cauldron at times, but Frank and Lila have found that allowing their children the opportunity to feel their emotions so fully has resulted in a natural moderation of those emotions as they have gained experience in their emotional lives.

Martha has always found that her daughter Amanda's emotions burn hot, and at the same time, that Amanda is unusually sensitive to her mother's emotional state. The downside to this is that when Martha is stressed out or upset, then Amanda's emotional "furnace" burns even hotter. The upside is that when Martha is relaxed and centered, that furnace cools down quickly. So to help both Amanda and herself settle down, Martha created the catchphrase "cool and calm." When either (or both) of them are upset, she says in a soothing voice, "cool and calm," and she notices that the emotional temperature in the room drops considerably. What really makes Martha smile on those tough days that all parents have is when Amanda sees her mother's tension, and applying the catchphrase to her, says, "cool and calm." It's difficult for Martha to continue to feel bad when she hears those words of wisdom from her young daughter.

Mark has been a big fan of Dr. Seuss's *How the Grinch Stole Christmas* since he was a child. As a boy, he loved the characters and the story, but as the father of three children, he came to see a powerful message about emotions in the narrative. Mark and his wife, Rachel, introduced their children to this classic tale at an early age.

As every parent knows, there are a lot of negative emotions flying around families, particularly those with young children; it's just part of experiencing and learning about their emotional lives. At the same time, Mark and Rachel really wanted their kids to see that there are a lot of wonderfully positive emotions that the family can experience. So they created two catchphrases, borrowing from Dr. Seuss, to capture the emotional highs and lows of family life: When their children are down, their catchphrase is "There is no joy in Whoville," to reflect and empathize with the current mood, and when they are up, their catchphrase is "There is once again joy in Whoville!" to get their children to acknowledge the upbeat mood.

An essential lesson that Ike and Lisa want to teach their daughter, Kaylie, is that how she responds to her emotions is a choice over which she has control. So their catchphrase for Kaylie is "Your emotions, your choice." When Kaylie is confronted with a potentially "combustible" situation, they gently say their catchphrase. Though when Kaylie was young, her emotional reactions were far from under her control, with this catchphrase and consistent emotional coaching from her parents, she has gradually learned that she actually can control her emotions and choose how to respond in emotional situations.

ROUTINES AND RITUALS FOR EMOTION

One of Catie and Gracie's favorite games is what we call Funny Faces. At least once a week, usually after dinner, the four of us sit around our kitchen table and take turns choosing an emotion. Then each of us gets to make a face that expresses the emotion. We run the gamut of emotions from sadness, fear, anger, frustration, and disgust to happiness, excitement, contentment, and pride. Even when we are making faces for the most unpleasant of emotions, we always end up with a very different emotion as we quickly dissolve into hysterical laughter because of the fun we are having.

ROUTINES AND RITUALS FOR EMOTION

- Play "Funny Faces."
- Breathe deeply
- Center on the heart.
- Rate emotional situations.
- Recognize teachable moments after upset.
- Talk to your children about emotions.

But this ritual isn't just for grins and giggles. Research has shown that children are wired to be attuned to facial expressions and practice at this can actually teach children empathy and emotional understanding by helping them feel different emotions in themselves and recognize different emotions in others. This game also strengthens our girls' emotional vocabulary and connects the vocabulary of emotion with others' expressions and with the feeling of making those expressions themselves.

Marcy and Cameron are Zen Buddhists who meditate every day and attend evening and weekend retreats as a means of finding an enduring state of inner peace and family harmony. Zen meditation, which includes deep breathing and centering exercises, is a regular part of their family life. To begin dinner, they and their two daughters, Sami and Jessie, hold hands, close their eyes, take several deep breaths, and center their focus on their hearts. Before reading books, taking naps, and bedtime, they share deep breaths and centering with their girls. When their lives get busy and stressed, Marcy and Cameron use deep breathing and centering as their mantra to calm down and be in the moment. When their daughters are upset, Marcy and Cameron encourage them to take deep breaths and center themselves to settle down. Marcy and Cameron have woven this ritual into their daughters' lives because they believe that if deep breathing and centering can become habits, this will provide their daughters with a powerful tool for regaining control of their emotions and their physical state when they are feeling out of control.

Dave's daughter, Patrice, is one sensitive gal. It seems just about anything that doesn't go her way can set her off, no matter how unimportant it seems from the outside. When Patrice turned four, Dave felt she was ready to start learning how to judge what was worth getting upset about and what wasn't. He read about a strategy in which he would ask Patrice to rate the importance of the situation causing the upset on a 1 to 5 scale (where 1 is not very important and 5 is very important). He introduced Patrice to the "Upset Scale" and made it one of their emotional rituals to help her gain perspective on her distress. Though it was certainly not a panacea for her sensitivity, Dave noticed that over the ensuing months, Patrice seemed to get upset less often, and when she did, and applied the Upset Scale, she would settle down more quickly.

Debbie and Armand believe in teachable moments, and, when it comes to emotions, they have experienced plenty from their eight- and four-year-old sons, Kenny and Jed. They know that they can't talk reason with their boys when they are in a bad place emotionally; they have learned that the hard way. But Debbie and Armand find that once their sons calm down, they are usually receptive to a conversation about emotions. So they make it a family ritual to talk to Kenny and Jed after a period of upset. In these discussions, Debbie and Armand probe their sons as to what emotion they were feeling and what caused it. They also explore what makes them feel better and make sure that their boys remember what worked. Most important, they talk about ways in which Kenny and Jed can avoid their upset altogether and come up with several new strategies their boys can use the next time they are set off.

ACTIVITIES FOR EMOTION

Sarah and I often wonder how Catie and Gracie (or any children, for that matter) figure out their emotional lives at all. Just think what it's like for them. They feel so many different emotions so strongly in their hearts, bodies, and minds, yet have no context to put them in, no perspective from which to understand them, and no strategies to deal with them. It is truly trial-and-error learning, and given the incredible impact of emotions on children, that just doesn't seem like a good way to learn about them.

There are two things that we do to provide our children with context, perspective, and strategies for their emotional-learning process. First, we connect emotions to our daily lives. When we are doing something as a normal part of our day that elicits an emotion, positive or negative, we label and mirror it. For example, if the girls are having a great time riding their bikes, we'll say something like

"You seem so happy riding your bikes!" in a tone that reflects that happiness. Conversely, when we are in situations that evoke a negative emotion, for instance, if I'm struggling to fix a leak in our garden's irrigation system, I will say "I get so frustrated when things don't work the way I want them to!" in a tone that expresses my consternation and irritation. This activity allows Catie and Gracie to understand that all emotions are just part of life. It also shows them that their parents experience the same sorts of feelings they do.

ACTIVITIES FOR EMOTION

- Connect emotions to your daily lives.
- Offer constructive ways to express emotions.
- Ask your children what will make them feel better.
- Stay calm and composed in the face of tantrums.
- Be empathic, yet firm.
- Don't yell.
- Understand the underlying cause of tantrums.
- Teach your children the vocabulary of emotions.
- Praise good emotional choices.
- Don't forget the positive emotions.

Second, Sarah and I guide Catie and Gracie to deal with their emotions in healthy ways, particularly negative emotions, such as anger or sadness, that make them feel bad and often aren't expressed well. We give them examples of constructive ways to deal with their emotions. For example, if Catie or Gracie are sad, one of us might say "When I feel sad about something, I like to sit by myself for a while till I figure it out and then I like to be with people because that makes me happier," or "I don't like to feel sad, so I do something that makes me happy, like go for a run. What could you do when you're sad that would make you feel better?" Or, using the example of frustration above, "When I'm frustrated, I stop doing what is frustrating me, take a deep breath, and ask for help." We also ask our girls what they like to do to feel better when they don't feel happy. Catie likes to paint or draw, play dress-up, read books, and bounce on her bed. Gracie likes to run around outside, play with Catie, and snuggle with her mom or dad.

Terry and Jaime find that their biggest emotional challenge with their children, Casey and Ivy, is when one of them throws a temper tantrum. Terry and Jaime are always conflicted about how to respond. On the one hand, tantrums can be messages that all is not right in their children's world, that they are sad, frustrated, afraid, tired, hungry, or sick. In this case, Terry and Jaime want to be empathetic and responsive. On the other hand, temper tantrums can be indications of being spoiled, wanting immediate gratification, or attempting to manipulate parents. In this case, if Terry and Jaime give in, their kids learn that they can get anything they want if they just "burn really hot." And it is often impossible to tell which is which!

Their strategy for tantrums starts with staying calm. If Terry or Jaime get upset, then it can turn into a mixed-martial-arts cage match in which everyone loses. When Terry and Jaime are composed, they avoid "feeding the fire" and their calm may actually rub off on their children. Their reaction involves being both empathic ("I feel your pain.") and firm ("No, you can't have that cookie."). Regardless of the reason for the tantrum, when their kids are really upset, Terry and Jaime want to send messages that respect and acknowledge those intense feelings. At the same time, in the event that their children are trying to "play them," they convey the message that such attempts at manipulation will not be rewarded.

Blair has quite a temper. When she gets angry, she has, in the past, just let her emotions explode. Her husband Anthony understands Blair and is able to accept the outbursts. He figures that Blair lets it out, lets it go, and then it's over. Blair also knows where she got her temper, namely, from her mother who could yell and scream with the best of them, so that Blair and her siblings were often the victims of their mother's wrath. But Blair didn't want to teach her two sons, Everett and Jude, that yelling was acceptable, so she was committed to tempering her temper. This was no small task given her history and the fact that it seems as if impatience, frustration, and anger are part and parcel of being a parent. So she is ever vigilant of her emotions when her children are acting up. Her knee-jerk reaction is to respond with anger, so controlling her temper has been perhaps the greatest challenge of her life. But she sees the value of her efforts when her sons are able to get frustrated or angry without blowing up. And she feels better about herself as a mother, wife, and person for her newfound ability to control her anger and express it in healthier ways.

Randy and Christina found it easy to get frustrated and irritated (and angry!) with their first child's tantrums and whining. And they didn't win any Parent of the Year awards with their reactions either. It took Randy and Christina quite a while to figure it out, but they finally realized that when their children are really upset, whatever emotion is most apparent is not usually the real emotion causing the problem. For example, when children have temper tantrums, anger is rarely the underlying emotion. Anger, in reality, is a defensive emotion aimed at protecting children (and adults, for that matter) from more painful emotions such as sadness, hurt, and humiliation. Whininess, in turn, is the outward expression of children feeling frustrated, not getting their needs met, or feeling out of control (all of which, I might add, are normal parts of being a kid). Or children may just be hungry, tired, or too cold or hot, and as a result, more emotionally sensitive. When Randy and Christina take the time to understand the underlying emotion or issue their children are expressing, they find that they are much more empathetic and are in a better position to send their children messages of understanding and support.

Dede believes in the power of words to shape the way people think and feel. With this in mind, she and her husband, Thad, felt that a great way to help their three children develop good emotional habits was to give them a large vocabulary of words to help them identify and describe the emotions that they feel. Dede and Thad first made a list of all of the emotions that they could think of, but found themselves stuck on the obvious ones such as love, happiness, sadness, anger, excitement, joy, and frustration. So they did a search online and found a veritable treasure trove of emotions that caused them to think "Of course, why didn't we think of those before?": courage, confusion, curiosity, disappointment, embarrassment, jealousy, surprise, contentment, inspiration, relief, loneliness, impatience, silliness, worry, shyness, satisfaction, compassion, empathy, friendliness, boredom, anxiety, and pride. At dinner several times a week, they introduce a different emotion to their children and have a discussion about what the emotion is, how it feels, the facial expressions that it provokes, and how it is expressed.

The key to emotional maturity for Alma is the ability to express negative emotions in a constructive way. Yet, such constructive expressions don't seem to come naturally or easily to children, and certainly not to her son Rex. Though it is easy to tell him what she doesn't think worked well (as it is to tell kids what they shouldn't do), Alma wants to focus him on what he does right. So whenever Rex responds to a potentially negative emotional situation by staying calm and collected, she praises him for the emotional choice he made ("You could have gotten really upset there, but you decided that being positive would work better, and it did!").

Gloria grew up in a family where the emotional tone was always negative, filled with pessimism, criticism, and conflict. And it was stifling. When she got married and had children, Gloria was determined to create a very different emotional tone in her family. Sure, some negativity is a natural part of family life, but she wanted to make positivity the "coin of the realm."

To that end, Gloria and her husband, Dennis (who was a very positive fellow), made positive emotions, such as happiness, excitement, pride, gratitude, and empathy, a regular part of their daily life. They wanted to highlight the presence of positive emotions for their children. So when their kids were clearly feeling upbeat, they would simply reflect back what they saw, for example, "You look like you're having so much fun playing together" or "You seem so excited about your school project." Gloria and Dennis also wanted to model positive emotions. So when they were feeling a particular positive emotion, they would share it with their kids. For example, after a productive day at work, Gloria might say, "I accomplished so much at work today and I am really proud of my efforts." Or if Dennis was feeling really contented, he would share this feeling with his family by saying, "I'm sitting here with my favorite people in the world, and I'm one happy guy."

Afterword

There were three central messages I wanted to communicate to you in *Your Children Are Listening*. The most important is that *your children become the messages they get the most*. Now, more than ever before, you must be intentional and persistent in the messages you send to your children. The reason is that, due to the proliferation of new technology and media, other forces in your children's world are conveying messages that are not the least bit healthy for them. If you don't transmit clear, consistent, and healthy messages about what you value and what you want your children to become, they will be shaped by the messages from those less benevolent forces in our society. Part of being deliberate about the messages you send to your children is understanding the many "conduits" through which you convey messages and the "message blockers" that can prevent your messages from getting through to them.

Second, I described nine messages—love, competence, security, compassion, gratitude, Earth, respect, responsibility, and emotion—that I believe are most essential for your children to hear early in their lives before your influence diminishes and that of outside pressures grows. These messages focus on how children feel about themselves, how they feel about others, and how others feel about them. I also encourage you to ask yourself what messages, other than mine, you want to communicate to your children.

Third, the payoff for sending positive messages to your children early and often is immense. These messages provide the foundation for your children to become the confident, caring, responsible, and contributing people that I'm sure you want them to be. You will set the stage for your children to find meaning, happiness, healthy relationships, and success in their lives. You will instill in your children the necessary capabilities to, when they leave the comfort and security of your family, fully engage with and thrive in a world that can be scary and scintillating, inhospitable and inviting, and frustrating and fascinating. And you will leave your children a legacy of being able to accept the healthy messages and reject the unhealthy ones they will surely receive every day from their expanding world. You will also show your children how to be conduits of positive messages to all those around them.

Because you are reading *Your Children Are Listening*, you probably have children who are pretty young, like our daughters. We certainly have a long way to go in raising Catie and Gracie. And it is *so* difficult sometimes: overwhelming, frustrating, exhausting, uncertain, and just plain terrifying. A friend of mine who has older children once told me: "The years are short, but the days are long." And there are many days when Catie and Gracie just don't seem to be getting our messages, and Sarah and I look at each other and wonder whether it will ever get any easier. But then something truly remarkable happens. Our girls say or do something that tells us they are, in fact, getting our messages. Then we look at each other and say, with a combination of pride and relief, "Our children are listening."

References

Adams, C. C. (2009). *The Self-Aware Parent: 19 Lessons for Growing with Your Children*. Charleston, SC: BookSurge.

Adderholdt-Elliott, M. (1991). Perfectionism and the gifted adolescent. In M. Bireley, & J. Genshaft (Eds.), *Understanding the gifted adolescent: Educational, developmental, and multicultural issues*. Education and psychology of the gifted series (pp. 65–75). New York: Teachers College Press.

Agliata, A., & Renk, K. (2008). College students' adjustment: The role of parent-college student expectation discrepancies and communication reciprocity. *Journal of Youth and Adolescence*, 37(8), 967–982.

Ainsworth, M.D., Blehar, M., Waters, E., & Wall, S. (1978). *Patterns of Attachment: A Psychological Study of the Strange Situation*. Hillsdale NJ: Lawrence Erlbaum.

Anderson-Butcher, D. A., & Cash, S. J. (2010). Participation in Boys & Girls Clubs, vulnerability, and problem behaviors. *Children and Youth Services Review*, 32 (5), 672–678.

Answerbag. (January 26, 2010). What is generosity of spirit? http://www.answerbag.com/q_view/1905071.

Antony, M. M., & Swinson, R. P. (1998). *When perfect isn't good enough: Strategies for coping with perfectionism*. Oakland, CA: New Harbinger Publications.

Armstrong, M., Birnie-Lefcovitch, S., & Ungar, M. (2005). Pathways between social support, family well-being, quality of parenting, and child resilience: What we know. *Journal of Child and Family Studies*, 14(2), 269–281.

Assor, A. Roth, G., & Deci, E. L. (2004). The emotional costs of parents' conditional regard: A self-determination theory analysis. *Journal of Personality*, 72, 47–89.

Bandura, A., Barbaranelli, C., Caprara, G. V. & Pastorelli, C. (2001), Self-Efficacy Beliefs as Shapers of Children's Aspirations and Career Trajectories. *Child Development*, 72, 187–206.

Bennett, C. (1984). "Know thyself." *Professional Psychology: Research and Practice*, 15(2), 271–283.

Bratton, S., Ray, D., Rhine, T., & Jones, L. (2005). The efficacy of play therapy with children: A meta-analytic review of the outcome research. *Professional Psychology: Research and Practice*, 36(4), 376–390.

Brotherson, S. (April, 2006). Keys to building attachment in young children. http://www.ag.ndsu.edu/pubs/yf/famsci/fs631w.htm.

Center for Advancing Health (2010, September 26). In cyber bullying, depression hits victims hardest. http://www.sciencedaily.com/releases/2010/09/100925115115.htm.

Center for a New American Dream. (May, 2002). Kids and commercialism. http://www.newdream.org/campaign/kids/press-release2002.html.

The Center on the Social and Emotional Foundations for Early Learning. Teaching your child to: Identify and Express Emotions. http://csefel.vanderbilt.edu/familytools/teaching_emotions.pdf.

Cherry, K. Attachment styles. http://psychology.about.com/od/loveandattraction/ss/attachmentstyle_4.htm.

Chislett, G., & Kennett, D. (2007). The effects of the Nobody's Perfect Program on parenting resourcefulness and competency. *Journal of Child and Family Studies*, 16(4), 473–482.

Collins, W., Maccoby, E., Steinberg, L., Hetherington, E., & Bornstein, M. (2000). Contemporary research on parenting: The case for nature and nurture. *American Psychologist*, 55(2), 218–232.

Cook, C. R., Williams, K. R., Guerra, N. G., Kim, T. E., & Sadek, S. (2010). Predictors of bullying and victimization in childhood and adolescence: A meta-analytic investigation. *School Psychology Quarterly*, 25 (2), 65–83.

Council of Economic Advisers to the President. (May, 2000). Teens and their parents in the 21st century: An examination of trends in teen behavior and the role of parental involvement.

Dateline. Is your phone addiction hurting your kids? http://www.msnbc.msn.com/id/21134540/vp/39172696#39105588

Declerck, C. II., & Bogaert, S. (2008). Social value orientation: related to empathy and the ability to read the mind in the eyes. *Journal of Social Psychology*, 148(6), 711–26.

Dehue, F., Bolman, C., & Völlink, T. (2008). Cyberbullying: youngsters' experiences and parental perception. *CyberPsychology & Behavior*, 11, 217–23.

DeNoon, D. J. (April 3, 2006). Media messages harm child, teen health. http://www.webmd.com/parenting/news/20060403/media-messages-harm-child-teen-health.

Economic and Social Research Council (ESRC) (2009, May 8). Mother's talk about feelings and intentions help children develop social understanding. ScienceDaily. http://www.webmd.com/parenting/news/20060403/media-messages-harm-child-teen-health.

Ekman P. (1973). Cross-cultural studies of facial expression. In P. Ekman (ed): *Darwin and facial expression: A century of research in review*. New York: Academic Press.

El Nokali, N. E., Bachman, H. J., & Votruba-Drzal, E. (2008). Parent involvement and children's academic and social development in elementary school. *Child Development*, 81(3), 988–1005.

Elliot, A., & Thrash, T. (2004). The intergenerational transmission of fear of failure. *Personality and Social Psychology Bulletin*, 30(8), 187–221.

Emmons, R. A., & McCullough, M. E. (2003). Counting blessings versus burdens: Experimental studies of gratitude and subjective well-being. *Journal of Personality and Social Psychology*, 84, 377–389.

Epstein, R. (2010, November/December). What makes a good parent? *Scientific American Mind*, 46–51.

Ericsson, A. K., Charness, N., Feltovich, P., & Hoffman, R. R. (2006). *Cambridge handbook on expertise and expert performance*. Cambridge, UK: Cambridge University Press.

Everett, G. E., Hupp, S. D., A., & Olmi, D. J. (2010). Time-out with parents: A descriptive analysis of 30 years of research. *Education & Treatment of Children*, 33(2), 235–259.

Farkas, S., Johnson, J., Duffett, A., Wilson, L., & Vine, J. (2002). A Lot Easier Said than Done: Parents Talk about Raising Children in Today's America. http://www.publicagenda.org/files/pdf/easier_said_than_done.pdf.

Fleming, N. D. & Mills, C. (1992). Not another inventory, rather a catalyst for reflection. *To Improve the Academy*, 11, 137.

Flett, G. L., Hewitt, P. L., Blankstein, K. R., & Mosher, S. W. (1991). Perfectionism, self-actualization, and personal adjustment. *Journal of Social Behavior and Personality*, 6, 147–160.

Flett, G., Hewitt, P., Blankstein, K., & Gray, L. (1998). Psychological distress and the frequency of perfectionistic thinking. *Journal of Personality and Social Psychology*, 75(5), 1363–1381.

Flett, G. L., Hewitt, P. L., Endler, N. S., & Tassone, C. (1994). Perfectionism and components of state and trait anxiety. *Current Psychological Research and Reviews*, 13, 326–350.

Friedman, E. (September 29, 2010). Victim of secret dorm sex tape posts Facebook goodbye, jumps to his death. *ABC News*. http://abcnews.go.com/US/victim-secret-dorm-sex-tape-commits-suicide/story?id=11758716.

Froh, J., Sefick, W. J., & Emmons, R. A. (2008). Counting blessings in early adolescents: An experimental study of gratitude and subjective well-being. *Journal of School Psychology*, 46, 213–233.

Frost, R. O., Marten, P. A., Lahart, C., & Rosenblate, R. (1990). The dimensions of perfectionism. *Cognitive Therapy and Research*, 14, 449–468.

Gardner, A. (January 26, 2009). Recess makes for better students. *The Washington Post*. http://www.washingtonpost.com/wp-dyn/content/article/2009/01/26/AR2009012600948.html.

Goldberg, S. (2000). *Attachment and Development*. Hillsdale, N.J.: The Analytic Press.

Goldsmith, D. (2010). The emotional dance of attachment. *Clinical Social Work Journal*, 38(1), 4–7.

Gottman, J. M., Katz, L. F., & Hooven, C. (1997). *Meta-emotion: How Families Communicate Emotionally*. Mahwah, NJ: Lawrence Erlbaum.

Grant, T., & Littlejohn, G. (2005). *Teaching Green: The Elementary School Years*. Portland, ME: Stenhouse.

Grinspan, D., Hemphill, A., & Nowicki, S., Jr. (2003). Improving the ability of elementary school-age children to identify emotion in facial expression. *Journal of Genetic Psychology*, 164(1), 88–100.

Harris, J. R. (1999). *Nurture Assumption: Why Children Turn Out the Way They Do*. New York: Free Press.

Hesch, B. John. (1992). Fostering the development of compassion in young children. *Journal of Pastoral Psychology*, 41(1), 31–37.

Hewitt, P. L., & Flett, G. L. (1991). Perfectionism in the self and social contexts: Conceptualization, assessment, and association with psychopathology. *Journal of Personality and Social Psychology*, 60, 456–470.

Hewitt, P. L., & Flett, G. L. (1990). Perfectionism and depression: A multidimensional analysis. *Journal of Social Behavior and Personality*, 5, 423–438.

Hewitt, P. L., Flett, G. L., & Endler, N. S. (1995). Perfectionism, coping, and depression symptomatology in a clinical sample. *Clinical Psychology and Psychotherapy*, 2, 47–58.

Huggins, C. E. (January 13, 2007). Competence, self-esteem keys to happiness. http://www.bnet.com/blog/ceo/competence-self-esteem-keys-to-happiness/38.

Jambunathan, S., & Hurlbut, N. (2002). Influence of Parenting Attitudes about Childrearing on the Perception of Self-Competence among Four-Year-Old Children. Issues in Education. *Journal of Early Education and Family Review*, 9(4), 17–25.

Kamins, M. L., & Dweck, C. S. (1999). Person versus process praise and criticism: Implications for contingent self-worth and coping. *Developmental Psychology, 35*, 835–847.

Kerns, K. A. (2008). "Attachment in Middle Childhood" in Cassidy J., Shaver P. R. *Handbook of Attachment: Theory, Research and Clinical Applications.* New York and London: Guilford Press. 366–382.

Kettman, S. M. (1999). *The 12 Rules of Grandparenting: A New Look at Traditional Roles and How to Break Them.* New York, NY: Facts on File.

Kiefer, R., Worthington, E., Myers, B., Kliewer, W., Berry, J., Davis, D., et al. (2010). Training parents in forgiving and reconciling. *American Journal of Family Therapy, 38*(1), 32–49.

Klass, P. (2002). Should you be friends with your child?. *Parenting, 16*(5), 102.

Klomek, A., Marrocco, F., Kleinman, M., Schonfeld, I., & Gould, M. (2007). Bullying, depression, and suicidality in adolescents. *Journal of the American Academy of Child and Adolescent Psychiatry, 46*(1), 40.

Kohn, A. (September 14, 2009). When a parent's 'I love you' means 'Do as I say.' http://www.nytimes.com/2009/09/15/health/15mind.html?_r=2.

Lewin, T. (October 23, 2009). No Einstein in your crib? Get a refund. *New York Times.* http://www.nytimes.com/2009/10/24/education/24baby.html?_r=1.

Luthar, S. S., & Becker, B. E. (2002). Privileged but pressured?: A study of affluent youth. *Child Development, 73*, 1593–1610.

Maag, C. (December 16, 2007). When the bullies turned faceless. *New York Times.* http://www.nytimes.com/2007/12/16/fashion/16meangirls.html?_r=1&ref=megan_meier.

Main, M., & Hesse, E. (1990). Parents' unresolved traumatic experiences are related to infant disorganized attachment status: Is frightened/frightening parental behavior the linking mechanism? In M. T. Greenberg, D. Cicchetti, & E. M. Cummings (Eds.), *Attachment in the Preschool Years: Theory, Research, and Intervention,* pp. 161–182. Chicago, IL: University of Chicago Press.

Main, M., & Solomon, J. (1986). Discovery of an insecure disoriented attachment pattern: procedures, findings and implications for the classification of behavior. In Brazelton, T. & Youngmann, M. *Affective Development in Infancy.* Norwood, NJ: Ablex.

Marsh, A. A., Kozak M. N., and Ambady N. (2007). Accurate identification of fear facial expressions predicts prosocial behavior. *Emotion, 7*(2), 239–51.

Massaro, G. (December 24, 2008). Drug Abuse Amongst Teenagers. http://www.associatedcontent.com/article/1309872/drug_abuse_amongst_teenagers.html?cat=5.

Mccarthy, G. (1999) Attachment style and adult love relationships and friendships: A study of a group of women at risk of experiencing relationship difficulties. *British Journal of Medical Psychology*, 72(3), 305–321.

McChesney, S. Respect: How to teach it and show it. http://www.familyresource .com/parenting/character-development/respect-how-to-teach-it-and-show-it

McCraty, R., Barrois-Choplin, B., Rozman, D., Atkinson, M., & Watkins, A. D. (1998). The impact of a new emotional self-management program on stress, emotions, heart rate variability, DHEA and cortisol. *Integrative Physiological and Behavioral Science*, 33(2), 151–171.

McCraty, R., & Childre, D. (2004). The appreciative heart: The psychophysiology of positive emotions and optimal functioning. In R. A. Emmons & M. E. McCullough (Eds.), *The Psychology of Gratitude*. New York, Oxford University Press, pp 230–255.

McCullough, M. E., Emmons, R. A., & Tsang, J. (2002). The grateful disposition: A conceptual and empirical topography. *Journal of Personality and Social Psychology*, 82, 112–127.

McCullough, M. E., Tsang, J., & Emmons, R. A. (2004). Gratitude in intermediate affective terrain: Links of grateful moods with individual differences and daily emotional experience. *Journal of Personality and Social Psychology*, 86, 295–309.

McGregor, H. A., & Elliot, A. J. (2005). The shame of failure: Examining the link between fear of failure and shame. *Personality and Social Psychology Bulletin*, 31 (2), 218–231.

Mueller, C. M., & Dweck, C. S. (1998). Praise for intelligence can undermine children's motivation and performance. *Journal of Personality and Social Psychology*, 75, 33–52.

Nelsen, J. (1999). *Positive time-out: And over 50 ways to avoid power struggles in the home and the classroom*. Roseville, CA: Prima.

Oregon State University (2009, September 1). Impact of positive parenting can last for generations. ScienceDaily. Retrieved November 19, 2010, from http://www .sciencedaily.com/releases/2009/09/090901082526.htm.

Park, A. (August 6, 2007). Baby Einsteins: Not so smart after all. *Time*. http://www .time.com/time/health/article/0%2C8599%2C1650352%2C00.html?cnn=yes.

Patterson, C., Cosgrove, J., & O'Brien, R. (1980). Nonverbal indicants of comprehension and noncomprehension in children. *Developmental Psychology*, 16(1), 38–48.

Paul, P. (October, 10, 2010). The playground gets tougher. *New York Times*. http://www.nytimes.com/2010/10/10/fashion/10Cultural.html?_ r=1&scp=2&sq=mean%20girls&st=cse.

Payne, K. J. (2010). *Simplicity Parenting: Using the Extraordinary Power of Less to Raise Calmer, Happier, and More Secure Kids*. New York, NY: Ballantine.

Pinquart, M., & Teubert, D. (2010). Effects of parenting education with expectant and new parents: A meta-analysis. *Journal of Family Psychology*, 24(3), 316–327.

Pinsky, D., S., & Young, M. (October 2006). "Narcissism and celebrity." *Journal of Research in Personality* 40(5): 463–471.

Quindlen, A. (2005). The good enough mother. *Newsweek*, 145(8), 50–51.

Raeff, C. (2010). Independence and interdependence in children's developmental experiences. *Child Development Perspectives*, 4, 31–36.

Rauh, S. (2006). 10 signs you're a micromanaging parent. http://www.webmd.com/parenting/features/10-signs-micromanaging-parent.

Rein, G., Atkinson, M, & McCraty, R. (1995). The physiological and psychological effects of compassion and anger. *Journal of Advancement in Medicine*, 8(2), 87–105.

Reis, H. T., Sheldon, K. M., Gable, S. L., Roscoe, R., & Ryan, R. (2000). Daily well being: The role of autonomy, competence, and relatedness. *Personality and Social Psychology Bulletin*, 26, 419–435.

Richtel, M. (November 21, 2010). Growing up digital, wired for distraction. *New York Times*. http://www.nytimes.com/2010/11/21/technology/21brain.html.

Ridley, M. (2003). *Nature Via Nurture: Genes, Experience, and What Makes Us Human*. New York: HarperCollins.

Rock, A., Trainor, L., & Addison, T. (1999). Distinctive messages in infant-directed lullabies and play songs. *Developmental Psychology*, 35(2), 527–534.

Rodewalt, F. & Tragakis, M. W. (2003). "Self-esteem and self-regulation: Toward optimal studies of self-esteem." *Psychological Inquiry*, 14(1), 66–70.

Romina, M., Barros, M. D., Silver, E. J., & Stein, R. E. K. (2009). School recess and group classroom behavior. *Pediatrics*, 123(2), 431–436.

Rosenthal, R. (1999, January). Young children's representations of self and parents: Are they related to experiences with mothers and fathers? (attachment). *Dissertation Abstracts International*, 60, Retrieved from PsycINFO database.

Schmalt, H. D. (1982). Two concepts of fear of failure motivation. In R. Schwarzer, H. M. van der Ploeg, & C. D. Spielberger (Eds.), *Advances in test anxiety research* (Vol. 1) (pp. 45–52). Lisse, The Netherlands: Swets & Zeitlinger.

Sheldon, K. M., Ryan, R. M., & Reis, H. R. (1996). What makes for a good day? Competence and autonomy in the day and in the person. *Personality and Social Psychology Bulletin*, 22, 1270–1279.

Singh, S. (1992). Hostile Press measure of fear of failure and its relation to child-rearing attitudes and behavior problems. *Journal of Social Psychology*, 132, 397–399.

Society for Research in Child Development (2008, February 7). Good parenting helps difficult infants perform as well or better in first grade than peers. *ScienceDaily*. http://www.sciencedaily.com/releases/2008/02/080207085631.htm.

Soenens, B., Luyckx, K., Vansteenkiste, M., Luyten, P., Duriez, B., & Goossens, L. (2008). Maladaptive perfectionism as an intervening variable between psychological control and adolescent depressive symptoms: A three-wave longitudinal study. *Journal of Family Psychology*, 22(3), 465–474.

Spagnola, M., & Fiese, B. H. (2007). Family routines and rituals: A context for development in the lives of young children. *Infants & Young Children*, 20(4), 284–299.

Stiffelman, S. (September 23, 2008). Positive discipline: Why time-outs don't work. http://www.sheknows.com/parenting/articles/805746/positive-discipline-why-timeouts-dont-work.

Stoolmiller, M., Gerrard, M., Sargent, J. D., Worth, K. A., & Gibbons, F. X. (2010). R-rated movie viewing, growth in sensation seeking and alcohol initiation: Reciprocal and moderation effects. *Prevention Science*, 11, 1–13.

Stright, A., Gallagher, K., & Kelley, K. (2008). Infant temperament moderates relations between maternal parenting in early childhood and children's adjustment in first grade. *Child Development*, 79(1), 186–200.

Sturge-Apple, M., Davies, P., & Cummings, E. (2006). Hostility and withdrawal in marital conflict: Effects on parental emotional unavailability and inconsistent discipline. *Journal of Family Psychology*, 20(2), 227–238.

Taffel, R. (1998). What your child wants most. *Parents*, 73(10), 63–66.

Tanski, S. E., Dal Cin, S., Stoolmiller, M. & Sargent, J. D. (2010). Parental R-rated movie restriction and early-onset alcohol use. *Journal of Studies on Alcohol and Drugs*, 71 (3), 452–459.

Teevan, R. (1983). Childhood development of fear of failure motivation: A replication. *Psychological Reports*, 53, 506.

Tresch Owen, M., & Mulvihill, B. (1994). Benefits of a parent education and support program in the first three years. *Family Relations*, 43(2), 206–212.

Twenge, J. M. & Campbell, W. K. (2009). *The Narcissism Epidemic: Living in the Age of Entitlement*. New York, NY: Free Press.

University of Gothenburg (2010, February 22). Cyberbullying: A growing problem. *ScienceDaily*. http://www.sciencedaily.com/releases/2010/02/100222104939.htm.

UT Southwestern Medical Center (2006, March 23). Successful treatment of mothers with depression helps their children, too. ScienceDaily. http://www.sciencedaily.com/releases/2006/03/060322184420.htm.

Van der Zande, I. (November 23, 2010). Generous gratitude: The art of giving thanks. http://www.kidpower.org/resources/articles/gratitude.html.

Vigdor, J., & Ladd, H. (2010, June). Scaling the digital divide: Home computer technology and student achievement. Working Paper 48. *National Center for Analysis of Longitudinal Data in Education Research.*

Wang, J., Nansel, T. R., & Iannotti, R. J. (2010). Cyber and traditional bullying: Differential association with depression. *Journal of Adolescent Health*, 16(2), 124–135.

Waters, E., Hamilton, C. E., & Weinfield, N. S. (2000). The stability of attachment security from infancy to adolescence and early adulthood: General introduction. *Child Development*, 71(3), 678–683.

WebMD Health News. (March 21, 2004). Kids not getting enough sleep. http://www.webmd.com/sleep-disorders/news/20040331/kids-not-getting-enough-sleep.

Webster-Stratton, C. (1998). Preventing conduct problems in Head Start children: Strengthening parenting competencies. *Journal of Consulting and Clinical Psychology*, 66(5), 715–730.

Weissman, M., Pilowsky, D., Wickramaratne, P., Talati, A., Wisniewski, S., Fava, M., et al. (2006). Remissions in maternal depression and child psychopathology: A STAR*D-Child Report. *JAMA: Journal of the American Medical Association*, 295(12), 1389–1398.

Whitham, C. (1994). Time-out: A discipline technique that works when used correctly. *PTA Today*, 19(3), 14–16.

Widen, S., & Russell, J. (2010). The "disgust face" conveys anger to children. *Emotion*, 10(4), 455–466.

Wilson, B. (2008). Media and children's aggression, fear, and altruism. *Future of Children*, 18(1), 87–118.

Wood, A. M., Joseph, S, & Linley, P. A. (2007). "Gratitude: Parent of all virtues." *The Psychologist* 20(1) 18–21.

Wood, A. M., Joseph, S., & Linley, P. A. (2007). Coping style as a psychological resource of grateful people. *Journal of Social and Clinical Psychology*, 26, 1108–1125.

Wood, A. M., Joseph, S., Lloyd, J., & Atkins, S. (2009). Gratitude influences sleep through the mechanism of pre-sleep cognitions. *Journal of Psychosomatic Research*, 66, 43–48.

Wood, A. M., Joseph, S., & Maltby, J. (2008). PersonalPages.Manchester.ac.uk, Gratitude uniquely predicts satisfaction with life: Incremental validity above the domains and facets of the Five Factor Model. *Personality and Individual Differences*, 45, 49–54.

Wood, A. M., Joseph, S. & Maltby J. (2009). Gratitude predicts psychological well-being above the Big Five facets. *Personality and Individual Differences*, 45, 655–660.

Wood, A. M., Maltby, J., Gillett, R., Linley, P. A., & Joseph, S. (2008). The role of gratitude in the development of social support, stress, and depression: Two longitudinal studies. *Journal of Research in Personality*, 42, 854–871.

Wu, T. F., & Wei, M. (2008). Perfectionism and negative mood: The mediating roles of validation from others versus self. *Journal of Counseling Psychology*, 55(2), 276–288.

Yuill, Nicola, et al. (2007). The relation between parenting, children's social understanding and language: Full Research Report ESRC End of Award Report, RES-000-23-0278. Swindon: ESRC.

Zilca, Ran (June 26, 2009). Immerse yourself in the gratitude stream. *Psychology Today*. http://www.psychologytoday.com/blog/confessions-techie/200906/immerse-yourself-in-the-gratitude-stream.

Acknowledgments

Special thanks to Kären Abbe, my stepmother-in-law, for doing what no one else was able to do, namely, come up with a compelling title for this book. Your time, effort, and creativity are indelibly printed on every copy of *Your Children Are Listening*.

I would also like to express my thanks to Stephanie Dargoltz and Paige Dunn for their outstanding work as my research assistants. Their commitment of time and energy helped make *Your Children Are Listening* a much better book.

Index

About the Author

JIM TAYLOR, PHD, a practicing psychologist, has consulted with young people, parents, and educators for more than 25 years. He has been a speaker at numerous elementary and secondary schools, youth sports programs, and performing arts organizations around the country.

Dr. Taylor's previous parenting books include *Positive Pushing: How to Raise a Successful and Happy Child*. He writes *Prime Family Alert!*, a bimonthly video and e-newsletter, and blogs on parenting for psychologytoday.com, huffingtonpost.com, and other Web sites around the U.S.

He lives north of San Francisco with his wife, Sarah, and their daughters, Catie and Gracie.

Dr. Taylor can be followed on Facebook (Dr. Jim Taylor) and Twitter (DrJimTaylor), and his interviews and video newsletters can be viewed on his YouTube channel (JimTaylorPhD). To learn more, visit www.drjimtaylor.com.